CONSUMPTION CHALLENGED

Consumption Challenged
Food in Medialised Everyday Lives

BENTE HALKIER
Roskilde University, Denmark

ASHGATE

Published by
Ashgate Publishing Limited
Wey Court East
Union Road
Farnham
Surrey, GU9 7PT
England

Ashgate Publishing Company
Suite 420
101 Cherry Street
Burlington
VT 05401-4405
USA

www.ashgate.com

British Library Cataloguing in Publication Data
Halkier, Bente.
Consumption challenged : food in medialised everyday lives.
1. Food consumption. 2. Food consumption--Research.
3. Nutrition surveys. 4. Food consumption--Environmental aspects. 5. Food habits. 6. Food consumption--Denmark--Case studies.
I. Title
339.4'86413-dc22

Library of Congress Cataloging-in-Publication Data
Halkier, Bente.
Consumption challenged : food in medialised everyday lives / by Bente Halkier.
p. cm.
Includes index.
ISBN 978-0-7546-7476-4 (hardback) -- ISBN 978-1-4094-1022-5 (ebook)
1. Food preferences. 2. Food consumption--Social aspects. 3. Consumer education--Social aspects. 4. Food habits--Social aspects. 5. Food--Social aspects--Denmark--Case studies. I. Title.
TX357.H26 2010
394.1'209489--dc22

2010011715

ISBN 9780754674764 (hbk)
ISBN 9781409410225 (ebk)

Mixed Sources
Product group from well-managed forests and other controlled sources
www.fsc.org Cert no. SGS-COC-2482
© 1996 Forest Stewardship Council
FSC

Printed and bound in Great Britain by
TJ International Ltd, Padstow, Cornwall

Contents

List of Tables

Preface

This book is intended to participate in discussions about the agency of ordinary food consumers: What can ordinary consumers do about societal problems such as the climate challenge and the obesity epidemic? A central analytical contention of this book is that nowadays food consumption routines become questioned via media campaigns and debates, and that such discourses typically individualise and privatise the responsibility for doing something about problems such as the environment and health. Therefore it is possible to see food consumption as challenged. The primary aim of this book is to provide empirical analyses of the varieties and complexities of how people respond to such contestations as consumers in their everyday lives. Thus, the arguments comment upon discussions about political consumption as well as discussions about communication for social change. Another of the aims of the book is to build more bridging between the sociology of consumption and user-oriented communication research.

This book is written from a particular theoretical perspective that highlights the performative character of social life and argues against methodological individualism as well as analytical structuralism. Practice theory has been discussed intensely among European sociologists researching consumption and consumer cultures in recent years, and yet another aim of this book is to discuss the usefulness and the implications of a practice theoretical perspective in consumption research.

Perhaps we associate the writing of a book with long lonely hours of struggle in front of the computer. In fact, writing a book is an inherently social process where many people should be thanked for their participation and contributions.

First of all, writing a book that is mainly empirical requires empirical data materials. I would like to thank all the people who have volunteered to be interviewed, to participate in focus groups, and to take photos of their food and cooking over the years. Without your generous spending of time and energy, it would not be possible to do empirical research on food consumption issues, and I am thoroughly grateful for your participation and our dialogues. Likewise, writing a book based on empirical research requires financed time. Thus, I would like to thank the Department of Communication, Business and Information Technologies at Roskilde University, the National Danish Strategic Environmental Research Programme and the National Danish Social Scientific Research Council (FSE) for financing some of this research and writing time. Furthermore, one of the empirical research projects has been carried out in partnership with my good colleague Iben Jensen at the Department of Communication, Business and Information

Technologies, Roskilde University. Much thanks to you for inspiring and dynamic cooperation.

Writing a book begins with vague ideas that are developed over cups of tea in front of the computer and with the cat snoozing on the sofa. But the ideas certainly also develop through sharing, discussion and reflection with others. I am thoroughly grateful to Neil Jordan from Ashgate for suggesting the idea of writing such a book to me back at the 2007 European Sociological Association Conference in Glasgow. Likewise, I would like to thank Jukka Gronow, Alan Warde and two referees for commenting on the book proposal. The actual writing of bits and pieces of the manuscript has in particular benefitted from my participation in five academic settings: The Research Network on Sociology of Consumption under the European Sociological Association; the Nordic network on consumers and sustainability; my own research group, 'Knowledge production and Communication'; other colleagues at the Department of Communication, Business and Information Technologies, Roskilde University; and the sociology group at the Department of Human Nutrition, Copenhagen University. Many national and international colleagues have provided useful comments and reflections for different parts of the book at different stages. Without any other order than an alphabetical one, I would like to express my gratitude to: Pernille Almlund, Nina Blom Andersen, Magnus Boström, Tim Dant, Arne Dulsrud, David Evans, Kirsten Gram-Hanssen, Jukka Gronow, Henrik Halkier, Tom Hargreaves, Pernille Hohnen, Lotte Holm, Iben Jensen, Katherine O'Doherty Jensen, Sisse Siggaard Jensen, Tally Katz-Gerro, Margit Keller, Unni Kjärnes, Mikael Klintman, Sanne Knudsen, Jesper Lassen, Johanna Mäkela, Lydia Martens, Mara Miele, Annemette Nielsen, Birgitte Ravn Olesen, Christina Hee Pedersen, Karsten Pedersen, Louise Phillips, Ursula Plesner, Inge Røpke, Kim Schrøder, Dale Southerton, Gert Spargaaren, Pål Strandbakken, Eivind Stö, Pekka Sulkunen, Laura Terragni, Lisbeth Thorlacius, Harald Throne-Holst, Monica Truninger, Gunnar Vittersø, Alan Warde, Terhi-Anna Wilska, Mark Ørsten, and Per Østergaard.

Some people have taken the time to read and comment upon whole chapters, and I thank Nina Blom Andersen, Henrik Halkier, Iben Jensen and Per Østergard for this. But I am particularly indebted to Lotte Holm and Alan Warde who spent their time and academic energy on reading the entire manuscript. Without your heroic efforts and constructive suggestions, the arguments in this book would have been considerably less clearly presented. The same type of thanks go to my English language editor, Marianne Stein. Also, I would have never completed the book without the consistent enthusiasm and optimism of my editor at Ashgate, Neil Jordan. All shortcomings of the book are, of course, my responsibility.

However, as the content of the book hopefully reflects, all practices take place in complex social relations. This is also the case for book-writing practices. Therefore I am particularly indebted to my family who have been putting up with me being there in my everyday life but at times not really being present while working on this book. Thanks to my daughters Rosa and Liva for insisting on dragging me into playing with fairy figures, jumping into swimming pools and losing card games with you. Thanks to my husband Søren for all possible kinds of practical and emotional support.

Bente Halkier, Copenhagen.

Chapter 1
A Field of Challenged Consumption

Challenging Consumption

> But I am also tired of the media in the way that … they bring something up, right, and then I sit and work myself all up about it and saying that it's too bloody bad … but my possibilities for doing ANYTHING about it are not really there, are they? You know … the fish doesn't get better from them making such a television show, right? I've just got yet another problem thrown into my face, right? (Danish food consumer)

Most of us living in modern globalised and medialised large-scale societies will probably be able to recognise the type of experience expressed above by this Danish food consumer. He talks about what he can do when television suddenly represents fish as potentially dangerous to eat because of its content of mercury or dioxin, whereas fish has otherwise typically been represented as healthy to eat. What are we as consumers going to do about all the different kinds of knowledge and opinions about what we eat and how we eat that we get from the media discussions about food? Do we as consumers have a responsibility for helping to solve societal problems such as the quality of food, the climate crisis, or the obesity epidemic? We cannot entirely escape discussions in the media that question our consumption routines, but how do we react to this constant questioning on a daily basis? The primary purpose of this book is to show the variety in consumer reactions in everyday life to such questioning of food consumption routines.

One of the assumptions made in this book is that everyday consumption activities become contested because we live in a thoroughly medialised society (Thompson, 1995). That society is medialised means that most of us use and relate to insights from media as an integrated part of many of our daily activities. We cannot directly experience everything we need to know or get to know what we need to know through sharing the experiences of people we know personally. Significant parts of our understandings are based upon representations in media of knowledges, experiences and discourses. Such representations are called medialised knowledges, medialised experiences and medialised discourses.

The quote at the beginning of the chapter, in which the male consumer is talking about a television programme on the quality of fish, refers to discourses in the media that question the consumer's fish consumption and suggest that he should change his eating habits in relation to fish. The same type of discourse in the media can be seen in relation to a number of societal food issues: environmental problems, health problems, food safety problems, ethical problems, problems related to cooking skills, and problems of social inequality. The primary message in such media discourses and communication campaigns is that we, as food consumers, ought to change our routines of shopping, cooking and eating in order to act as morally good consumers, who help to solve collective problems in society. We can react in many different ways to the suggestions in this type of media discourse and communication campaigns. We can, for example, comment upon, reflect upon, ignore, discuss, and/or act upon such suggestions for changing our food consumption routines. When we as consumers react in these various ways, we are already interacting with the discourses that contest our food consumption.

Ordinary routinised, unnoticeable consumption activities become normatively[1] challenged as a result of such media discourses (Adams and Raisborough, 2008: 1178; Clarke et al., 2007; Ehn and Löfgren, 2009: 106; Sulkunen, 2009: 8). The whole point of the majority of the media discourses on consumer responsibility is that a large amount of consumption activities ought to be noticed, reflected upon and changed – e.g. into more sustainable, healthy, ethical and safe patterns. The discourses of communication campaigns (Windahl et al., 1992) are meant to make consumers mindful of their unnoticed routines in consumption, although such reflexivity has been shown on many occasions to be both demanding and difficult (Wilk, 2009: 146).

This book aims to show similarities and differences in consumers' handling of such normative challenging of their consumption activities across four specific issues where food habits are being contested through media discourses: the environmental issue, the issue of food safety, the issue of cooking from scratch, and the issue of nutrition.

During the last twenty years, there has been an increased ascription of societal responsibility and agency to ordinary citizens in their capacities as private individual consumers.[2] Expectations as to what ordinary consumers themselves can do to solve societal problems have risen significantly. In public debates, communication campaigns and public policies, consumers are being called upon to help solving a broad array of societal problems. The UN Brundtland Report in 1987 and the following Rio Conference in 1992 framed individual ordinary consumers as

1 I am using the terms 'normative', 'normativised', 'normatively' and 'normativity' instead of 'moral', 'moralised', 'morally' and 'morality' because 'normative' is related to social norms. Social norms are more specific, practical and flexible ways of regulating human conduct than moral values that are often more general and abstract and tend to be treated as more rule-bound (Mortensen, 1992). For example, a moralising discourse in the media would claim that consumers have a co-responsibility for helping to solve the climate problems, whereas a normative discourse in everyday life would suggest practical and socially acceptable ways of acting climate responsibly. In this sense, 'normativity' means practical morality.

2 This is different from the ascription of societal responsibility to consumer organisations and bodies of experts, speaking on behalf of consumers, which began much earlier (see e.g. Chatriot et al., 2006) and is of course still taking place, parallel to the more individualising process focused on in this book.

co-responsible for solving environmental problems (Christensen et al., 2007: 94–95). Max Haavelaar introduced the first Fairtrade labeeling scheme in 1988, presenting ordinary consumers in supermarkets with the choice of ethical consumption (Nicholls and Opal, 2005: 10). The institutional changes in food safety policies in the wake of Europe's hitherto largest food scandal, the BSE crisis, beginning in 1996, led to attempts to involve ordinary consumers in the societal regulation of food risks (Holm and Halkier, 2009). The global so-called obesity epidemic at the beginning of the twenty-first century led to media products confronting ever-younger consumers with discourses about healthy eating practices (Kline, 2005).

The development of ascribing societal responsibility to individual consumers and thereby challenging everyday consumption practices is reflected in the social scientific field. In recent years, a number of international journals publishing about consumers and consumption have devoted special issues to the theme of challenging consumption. The *International Journal of Consumer Studies* published a special issue on political consumerism in 2006, the *Journal of Consumer Culture* ran an issue on ethical consumption in 2007, the *Journal of Business Research* published an issue on anti-consumption in 2009, and *Anthropology of Food* published one on sustainable consumption in 2009.

In the sociology of consumption and studies of consumer culture, this tendency can be observed, for example, in the discussions about the agency of consumers. In 1995, a much-quoted book by Yiannis Gabriel and Tim Lang, called *The Unmanageable Consumer*, discussed different conceptualisations of consumers. The aim of their book was on the one hand to give theoretical importance to an understanding of the concept of the consumer across the various research traditions that tried to make it their own, and on the other hand, to signal something about the unpredictability of processes of consumption (Gabriel and Lang, 1995: 4).

In a recent article, Gabriel and Lang reflect upon this category of the unmanageable consumer and conclude:

> The consumer, then, is unmanageable, both as a concept, since no-one can pin it down to one specific conceptualization at the expense of all others, and as an entity, since attempts to control and manage the consumer result in mutations from a stable consumer concept to an unstable one. (Gabriel and Lang, 2007: 333)

However, they also highlight that in spite of the unmanageability of consumers, concrete consumption activities and patterns are constantly attempted, influenced, managed, controlled, and changed, and they mention environmental problems and demographic problems as legitimate grounds for challenging consumption (ibid.: 335). This type of argumentation brings Gabriel and Lang in line with several other contributions to the field which debate how consumption is a complicated and even ambivalent social phenomenon that cannot be held apart from societal moralisations (Adams and Raisborough, 2008: 1170–71; Wilk, 2001: 253) but needs to be discussed in relation to agency and citizenship (e.g. Boström and Klintman, 2008; Soper and Trentmann, 2008).

In communication and media research, consumers are also seen as communication users, and the main debate has focused on an expansion of the concept of citizenship into a more culturally based understanding (e.g. Dahlgren, 2006; Dodds et al., 2008; Keum et al., 2004), probably because consumption typically is seen as cultural consumption in communication and media research (Storey, 1999; Hermes, 2005). Dahlgren argues that the boundaries between the traditionally differently conceived spheres of society such as the public and the private are fluid, and that understandings of current, more culturally based citizenship must include the everyday life experiences of ordinary communication users: *'In short, to understand the origins of civic competence, we need to look beyond the public sphere itself into the terrain of the private – or expressed alternatively, into the experiential domain of everyday life or civil society'* (Dahlgren, 2006: 276). Contributions that express more scepticism in relation to the agency potential of ordinary communication users and consumers point to the conditions under which it is assumed that such a culturally broader civic engagement is supposed to be carried out (e.g. Phillips, 2000). But it seems to be a shared assumption across the more optimistic and the more sceptical approaches that the development towards expansion of citizenship via consumption and other ordinary life activities is taking place as a kind of social conditioning in itself.

In business studies and marketing, the topic of challenging consumption has been discussed as an additional symbolic dimension of consumer choice (e.g. Aspers, 2008; Belk et al., 2005; Hanpää, 2007; Sandikci and Ekici, 2009), in which the symbolic gratifications and identifications can be grounded for ordinary consumers. The contributions to this discussion have not necessarily involved the potential element of changes of consumer choice. Another type of discussion in business and marketing (overlapping with parts of communication research) has focused more on the element of change. This is the debate about the potentials and pitfalls of social marketing as a strategy for behavioural change (e.g. McKenzie-Mohr, 2000; Peattie and Peattie, 2003; Pechmann and Slater, 2005). Social marketing is the use of marketing methods to change consumer behaviour in relation to a social goal and not a business goal. Reflecting one of the issues of this debate Pechmann and Slater conclude: *'In sum, social marketers should not assume that any message is better than no message. At minimum, messages should be quantitatively pretested prior to airing using methods that are sensitive to adverse effects'* (Pechmann and Slater, 2005: 202). In other words, social marketing can also unintendedly push consumers away from an issue.

Finally, the ascription of societal agency to individual consumers has also become part of political science and policy studies. There are more general conceptual discussions about whether and how activities of individual consumers can be understood as political participation (e.g. Bang and Sørensen, 2001; Michelletti, 2003). There are also a number of contributions where empirical case studies are seen as examples of the politicisation of consumption in as different areas as, for example, public health services, biotechnology and animal welfare (Newman and Kuhlmann, 2007; Schibecci and Harwood, 2007; Wahlström and

Peterson, 2006). Furthermore, consumption activities now form part of standard batteries of questions in surveys about political participation and civil audits (e.g. Goul Andersen and Tobiassen, 2004; Pattie et al., 2003), reflecting that the ascription of political agency to individual consumers is taken for granted on a par with citizens voting and becoming members of organisations.

Why Food?

This book focuses on food as an area of challenged consumption and thus as an example of the development of the discourse. It is necessary to focus on one type of consumption, since consumption is an aspect of nearly all of our activities in modern, medialised, large-scale societies. Food is chosen for two reasons. First, food as type of consumption is a multifaceted phenomenon, which allows for complex analytical discussions about the consequences of challenging consumption activities. We must consume food every day, which means that everybody in society has a vast amount of experiences with this type of consumption. Food provision and eating are intimate bodily sensate activities, during which objects are handled with all senses and taken directly into the body or, indeed, kept out of it (Falk, 1994; Fischler, 1988). At the same time, food, shopping for food, cooking, and eating are highly symbolic activities, interpreted carefully, represented in numerous different ways, and used for social distinctions (Lupton, 1996; Mennell et al., 1992; Warde, 1997). Food is a private matter, often decided upon and carried out by individuals and/or in families and households. At the same time, food is a societal and institutionalised matter, integrated in large chains of production, science, marketing, retailing and public regulation (Kjærnes et al., 2007).

The second reason for focusing on food as an area of consumption is that the discourse of challenging consumption seems to be particularly salient in regards to food. In general, when food at the same time is a bodily-bound, everyday life activity and an institutionalised field in large-scale societies, this suggests the importance of power relations in play and political conflicts about managing the field of food. This has been exacerbated by processes of globalisation and the blurring of boundaries between public and private in the governance of food (Halkier and Holm, 2006; Lien, 2004). Furthermore, food is an area of consumption where there are many obvious examples of groups of consumers themselves stepping into character and taking societal agency upon themselves (e.g. Blue, 2009; Halkier and Holm, 2008; Kjærnes et al., 2007).

Mapping an Analytical Field of Challenged Consumption

The rest of this chapter focuses on mapping the different analytical positions in the emerging research field around societally challenged consumption. It is argued that this emerging field can be mapped around four positions. In the first position, contributors are primarily interested in contributing to attempts to direct and control consumption. In the second and the third positions, contributors are interested in the powers of everyday life agency of consumers, but there seems to be an optimistic as well as a pessimistic version. And finally, the last position tries to strike a balance and underlines the complexities of everyday life agency and the consequences of the development of ascribing societal agency to ordinary consumers.

The primary purpose of this book is – as mentioned earlier – to empirically show the varieties in consumers' handling of such normative challenges to their consumption activities. A secondary purpose is to participate in the social scientific discussions about consumer agency on the basis of theoretically informed empirical analysis. My own empirical analyses in this book are written from a practice theoretical perspective (see Chapter 2) on everyday life and consumption. Thus, the book also serves as a way of discussing the usefulness of a practice theoretical approach in this field. However, this is *not* meant as some puritan theoretical statement on behalf of practice theory. Rather, I see a practice theoretical perspective as merely one of an everyday life analytical family of approaches to sociology of consumption and consumer culture that are capable of analysing some of the current complexities in consumption. This everyday life analytical family of approaches is reflected in the fourth analytical position ('Everyday complexities of consumption') outlined in this chapter, and it is also discussed in its more general version in Chapter 2 under the heading 'Consumption as everyday practices'.

The First Position: Steering Consumers

The main assumption in this position in the debate is that it is legitimate to try to make consumers change their behaviours, because consumers contribute to all sorts of societal problems just by carrying out their daily consumption choices and activities. We drive our cars to work and contribute to climate change. We drink coffee at work and contribute to the socially unequal distribution of resources in the world. We help our daughter buy a birthday present for her kindergarten friend and contribute to violations of human rights in China. We serve ready-made pizzas to our families and contribute to the obesity epidemic. Thus, the aim of most of the analytical contributions in this position is to produce knowledge about the most efficient and the most socially acceptable ways of influencing consumers into changing their behaviours in order to allegedly improve society.

There is a relatively *rationalist informed version* of the steering position. Here, it is analysed empirically how different target groups of consumers perceive and behave in relation to public communication initiatives in the different areas of challenged consumption. There is often a particular emphasis on measuring the relations and gaps between knowledge, attitudes and behaviour among consumers, in line with, for example, the theory of planned behaviour (e.g. Ajzen, 1991; Fishbein and Cappella, 2006), and it is assumed that influencing knowledges and attitudes will have a bearing on behaviour. A typical part of a theoretical section in such contributions follows here: *'The three main determinants of behavioural intentions with relevance to sustainable consumption are values, needs, and motivations, information and knowledge, and behavioural control'* (Vermeir and Verbeke, 2006). The analytical conclusion here is that if we want to know whether and how consumers can act more sustainably, then the key parameters are individual cognitive characteristics such as values, motivations and information.

This rationalistic version is particularly abundant in the areas of environmentally challenged consumption (e.g. Fraj and Martinez, 2007; Hustvedt et al., 2008; Vermeir and Verbeke, 2006) and in risk-challenged consumption (e.g. Frewer et al., 2002; Qin and Brown, 2007). Thus, empirical studies in the rationalistic version of the steering position analyse, for example, conditions for so-called informed choice in relation to food risks (Frewer et al., 2002), willingness among consumers to pay for sustainable products (Hustvedt and Bernard, 2008), the gap between attitudes and behavioural intentions in relation to food choices and sustainability (Vermeir and Verbeke, 2006), and the effects of communication format differences on the learning from information on genetically modified food risks (Qin and Brown, 2007).

A slightly less rationalistic version of the steering position is *social marketing,* as empirical social marketing analyses often involve a stronger orientation towards the perspective of the consumer audiences themselves. Social marketing constitutes a field in itself, and an oft-quoted definition of social marketing is *'the use of marketing principles and techniques to influence a target audience to voluntarily accept, reject, modify or abandon a behaviour for the benefit of individuals, groups or society as a whole'* (Kotler et al., 2002). Social marketing focuses on the methods themselves or the social technologies of attempting to change consumer behaviour. One of these methods is to direct the analysis towards the consumers' own perspectives in order to know how to frame the communication, equivalent to target group analysis conducted for public and private communication campaigns in communication and media research (Windahl et al., 1998). Apart from the orientation towards consumer audience perspectives, principles in social marketing typically include analysis of different types of societal stakeholders and partnerships, as well as a focus on how consumers can maintain behavioural changes (Peattie and Peattie, 2009: 263).

Hence, the discussions about social marketing in relation to changing consumers' patterns of activities reflect upon procedures for influencing ordinary consumers in the overlapping areas of marketing and communication. There are, for example, discussions about the uses of new media technologies (Lefebvre, 2007), about the uses of negative emotional appeals (Brennan and Binney, 2010), and about the potential adverse effects of social marketing – the possibility that consumers will counter-react upon campaigns (Pechmann and Slater, 2005). Thus, there are many examples of the uses of a social marketing perspective in empirical analyses of the potentials for changing individual consumers' behaviour, particularly in the areas of environmentally challenged consumption and health-challenged consumption. Contributions include, for example, analysis of how to enhance the ethical dimension of consumers' motives for buying organic food (McEachern and McClean, 2002), analysis of how consumer science can contribute to developing effective social marketing strategies for sustainability goals (Frame and Newton, 2007; Sibbel, 2008), analysis of the implementation of social marketing strategies in alcohol abuse prevention (Thomas, 2008), in consumption reduction in relation to sustainability (Peattie and Peattie, 2009), in anti-obesity measures in relation to food choice (Piggford et al., 2008) and in nutrition (Bellows et al., 2006).

Participatory involvement is the last version of the steering position. In this kind of analysis, consumers are understood as societal stakeholders for interaction about problem solving. It is typically assumed that a more dialogical and participatory format in engaging and interacting with ordinary consumers as citizens will produce societally more legitimate ways of changing perceived problematic patterns of consumer activities. This type of analysis is particularly influential in relation to issues of challenged consumption where communications of new technologies and science are involved. Here is a typical quote from the theoretical section of such an article:

> We locate this analysis within the frame of efforts to engage citizens directly on issues of technology for policy-making. This process has been referred to as participatory technology assessment, a description that reflects the intent of direct citizen engagement in the policy process (as opposed to the involvement solely of experts). (Einsiedel et al., 2001)

There are examples of overlaps between this type of analysis and social marketing (e.g. Frame and Newton, 2007), but the majority of contributions focus on the variations in types of participatory processes whereby consumers can become actively involved in determining the aims of changing consumption activity patterns. Examples of empirical contributions are analysis of the workings of consensus conferences in relation to food biotechnology (Einsiedel et al., 2001), analysis of social experiments to construct the scientific citizen in the food area (Irwin, 2001), analysis of dialogue as strategy in challenged consumption areas (van der Sanden and Meijman, 2008), analysis of processes of establishing issue-based publics in relation to challenged-consumption issues such as climate change (Featherstone et al., 2009) and analysis of experiments with involvement of consumers in food research funding priority setting (Rowe et al., 2009).

All three versions of the steering position – the rationalistic, the social marketing and the participatory involvement – analyse aspects of how patterns of ordinary consumption activities can be challenged and potentially changed. But the three types of analysis can also be interpreted as directly contributing to the ways in which ordinary consumption becomes challenged from various moral and political issues. Ordinary food consumers point to the huge amount of public and private communication campaigns and citizen involvement attempts as pushing demands for consumer change (Halkier, 1999: 30–32; Halkier, 2001b: 806–10). Although there are big theoretical differences between a rational choice-inspired social marketing approach and a dialogical participatory approach to consumer involvement, both can be said to constitute contributions to the attempts to control and direct consumers by challenging ordinary consumption activities. The question is how consumers react to all these initiatives to make them use their societal agency. The positions, possibilities and conditions for societal everyday life consumer agency are topics for the next section of this chapter.

The Second and Third Positions: Empowering and Disempowering Consumers

Discussions in the social sciences that deal with questions of consumers' own understandings, initiatives and actions oriented towards taking societal responsibilities include the topics of political consumers, political consumerism and political consumption (e.g. Boström et al., 2005; Klintman and Boström, 2006; Micheletti, 2003; Micheletti et al., 2004; Spaargaren and Mol, 2008). The main assumption in these discussions is that particular types of individual consumption activities can be understood as a kind of political participation and therefore analysed as expressions of societal or political agency, similar to studies of voting behaviour, membership of interest organisations, involvement in grassroots movements, and ad hoc bottom-up direct actions. These discussions also parallel what is studied and debated as boycotts (e.g. Friedman, 1996; Greenberg, 2004), ethical consumption (e.g. Belk et al., 2005; Gulyas, 2008; Terragni and Kjærnes, 2005) and the citizenship of consumers (e.g. Holzer, 2006; Stevenson, 2002). The discussions also resonate with a more general level of social scientific theory. Anthony Giddens' concept of life politics (Giddens, 1991: 214–31) argues in favour of seeing individual, practical everyday life choices as expressions of living responsibly towards each other in a globalised world. Ulrich Beck's concept of subpolitics (Beck, 1992: 184–87) argues in favour of seeing ordinary consumers as producing politics from outside of the traditional, formal political channels.

In this framework, consumers who eat organic food regularly, buy Fairtrade products, use collective transportation, and give their old clothes away to recycling are exerting their societal everyday life agency. The concept of agency itself is the subject of a multitude of different debates in different corners of social science (e.g. see Alexander and Seidman, 1990; Archer, 2002; Giddens, 1984; Held, 1987; Hirschman, 1970; Mouzelis, 1995). But in this more specific context of looking at agency in everyday life consumption, the assumptions about agency have mainly evolved around two dimensions: intentionality and autonomy (Halkier and Holm, 2008: 668–69). The first dimension considers whether consumers themselves direct their consumption activities towards some societal responsibility (Dahlgren, 2006: 168–71; Micheletti, 2003: 18–24). The second dimension considers whether conditions of consumers and consumption allow sufficient space for such responsible activities (Bevir and Trentmann, 2008; Boström and Klintman, 2008: 33–45). Taking into account these two dimensions, an optimistic position on consumer everyday agency has developed, followed by its counterpart, a more pessimistic position on consumer agency.

The optimistic version assumes that in general an *empowering of consumers* is taking place. It is argued that the politicisation of consumption constitutes an enhancement of possibilities for democratic participation and influence in society. It is assumed that the recognition of politically and ethically based consumption choices opens a different space for citizens' participation in settings where citizens are already present; that is, in their everyday lives. At the same time, it is assumed that these types of consumption choices carry social responsibility as criteria into the market mechanism, influencing societal solutions in the economy directly without going the long way round through interest organisations, parliament and governmental administration. One of the influential contributors in the optimistic position, Michele Micheletti, defines this type of consumption as 'individualised collective action' in her book *Political Virtue and Shopping. Individuals, Consumerism and Collective Action* (2003). Her working definition is: *'The practice of responsibility-taking through the creation of everyday settings on the part of citizens alone or together with others to deal with problems which they believe are affecting what they identify as the good life'* (Micheletti, 2003: 35). One of the main arguments in relation to consumption agency in the book is that consumption practices can be both individual and collective, because by taking active responsibility for 'the good life', consumers can do something good for themselves at the same time as doing something good for a collective. In other words, public and private virtues are not necessarily mutually exclusive (ibid.: 18–24).

Magnus Boström and Mikael Klintman's book about labelling and so-called green consumerism ends on an optimistic note with regard to how to empower consumers through labelling. Like Micheletti, they do not see the private virtues of consumption as necessarily contradicting public virtues in everyday life. They argue, for example, that the simplicity and categorical character of eco-labelling does not match the reflective capacities of interested consumers, but that it is possible to go further and involve ordinary consumers in discussions about labelling criteria (Boström and Klintman, 2008: 194–95).

Gert Spaargaren shares the optimism of the potential empowering of consumers in his argumentation about the role of domestic consumption in environmental policies (Spaargaren, 2000). Building on a combination of ecological modernisation theory (Mol and Spaargaren, 2000) and structuration theory (Giddens, 1984), he contends that the potential for changing unsustainable patterns of consumption activities in domestic practices such as eating, cleaning and heating comes from involving ordinary consumers in changing their lifestyles. Consumers can participate in forming innovations in the provisions systems for such domestic practices as a kind of 'in-use involvement' (Spaargaren, 2000: 330–32).

The optimistic position of empowering consumers is expressed across a broad range of social sciences. Micheletti, Boström and Klintman, and Spaargaren refer to issues within political sociology. The analytical interests in this field aim to map quantitatively who consumers are as political participants (e.g. Goul Andersen and Tobiassen, 2004); why citizens use their consumption activities to try to influence societal decision-making (e.g. Pattie et al., 2003); and how political consumption activities are related to other important tendencies in politics such as political trust and distrust (e.g. Stolle et al., 2005). They also include specific policy discourses involving elements of political consumerism such as ecological citizenship (e.g. Jagers, 2009; Seyfang, 2006).

The optimistic position of empowering consumers is also represented by contributions that are particularly interested in the existence and diffusion of symbolic and social motives behind consumption choices that can work as driving forces behind ethical and political purposes (Hogg et al., 2009). In her article about anti-consumption discourses Helene Cherrier (2009) argues in favour of the centrality of identity-formation to the development of consumer resistance. A similar type of optimism is found in analyses of a form of consumer activism called 'culture jamming' (Carducci, 2006; Sandlin and Callahan, 2009) where market brands, logos and slogans are publicly deconstructed and rhetorically sabotaged by consumer activists in order to empower individual consumers to consume in more socially responsible ways. A concrete example of this is the well-known case where the sports apparel firm Nike offered its customers the opportunity to order a pair of individually customised shoes, and Jonah Peretti ordered such a pair with the inscription 'sweatshop' in order to protest against the working conditions of the firm, whereby he released massive media coverage on the Internet and elsewhere about Nike and sweatshops (Peretti, 2004).

This symbolically oriented version of the optimistic position mainly draws upon empirical research within marketing and communication research. Empirically, this version of the optimistic position has analysed consumption of organic food (Howard and Allen, 2006), Fairtrade consumption decision-making (Ozcaglar-Toulouse et al., 2006), religiously or nationalistically motivated brand rejection (Sandikci and Ekici, 2009) and branded political communication where well-known logos of goods and services are used in communication campaigns to consumers about various issues of corporate social responsibility (e.g. Bennett and Lagos, 2007).

The question is, however, whether this development of politicising ordinary consumption contributes to a *disempowering of consumers*? This is what the more pessimistic position in the discussions about individual consumer agency would contend. The pessimistic position focuses on the conditions and structuring of consumption and politicised consumption activities, and it is typically argued that the space for action of ordinary consumers is relatively limited or relatively controlled. Analyses inspired directly by a Foucauldian governmentality approach (Dean, 1999; Foucault, 1991; Hewitt, 1991) form a significant part of the contributions within the pessimistic position. Here, attempts to influence consumers to help solve societal problems such as sustainability, salmonella infections, or animal welfare is seen as a way of governing society by making ordinary people monitor and direct their own behaviours, bodies and thinking. Governing societal problems becomes 'the conduct of conduct' (Dean, 1999: 10). Such governing is seen as entailing citizens' controlling, disciplining and normalising their bodily practices in everyday life (Hewitt, 1991: 228–30).

Stewart Lockie reports an empirical study of how ordinary food consumers are encouraged to be involved in local production–consumption networks around organic foods in Australia (Lockie, 2002). His study is based on a governmentality approach combined with actor-network theory. He concludes that the ways in which consumers can influence market provision of organic foods are highly dependent upon the simplistic discursive constructions of what constitutes an organic consumer communicated by the market actors:

> This does not necessarily mean that potential consumers are disempowered and manipulated, but it does mean that despite the much wider consumption base identified for organics through survey techniques, some 'demands' are more visible and more likely to be met than others unless alternative knowledges and projects are brought to the fore. (Lockie, 2002: 289)

In other words, consumers try to exert their everyday life agency in social spaces highly strategically moulded by more powerful actors and relations; thus, consumers are at risk of becoming disempowered because of these strategically controlled framings of the space for action.

Pessimism can also be based on a societal situation of apparent lack of control. Such an argument comes from Pekka Sulkunen, who analyses different policies of prevention of lifestyle diseases in Finland from a Foucauldian perspective (Sulkunen, 2009). He argues that representatives of the public sector attempt both to involve the individual consumer-citizen in taking responsibility for improving their lives, and at the same time try to withdraw from normative responsibility themselves. Sulkunen calls this 'espistolary power' and explains how this consists of governing at a distance:

> Epistolary power shifts moral responsibility from the state to communities and citizens who are expected to operate without a centrally directed plan, to decide what is good for them, under the sole constraint that they should respect other peoples' rights. (Sulkunen, 2010: 8)

Such a situation where consumer-citizens are ascribed with responsibility for disciplining their consumption routines but with hardly any official help from other societal actors constitutes another way in which consumers can become disempowered.

Exactly this mixture of consumer elements and citizen elements in ascribing societal responsibility to consumers has fuelled a conceptual discussion where scepticism is expressed (Holzer, 2006; Stevenson, 2002; Trentmann, 2007; Zukin and Maguire, 2004). Kaela Jubas (2007) argues in her contribution on the basis of feminist theory and critical cultural studies in favour of being sceptical towards the conceptual coupling of consumption and citizenship, because consumption as a type of participation suffers from a severe lack of equality in opportunities, which is supposed to be a central aim of democratic citizenship in general:

> Citizenship remains more than consumption and, as Shiva argues, democratization involves a radical change in capitalist and other exclusionary structures rather than a new, politically charged consumerism. Today, the ideology of consumerism functions to conflate the concepts of consumption and citizenship and capitalism and democracy, as if consumption offered a resolution to social and political struggles. (Jubas, 2007: 251)

The most sharply drawn and well-known representation of this scepticism towards mixing consumer and citizen elements comes from the works of Zygmunt Bauman on consumerism and the 'liquid modern way of life' (Bauman, 2005). In his analysis of current modernity, Bauman depicts a process of individualisation of everyday life turned into living under constant uncertainty and self-reflexivity in order to construct 'do-it-yourself-identities', related to the marketised consumer culture, impinging on every detail of ordinary social living. Here, new social hierarchies of inclusion and exclusion from normality are established, and Bauman suggests that life-long education in citizenship is a necessity to counterbalance consumerism in politics: *'The consumer is an enemy of the citizen ... '* (Bauman, 2005: 126). Thus, including consumerism as part of political or societal participation constitutes disempowering in itself.

Finally, a number of contributions to specific policy fields focus on different conditions that impede upon the potentials for the successful performance of societal consumer agency in everyday life, and through this they contribute to a pessimistic picture of disempowering consumers. Some analyses place a co-responsibility upon consumer sciences and consumption research for establishing alliances with other stakeholders in society to further societal consumer agency, e.g. in the area of sustainability. The argument here is that otherwise the economic and political institutions in globalised societies will form a serious barrier to such agency (Cohen, 2006). A similar argument has recently been applied to communication sciences and communication research in relation to involving consumers in ethical and risk issues in the area of biotechnology (Fennell, 2009), and to so-called post-BSE food issues around risk, environment and ethics. In these discussions, transparency around the conditions of food production through legal frameworks and labelling are seen as key preconditions for consumer agency to be performed meaningfully and successfully (Buttel, 2000).

Are consumers becoming empowered or disempowered by the development of ascribing responsibility to consumers for solving societal problems by changing their own habits? The optimistic as well as the pessimistic positions in the debate about political everyday life consumer agency both put forward reasonable analytical claims about consumer reactions to challenges of consumption and the conditions of such reactions. However, both positions also seem to share one blind spot in their eagerness to assess consumption agency as political participation, societal influence and ethical symbolic motivations. Few of the contributors to these agency discussions acknowledge that domestic consumption activities in themselves are highly complex social everyday phenomena. Thus, it is underestimated how ordinary consumers' dealings with the different medialised normative challenges of consumption are embedded in the complicated configurations of their daily lives. The last section of this introductory chapter provides examples of contributions to the emerging field of handling challenged consumption that take into account the everyday complexities of such normatively contested consumption.

The Fourth Position: Everyday Complexities of Consumption

A number of contributions to the emerging analytical field of consumers dealing with challenged consumption acknowledge the complexities of consumption as everyday life phenomena and seek to unfold both agency capacities and the social conditioning of ordinary consumers in their argumentations and empirical studies. This position in the debate belongs to a broad everyday life analytical family of approaches, where the playing out of social life is understood as compound, conditioned and dynamic (see Chapter 2, Consumption as Everyday Practices). It is also the analytical position to which my own contribution belongs. Here, I will give a few examples of arguments within this position by other researchers before I unfold the main characteristics of my own argument through an outline of the contents of the rest of this book.

To acknowledge the complexities of consumption in relation to normatively challenged consumption activities entails working with an approach that includes and balances the importance of change and reproduction. When medialised discourses represent individual consumers as responsible for reducing their food miles to improve global climate problems, social dynamics in everyday food consumption (such as identification) enable consumers to react in multiple ways and the social institutionalisations of food consumption (such as retail availability) condition how these multiple ways of reacting are configured in people's everyday lives.

Matthew Adams and Jayne Raisborough call this a 'situated understanding of reflexivity' in their study of Fairtrade consumption in Britain (Adams and Rainsborough, 2008: 1169). They argue that ordinary consumers in their everyday lives are capable of reflecting upon their actions, understandings and conditions of these, while at the same time being bound and enabled by such conditions.

> What is demanded as a result is a more 'situated' understanding of reflexivity ... The tendency to separate self-reflexivity processes demeans the complex and ongoing relationship between subjectivity, agency and social structure, particularly as expressed via consumption practices, and provides us with a caricature portrait of the individual as rational actor ... It is scepticism towards

> the extended reflexivity thesis that informs our sociological approach to Fairtrade consumption. (Adams and Rainsborough, 2008: 1169)

Thus, the researchers achieve an analytical perspective that allows for contingent variations in consumer handling of the Fairtrade moral discourses as well as for the more structuralised conditionings of such variations. Their specific theoretical understanding builds upon current attempts to hybridise the theoretical assumptions around the concept of habitus (Bourdieu, 1990) and the concept of reflexivity (Giddens, 1991) in social theory (Adams, 2006).

Other researchers would perhaps describe Adams and Rainsborough's approach as dialectical, insofar as it invokes a mutually dependent relationship between two otherwise polarised or contradicting dynamics. A dialectical approach is used by a number of other contributors with an eye for the complexities of consumption in their analyses (Jacobsen and Dulsrud, 2007; Johnston, 2008; Soper, 2007; Thompson and Coskuner-Balli, 2007). The argument is that a dialectical approach helps avoiding the pitfalls of existing camps in the analysis of consumer-citizens; that is, the optimistic 'empowering consumers' position and the pessimistic 'disempowering consumers' position.

Kate Soper has studied the anti-consumerism phenomenon 'alternative hedonism' in Britain empirically. Alternative hedonism occurs when consumers begin to appreciate the pleasures of public goods and social relationships over private consumer goods. On the basis of this, she claims that 'alternative hedonism' has the potential of making consumption activities in everyday life acquire a citizenship dimension. She points out the weaknesses of both main camps of citizen-consumer research:

> Consumer behaviour that is treated as a matter of existential choice, through the one optic, is viewed through the other, as the altogether less voluntary effect of transcendent economic and social structures and their systemic pressures and forms of social governance. (Soper, 2007: 216)

Josee Johnston researches citizen-consumers' relations with whole foods markets in Canada. Johnston focuses his analysis theoretically on the contradictions of consumer spaces and methodologically through critical discourse analysis. He uses the term dialectical explicitly to describe his approach:

> A dialectical focus helps us avoid naïve optimism, or determinist pessimistic accounts of consumer-focused projects for social justice and sustainability. A dialectical approach recognizes that meaning and agency are present in consumption decisions, but takes seriously the structural conditions shaping consumer agency. (Johnston, 2008: 233)

This explicitness with regards to using the term dialectical also applies to Craig Thompson and Gokcen Coskuner-Balli in their research on uses of organic community-supported agriculture (CSA) in the United States (Thompson and Coskuner-Balli, 2007: 292–93).

In another example of the complexity position, Eivind Jacobsen and Arne Dulsrud from Norway come to a more radical analytical conclusion based on their critical review of the literature on political consumerism (Jacobsen and Dulsrud, 2007). They almost suggest that the field of consumer-citizen research should get rid of what they call 'the generic active consumer model' in which consumers are assumed to be active societal decision-makers and actors. Instead, they propose a perspective that takes into account how consumption is institutionalised interactively through market processes, governance structures, and everyday life dynamics: *'In stead of moralizations over consumers' lacking virtues, what is needed is therefore a renewed ideological debate on private versus public responsibilities'* (Jacobsen and Dulsrud, 2007: 479). This kind of argument resonates with recent comparative empirical results about the social and institutional conditions of consumers' trust in food in six European countries (Kjærnes et al., 2007).

Thus, to acknowledge the complex and compound character of consumption as a social phenomenon is a distinctive feature of the different analytical contributions to this last position in the analytical field of challenged consumption: the 'everyday complexities' position.

The Contents of the Book

In this first chapter, I have argued that there are societal processes taking place by which ordinary individual consumers in media discourses are framed as responsible for helping to solve a variety of political food problems by changing their own consumption patterns. This involves potential contestation of food habits with which consumers are confronted insofar that they live in thoroughly medialised societies. I call these processes the 'challenging of consumption'. The question is how consumers react to and deal with such challenges. There seems to be a rather large and complex analytical field of challenged consumption research, and in Chapter 1, I have mapped this field into four different analytical positions. The first position is called 'steering consumers', where the uniting feature is to assume that it is legitimate to try to direct consumers to change their behaviours. The second position is called 'empowering consumers', and here it is the optimism on behalf of the possibilities for consumer agency that the contributions have in common. The third position is called 'disempowering consumers' and constitutes the pessimistic counterpart of the second position. The last position is called 'everyday complexities of consumption', and the uniting feature is an acknowledgement of the complexities of consumption as a social phenomenon.

As I have explained earlier (p. 6), the purpose of this book is twofold. There is an empirical purpose in demonstrating the multiple complexities in the ways in which contested food consumption is dealt with in everyday life settings. There is also an analytical purpose of contributing to the discussions about consumer agency on the basis of these empirical results. For both of these purposes, a theoretical perspective is needed that is capable of acknowledging the complexities of consumption. The chosen theoretical perspective is a practice theoretical one. Chapter 2 is a theoretical chapter that outlines the development in different theoretical approaches and waves of the social scientific study of consumption and consumer culture. The practice theoretical perspective is described and discussed specifically in relation to analysing everyday dealings with challenged food consumption. Furthermore, Chapter 2 also contains a short section on methodological implications.

The empirical analyses of how ordinary people handle the normative challenges of food consumption are unfolded through four qualitative case studies from Denmark. The Danish cases are relevant in an international discussion of the consequences of ascription of societal consumer agency, because the Scandinavian countries are seen as comparative frontrunners when it comes to attempts to involve the ordinary consumers in politics (Boström et al., 2005: 10; Kjærnes et al., 2007: 188). However, the four Danish case studies are, of course, compared and discussed in relation to the specific international literature in each area. Hence, the bulk of the book consists of four empirical chapters, each dealing with one particular type of challenging of consumption. Chapter 3 deals with environmental contestation of food consumption and how this challenge is handled among young Danes. Chapter 4 covers risk contestation of food consumption and how this challenge is handled among Danish parents with young children. Chapter 5 analyses the contestation of food consumption coming from discourses that equate good food with food cooked from scratch, and how this challenge is dealt with among Danish readers of a particular lifestyle magazine. Chapter 6 looks into nutritionally contested food consumption and how this challenge is handled among Pakistani Danes.

Finally, Chapter 7 constitutes the conclusion to the book. The chapter pulls together the empirical similarities and differences in everyday dealings with contested food consumption across the four areas of challenged consumption. Furthermore, the conclusion sums up the analytical debate about consumer agency, as well as the usefulness and limitations of a practice theoretical perspective.

Chapter 2
Analysing Challenged Consumption from a Practice Theoretical Perspective

How to Conceptualise Consumption?

In the first chapter, it was argued that everyday consumption activities become normatively contested in contemporary societies, because ordinary consumers in medialised discourses are increasingly ascribed with responsibility for helping to solve a large number of societal difficulties, such as environmental and health problems. In this way, otherwise unnoticed routine-based types of consumption activities become potentially noticed and questioned in relation to the medialised discourses. These processes constitute challenges of ordinary consumption. The question is, which reactions to and ways of handling such normative challenges can be found in everyday life?

Using food as the specific area of consumption on which to base the discussion, Chapter 1 presented a mapping of four different analytical positions in the emerging research field around societally challenged consumption and how such processes are handled in everyday life. The first position, 'steering consumers', focuses on how to direct consumers into 'politically correct' changes of habits. The second and the third positions, 'empowering consumers' and 'disempowering consumers', focus on the character of consumer agency, the second being a more optimistic version and the third being a more pessimistic one. The last position, 'Everyday complexities of consumption', acknowledges the complexities of consumption in everyday life and focuses on embracing social conditions and agency capacities in one analytical movement. It is within this last position that the perspective of this book is located analytically.

In this chapter, general analytical approaches to consumption are presented and discussed from the perspective of how challenged consumption in the food area is handled in everyday life. The ways in which recent international overviews (Gronow and Warde, 2001; Paterson, 2006; Sassatelli, 2007; Soper and Trentmann, 2008; Warde, 2002) carve up the field of theoretical approaches to sociology of consumption are remarkably similar to a distinction of three main approaches made in 1990 (Featherstone, 1990) with the addition of a fourth approach, focusing on everyday practices. Thus, the first four sections of this chapter describe these four approaches and position them in relation to everyday handling of challenged consumption. These approaches are: consumption as a function of economy, consumption as a function of culture, consumption as creativity, and consumption as everyday practices.

The discussion of the four general approaches to consumption research is conducted with the purpose of placing the analytical positions mapped in Chapter 1 in a larger social scientific context. Furthermore, this discussion also serves as a way to position the theoretical framework of this book in relation to the trajectories of the general field of social scientific research on consumption and consumer culture. Thus, the first half of Chapter 2 outlines the four general approaches to consumption, while the second half of the chapter introduces the theoretical framework of this book – a practice theoretical perspective – and the analytical and methodological implications of this perspective.

Consumption as a Function of Economy

There are two different approaches to the conceptualisation of consumption as a function of economy. The first of these is the neoclassical understanding of the consumer as a relatively powerful and rational utility-maximising actor, who chooses goods and services on the basis of their needs, the information on the use-value of the goods and services, and their own budget constraints. Furthermore, this behaviour is seen as functional for the optimisation of the relations between supply and demand in the societal economy (Falk, 1994: 106–13; Gabriel and Lang, 1995: 27–28; Sassatelli, 2007: 57–64; Slater, 1997: 61–62).

This conceptualisation dominated the empirical studies of consumption until the end of the 1970s. One of the impacts of this conceptualisation in the studies of consumption has been the broad use of the rational actor-understanding of the consumer outside the fields of economics and marketing. The rational actor-understanding of the consumer has informed a considerable number of studies (Gronow and Holm, 2008), and it plays a key role in one of the versions of the 'steering consumers' position in Chapter 1. One example is the well-known Theory of Planned Behaviour in relation to consumption challenged by environmental, risk and nutrition discourses (Hansen et al., 2003).

The second approach is the critical theory conceptualisation of the consumer as a relatively powerless actor, who is becoming alienated from their authentic material and symbolic needs through the manipulations that producers exert in order to make consumers participate in ever more superfluous material consumption with their habits, choices and interpretations (Featherstone, 1991: 14–15; Gabriel and Lang, 1995: 136; Paterson, 2006: 58–86; Sassatelli, 2007: 74–82; Slater, 1997: 120–30).

This conceptualisation has existed alongside the rational actor-understanding of consumers, and it continues to have influential representatives in the discussions about consumption and consumer culture, although its influence has declined somewhat in recent years (Warde, 2002: 11). Probably the best known contemporary example is the 'McDonaldisation thesis' (Ritzer, 1993/2008), where the main argument is that consumption in modern, large-scale societies becomes homogenised through processes of efficiency, calculability, predictability and control, epitomised in the organisation of the McDonald's fast food outlets.

The position of the individual, ordinary consumer is constructed differently in the two conceptualisations of consumption: as the choosing hero in the rational actor-understanding, and as the dependent victim in the critical theory-understanding. But the two conceptualisations have one assumption in common that distinguishes them from the other three social scientific approaches to consumption. The consumers' activities and interpretations as well as the conditions and possibilities of consumption processes are understood as one-sidedly dependent upon economic rationalities (Sulkunen, 1997: 1). Thus the diversities of social dynamics involved in the constitution of consumption as social phenomenon are neglected.

This construction of consumption as dependent upon economic rationalities can be found in its two different versions in the analytical field of challenged forms of consumption (see Chapter 1). Under the 'steering consumers' position, a significant proportion of the studies on strategic communication to consumers, consumers' behavioural change and social marketing draw upon the rational actor-understanding, contending that consumers will choose 'morally correct' actions if they receive the information required to change their attitudes (e.g. Fishbein and Cappella, 2006; Frewer et al., 2002; Peattie and Peattie, 2009). An example of this type of reasoning would run along the following lines: if accurate knowledge is communicated to consumers about issues such as the climate effects of greenhouse gas emissions from cows, they will buy and eat less beef in order to make climate-friendly choices.

On the other hand, the 'disempowering consumers' position (e.g. Bauman, 2005; Lockie, 2002) presented in Chapter 1 seems to share its pessimism and some of the victim assumptions about consumer agency with the critical theory-understanding of ordinary consumers as dependent and manipulated. From this perspective, the above example regarding the knowledge of the effect of beef consumption on the climate problems would be seen as another way of steering citizens' intimate activities through disciplining their eating on environmentally rationalised grounds.

Consumption as a Function of Culture

This approach covers a range of conceptualisations, which have in common that they recognise consumption as a social phenomenon embedded in cultural dynamics. In comparison with the first approach, this perspective broadens the scope for diversity in consumption processes considerably. Consumers' material and symbolic uses of goods and services are seen as expressing cultural orders and social hierarchies that are reproduced through the specific patterns of their habits, choices and interpretations. Thus, this approach focuses on consumption as part of the demarcations of collective social identities and differences (Featherstone, 1991: 16–21; Gabriel and Lang, 1995: 39, 53,55; Paterson, 2004: 36–48; Sassatelli,

2007: 92–101; Slater, 1997: 153–63; Warde, 1997: 39–41). Classical contemporary representatives of this approach to consumption are the works of Pierre Bourdieu (1984) and Mary Douglas (Douglas and Isherwood, 1980).

The cultural approach has been influential in the sociology of consumption and consumer culture studies since the beginning of the 1980s. In particular, studies inspired by Bourdieu (1984) viewing consumption as reproduced status patterns of taste and lifestyle based on consumers' locations in the social structures related to habitus and forms of capital, have delivered steady contributions to theoretical discussions and empirical research, for example in the area of lifestyle segmentation. A widely discussed contemporary example is the'omnivore thesis' (e.g. Sullivan and Katz-Gerro, 2007) of cultural consumption, which argues that a segment of consumers can be identified in modern, large-scale societies, who gain high social status from engaging in cultural consumption activities that cut across traditionally different socially structured positions.

This approach clearly builds on an understanding of consumption as social and relational. However, the construction of the individual, ordinary consumer tends to underestimate the importance of the active aspects of consumption and position the individual consumer as a kind of victim of conditions. This is related to the conceptualisation of the social elements in consumption processes as dependent on relatively stable cultural structures, but this underestimates consumer agency and social change in consumption processes. This is absolutely *not* to say that all studies based on, for example, Bourdieu can be criticised for underestimating dynamics of agency and processes in consumption. However, there has been a tendency to draw upon the more structuralist interpretations of Bourdieu in this type of consumption studies.

The 'consumption as a function of culture' thinking seems to inspire parts of the 'disempowering consumers' position about challenged consumption outlined in Chapter 1. Scepticism towards consumer agency is a shared concern, and there are parallel theoretical understandings about the degree of structuring of consumption activities and consumer habits. To change the eating habits of groups of ordinary citizens into, for example, less fattening and more nutritious patterns would here be seen to stumble upon the tacit cultural structures governing everyday shopping, cooking and eating (Coveney, 2000; Holm, 2004).

Consumption as Creativity

This section discusses a range of studies which have in common their emphasis on consumers' symbolic agency. From this perspective, the symbolic and pleasurable aspects of consumption are given priority compared to material and practical aspects. Consumers are seen as competent, creative and playful social actors, who possess considerable freedom to engage in consumption activities as well as freedom to interpret and negotiate symbolic meanings of such activities (Featherstone, 1991: 21–26; Gabriel and Lang, 1995: 100–103; Sassatelli, 2007: 80–82; Warde,

1997: 16–17). Classic contemporary representatives of this approach include, for example, French postmodern cultural theory (Baudrillard, 1988; Maffesoli, 1996), British cultural studies and sociology (Campbell, 1987; Hebdige, 1988; Willis, 1990), American consumer culture theory (Holbrook, 1995; McCracken, 1988) and communication theory (Fiske, 1990).

This approach has been influential in the sociology of consumption and consumer culture studies since the end of the 1980s, and the understanding of consumption as individual choice, shopping, self-identity and symbolic bricolage has often been associated with the postmodern strand in social science (Paterson, 2006: 224–30). Consumer culture studies within marketing have been particularly inspired by this approach to consumption (e.g. Arnould and Thompson, 2005; Ratneshwar and Mick, 2005; Rindfleish, 2005; Ventakesh and Meamber, 2008).

The approach represents the bringing in (or bringing back) of the active agency of consumers to the sociology of consumption and the study of consumer culture. However, there is a voluntaristic tendency to exaggerate the freedom for consumers to choose both goods and symbolic meanings in the attempt to take the polysemic character of goods and services seriously, as well as the active character of consumption activities. Here, the construction of the individual consumer resembles a culturalist version of the neoclassical economic understanding of consumers.

A widely discussed contemporary example of this kind of approach in consumption studies is the reference to the concept of 'neo-tribes' (Maffesoli, 1996) for categorising specific groups of consumers (e.g. Cova and Cova, 2001; Johnson and Ambrose, 2006). Neo-tribes are social groups that are based on affections and aesthetical experiences, where the membership is individually chosen, and the collective ties of the group are characterised by dispersed and occasional gatherings. Examples are online communities and pop music fans.

The perspective of 'consumption as creativity' has theoretical assumptions about consumer agency in common with the 'Empowering consumers' position from Chapter 1. Here, challenged consumption forms are seen to create opportunities for ordinary consumers to accomplish empowerment in society on the basis of reflected and creative uses of their own everyday activities (Michelletti, 2003). According to this perspective, consumers can influence food risk policies in society through exercising their shopping choices and symbolically signalling that they do not accept, for example, processed food items with endless numbers of additives in the dinners they serve for their children.

Consumption as Everyday Practices

This last approach includes studies that view consumption as complex practical and symbolic processes, embedded in social and institutionalised contexts. The consumers are understood as socially and practically conditioned active agents who in their consumption activities handle conditions routinely and conventionally on the basis of their experiences. Consumption is seen as the broader uses of goods and services, not just the buying, and the individual consumer is constructed as carrying out these mundane practices in dynamic interdependency with a variety of social relations. Contemporary representatives of this approach are mainly located in European sociology (Bell and Hollows, 2005; de Certau, 1984; Chaney, 2002; Dant, 2008; Gronow and Warde, 2001; Martens et al., 2004; Miller, 1998; Slater, 1997; Warde, 2005).

This approach has been influential in the sociology of consumption and studies of consumer culture since the end of the 1990s. An important aspect of this approach is that it is positioned as different from both the 'function of culture' approach and the 'creativity' approach to consumption. This is expressed clearly by Don Slater in his book *Consumer Culture and Modernity* (1997):

> Consumption, then, is part of the cultural reproduction of social relations, a rather concrete process carried out through social practices in mundane life. This view of things can be mechanical, can imply that consumption is inevitably conformist as well as an agent for ensuring social conformity. Yet precisely because consumption is an everyday practice in which actual social agents skilfully use cultural resources (language, things, images) to deal with their needs, it necessarily involves reinterpretations, modifications, transgressions – and can be used to culturally challenge as well as culturally reproduce social order. (Slater, 1997: 148)

Another programmatic formulation of the approach can be found in the anthology *Ordinary Consumption* from 2001, edited by Jukka Gronow and Alan Warde. The introduction contains a critique of especially the 'creativity' approach to consumption, arguing that empirical research in consumer culture studies has been overly focused on, for example, purchase decisions rather than practical contexts of use, individual choice rather than contextual conditionings, and conspicuous rather than mundane consumption (Gronow and Warde, 2001: 4).

When consumption is understood predominantly as everyday practices, a middle position between optimistic and pessimistic argumentation regarding challenged consumption forms can be obtained (Soper and Trentmann, 2008: 8–13). For example, a reaction to the environmental challenges of ordinary food, such as choosing to eat organic food, can take many different situational and relational social forms at the same time or interchangeably: To act as the protective mother by feeding your young children presumably safer types of food; to indulge in much more tasteful kinds of dishes; to show friends how politically responsible you are; to use routinely what is available in your local supermarket; to consume nostalgically the same type of food that your grandmother picked in her garden and preserved; to fit socially into the lunch table interactions at work, etc.

At the same time, this food consumption is conditioned institutionally by the configuration of market and public structures, the different organised actors in the food sector, and the variety of medialised discourses on food (Kjærnes et al.,

2007): This includes, for example, which varieties of food are available through which types of market outlets; which types of public food control are working; which types of food labelling schemes are used; how different food issues are framed in the multiple medialised communications about food, etc.

The general everyday practice approach to consumption is able to embrace multiplicities and ambivalences of consumption processes, which is necessary when analysing consumption as cultural contestation processes in modern medialised societies. The empirical analyses in this book draw upon a particular version of the everyday practice approach, and it is to this theoretical framework that we now turn.

Practice Theory

The analytical perspective to consumption taken in this book is a practice theoretical one. Practice theory is not a coherent theory; rather it aims to develop a synthesis of elements in existing sociological theories in order to obtain a new analytical perspective on the constituting and conditioning of micro-processes in social life. The focus of practice theory is – not surprisingly – practices.

The international efforts to synthesise practice theory involve a particular reading of an assembly of theoretical elements concerning social practices, mainly drawn from early Pierre Bourdieu (1990), Judith Butler (1990), late Michel Foucault (1978), Harold Garfinkel (1967), early Anthony Giddens (1984), and Bruno Latour (1993). In the rest of this section, the general practice theoretical understandings from the synthesising attempts of Andreas Reckwitz and Theodore Schatzki are outlined.

Positioning Practice Theory among Cultural Theories

The sociologist Andreas Reckwitz (2002: 247–49) most strongly positions practice theory in relation to other grand theoretical ideal types of positions within cultural theory. Practice theory is, first, seen as different from what is labelled *cultural mentalism*, where the social is placed in mental repertoires of actors' consciousness and in mental activities such as common understandings and assumptions. Social life is understood as primarily connected to sense-making processes. Phenomenology can be seen as an example of cultural mentalism. Phenomenological studies are often preoccupied with analysing social actors' intentional interpretations of meaning in their life experiences (e.g. de Certau, 1984; Luckmann, 1989; Schütz, 1975).

Secondly, practice theory is seen as different from *cultural textualism,* which places the social outside of actors in larger chains of signs, symbols, language and discourses. Social life is understood as primarily connected to structures of meaning external to the social actors (in contrast to cultural mentalism). Various types of social constructivist and post-structuralist approaches can be seen as examples of cultural textualism in the sense that they primarily focus on how the social is expressed discursively (e.g. Fairclough, 1992; Foucault, 1972; Hall, 1997; Laclau, 1996; Luhmann, 1995; Phillips and Jørgensen, 2002).

Thirdly, practice theory is seen as different from *cultural intersubjectivism,* which places the social in the symbolic interactions between social actors. Thereby, actor subjectivity is recognised (in contrast to cultural textualism) but in a relational manner (in contrast to cultural mentalism). Reckwitz uses Jürgen Habermas' (1984; 1987) theory of communicative action as the most important example of cultural intersubjectivism. Habermas' version of an interaction approach focuses on formal language and the uses of different types of rationalities. In this way, Reckwitz delimits practice theory from social interaction approaches, but he seems to be doing so on the basis of a critique of one specific and narrow approach to interaction, namely the Habermasian one. Other types of approaches to social interaction (Berger and Luckmann, 1966/87; Goffman, 1967) are much less focused on language and include a broader range of social dynamics. I will return to this discussion about the social interaction element in the section on applying practice theory to consumption.

Reckwitz summarises his positioning of practice theory by highlighting where the social is *not* placed: *'Practice theory does not place the social in mental qualities, nor in discourse, nor in interaction'* (Reckwitz, 2002: 249). This brings him to the positive definition of practices and social life in practice theory:

> A practice … is a routinised type of behaviour which consists of several elements, interconnected to one other: forms of bodily activities, forms of mental activities, things and their use, a background knowledge in the form of understanding, know-how, states of emotion and motivational knowledge. A practice – a way of cooking, of consuming, of working, of investigating, of taking care of oneself or of others etc. – forms so to speak a 'block' whose existence necessarily depends on the existence and specific interconnectedness of these elements, and which cannot be reduced to any one of these single elements. (Reckwitz, 2002: 249–50)

In other words, social practices should be understood as configurations of bodily and mental activities, uses of things, knowledge (in the broadest sense) about activities, and emotional forms. Examples of social practices are working, transporting, eating, dancing, gardening, parenting, political participation, etc.

Reckwitz emphasises that all these different elements that go into the carrying out of practices are equally important, and they are mutually interdependent upon each other as elements of the organisation of a practice (Reckwitz, 2002: 250). This equality and mutual interdependence between the different elements of practices is why this theoretical thinking can be said to work with a multi-relational perspective on activities in social life.

Developing Micro-level Practice Theoretical Concepts

The philosopher Theodore Schatzki (1996; 2001; 2002) has developed his contribution to practice theory based on the work on practices and language games from the late work of Wittgenstein, but with clear references to a number of the sociological grand theory roots to practice theory, including early Bourdieu, Butler, late Foucault, early Giddens and Latour. Where Reckwitz is concerned with positioning practice theory in relation to other grand social theory perspectives, Schatzki is concerned with developing and fine-tuning the basic theoretical concepts. Schatzki defines a social practice in the following way:

> As indicated, practices are organized nexuses of actions. This means that the doings and sayings composing them hang together. More specifically, the doings and sayings that compose a given practice are linked through (1) practical understandings, (2) rules, (3) a teleoaffective structure, and (4) general understandings. Together, the understandings, rules and teleoaffective structure that link the doings and sayings of a practice form its organization. (Schatzki, 2002: 77)

The most basic assumption is that practices consist of combinations of sets of 'doings' and 'sayings', in which the bodily and material as well as the discursive parts of social action are equally included. As in Reckwitz' emphasis of multiple related elements in social practices, Schatzki also conceptualises practices as blocks of activities, dependent upon a variety of social forms to organise these blocks (Schatzki, 2002: 71, 77–86).

The two types of understandings within practices are divided into practical understandings and general understandings. The practical understandings come close to Bourdieu's concept of the practical sense (Bourdieu, 1990: 66–75) and to Giddens' concept of practical consciousness (Giddens, 1984: 5–14), i.e. practical knowledge and know-how. General understandings, on the other hand, are not only part of organising one kind of practice, and they seem to be slightly more explicit. Rules are explicit principles, definitions, procedures and instructions on how to do activities. Teleoaffective structures are a kind of open emotional and normative orientations for activities. Pervading the entire conceptualisation of practices as nexuses of actions is also the emphasis of the importance of the bodily and material elements in human agency, in continuous dialogue with Latour (1993) and the actor-network concept of actants (object-agency).

Another way in which Schatzki refines the conceptualisation of social practices is by defining how to distinguish one practice from another. The boundaries for each practice are constituted by the elements in the organising nexus:

> It is important to emphasize that the organization of a practice describes the practice's frontiers: A doing or saying belongs to a given practice if it expresses components of that practice's organization. (Schatzki, 2002: 87)

Part of this description of practices is also a distinction of several levels in which practices are done (Schatzki, 2002: 73–74). Practices consist of concrete activities (doings and sayings). For example cooking as a practice entails numerous concrete activities, such as shopping for milk, asking your spouse to take meat out of the freezer, rinsing vegetables, and putting bread in the oven. Groups of activities are labelled tasks, and in the case of cooking practices, one of the tasks is usually to produce a whole meal for the family to eat. Combinations of tasks within the same type of practice can form a project. In relation to cooking practices, one project could, for example, be to attempt to cook as many of the meals from scratch as possible.

Finally, Schatzki also distinguishes between different types of practices. Integrative practices are the complex kinds of practices described above, where multiple dynamics form the organisation of carrying out these practices, and the practices are grounded in some particular field of the social sphere, such as cooking practices, transportation practices, teaching practices etc. Another type of practices are dispersed practices, which cover only one type of action that is typically a part of other practices, e.g. describing, following a rule, sitting, answering, moving things, etc. (Schatzki, 2002: 88).

These two efforts to create a distinct approach out of the existing practice theoretical elements operate at a high level of generality, meaning they can be used for studying any kind of social practices.[1] The next section deals with the efforts to translate practice theoretical assumptions into a sociology of consumption. Briefly stated, the positioning of practice theory in relation to other approaches in social theory both fits and does not fit the everyday consumption approach. Practice theory can be distinguished from theoretical 'textualism', and this parallels the 'consumption as everyday practices' critique of the critical theory approach to consumption as well as the structuralist cultural approach to consumption. However, when practice theory is distinguished from theoretical 'mentalism', this critique can be aimed both at phenomenological studies in sociology of consumption as well as motives-based marketing research in consumer culture studies. Thus, a practice theoretical angle on consumption is narrower than the 'consumption as everyday practices' approach, due to specific analytical capacities in relation to studying consumption. It is to these capacities that we now turn.

---

1 There are of course other types of practice theory that I do not describe and discuss in this book due to the limitations of space but also for the sake of upholding the main line of argument. One example is the explicitly critical realism debate about practice theory (Archer, 2002; Gronow, 2008) and another example is the critique of practice theory from advocates of methodological individualism (Turner, 1994; 2001).

Applying Practice Theory to Consumption

In contemporary European sociology, practice theory and how to construct operative concepts in relation to consumption are discussed intensely (Burgess et al., 2003; Christensen and Røpke, 2005; Gram-Hansen, 2007; Halkier, 2006; Hargreaves et al., 2007; Helle-Valle, 2009; Mäkela and Timonen, 2007; Masullo, 2009; Shove, 2003; Shove et al., 2009; Shove and Pantzar, 2005; Southerton et al., 2004; Truninger, 2009; Warde, 2005).

Alan Warde (2005) constructs an overview and argumentation for the use of practice theory in the sociology of consumption. Specifically, he suggests an analytical translation of the concepts of practice from Reckwitz and Schatzki into the empirical study of consumption. Warde's goal, however, is not to argue for a homogenous practice theory. Rather, the purpose seems to be to show how an everyday life-oriented sociology of consumption can improve its conceptualisations and empirical analyses by using practice theory to inform its analyses of how consumption is organised and carried out. Following this, his definition of consumption becomes highly processual:

> I understand consumption as a process whereby agents engage in appropriation and appreciation, whether for utilitarian, expressive or contemplative purposes, of goods, services, performances, information or ambience, whether purchased or not, over which the agent has some degree of discretion. (Warde, 205: 137)

Warde argues that one of the consequences of analysing consumption through practice theory is to *not* see consumption as a practice in itself, but rather to see consumption as an element that forms part of almost any type of practice in our modern societies (ibid.: 137). This way of conceptualising consumption turns the idea of motives, wants and choices as preludes to consumption activities that is assumed in so many studies of consumer culture completely around: instead, it is practices that generate wants and occasions for choice. The question is whether this radical conceptualisation of consumption fits every type of consumption. I will return to this discussion in the next section of this chapter, where a practice theoretical perspective in relation to challenged consumption is unfolded.

Warde translates Schatzki's social philosophical concept of practice and the elements that organise a practice into sociological thinking, which makes the concept of practice slightly more manageable in relation to empirical research. Warde clarifies the concept of practice as constituting a nexus of practical activity and its representations (doings and sayings), which become coordinated by understandings, procedures and engagements (Warde, 2005: 134). Understandings are the practical interpretations of what and how to do; knowledge and know-how in a broad sense. Procedures are instructions, principles and rules of how to do. Engagements are emotional and normative orientations related to what and how to do. If we combine this analytical translation with Reckwitz's multi-relational understanding of practice, each of the three elements that coordinate practices

– both understandings, procedures and engagements – comprises both tacit as well as discursive processes, and they cover both bodily as well as mental processes. For example, eating practices such as the lunch activity of grabbing a sandwich on the way, are organised by understandings of eating (e.g. food is fuel for the body), by procedures for eating (using take-away, not sitting down) and by engagements in eating (e.g. to get it over and done with).

I want to highlight two more characteristics of Warde's practice theory perspective on consumption that have important consequences for empirical analyses of consumption processes. Both of these characteristics demonstrate how focus in a practice theoretical analysis of consumption is on the social dynamics, i.e. neither on the individual nor on the collectively structured.

The first characteristic is that practices at the same time are both coordinated phenomena and performed phenomena (Warde, 2005: 133–35). That practices are coordinated means that the different constitutive elements (understandings, procedures and engagements) relate systematically to the activities (doings and sayings) and to each other within a practice and organise the practice. In the above example of eating practices, the lunch activity of grabbing sandwiches on the way is systematically linked to the content of, for example, the procedures of using take-away and not sitting down. This activity is also linked systematically to an engagement in getting the eating done, and not necessarily an engagement in the pleasures of eating. Thus, the grabbing of sandwiches on the way activity is part of carrying out eating practices, because this lunch activity is fitted together by basic constituting elements that belong to eating practices.

That practices are performed means that practices come into being in the processes of activities carried out in front of, together with, and in relation to others. Everyday practitioners socially recognise a certain way of carrying out a practice (such as cooking) by experiencing the processes of performing cooking and connecting these to the coordinating elements (understandings, procedures and engagements that are done and said). Understandings of cooking go together with procedures for how to cook and engagements in cooking in order to know that now it is cooking that takes place. At the same time, everyday practitioners would not be able to recognise a practice (such as cooking) if this practice was not regularly performed by practitioners together with other practitioners. For example, to make porridge for breakfast, people have to have heard about it or seen it done in order to place it as a breakfast cooking activity. They will also have to have seen it done or participated earlier in order to make the porridge themselves without burning it in the bottom of the pot and thus to make edible or even tasty porridge. So, for cooking practitioners to know the details of the flow of cooking conduct, such flow of activities must be shown and shared socially as performances. The characteristics of a particular practice, such as cooking, are the qualities of the routinely repeated and performed activities and their coordinating elements, rather than the qualities of the individual cooking practitioner.

In my view, this underscores the importance of social interaction, which Reckwitz discards from practice theory a little too rashly. Social interaction does not necessarily have to be understood as exchanges between individually experienced intentionalities or linguistic symbolic interactions, but can instead be understood as productive habitual social processes.

The second characteristic that demonstrates the focus on the social in using practice theory to analyse consumption is the incorporation of dynamics and innovations in practices. Particularly interesting here is the concept of 'trajectories' of practices through time and space, and the concept of practitioners at intersections of multiple practices (Warde, 2005: 139–45). The ways in which particular practices (such as cooking and transporting) are carried out can potentially be changed through small adaptations, negotiations, improvisations and experiments, which happen in the trajectories of the practical performances of activities. For example, cooking is done in different ways when people move in with a partner, compared to how they cooked when living alone. A classic example is a woman who begins to include more meat in her dishes when moving in with a male partner. These trajectories of practices are at the same time interdependent with larger historical and institutional dynamics, such as technological and product innovations, organisational regulatory developments, and shifts in media discourses (Shove, 2003). For example, ways of cooking are also adapted to the supply of processed foods in supermarkets and to advice on healthy eating on Internet websites.

Likewise, each individual participates in a plethora of intersecting practices – for example, working practices, parenting practices and relationship practices – which necessitate planning, timing, scheduling, flexing and improvising in order to be carried out. In other words, coordinating between practices (and not just coordinating each practice) is an important part of everyday life (Shove, 2009: 27–28). When practitioners attempt to coordinate different practices, the expectations and conventions of performing each practice can challenge each other. This is because the different practices are not necessarily organised by understandings, procedures and engagements that fit together across practices. For example, the intersection of working practices and parenting practices often create dilemmas for the individual, because understandings and procedures for timing can be very different in the two kinds of practices. Parenting practices revolve around being attentive with the child, no matter how much time it takes, whereas working practices often involve hurrying in order to keep schedules. Thus, the placing of the individual practitioner in the intersection of many different practices can also bring about changes in practices.

In sum, consumption processes seen through the lenses of practice theory carry the following theoretical or analytical assumptions: first, consumption is understood as a part of all types of integrative practices, and therefore practices generate consumption. For example, parents of young children usually need to either carry or to buy little snacks on trips with the children, so the practice of family trips generates certain types of food consumption. Second, since the activities (doings and sayings) of practices are coordinated by understandings, procedures and engagements, consumption is also an element of these coordinating dynamics. For example, depending on the type of engagement in food practices and family trip practices, the snacks can be of many different types, such as sausages bought on the spot, fruit from the supermarket, home-made buns, etc. Third, to recognise a practice and its moments of consumption, the coordination of the doings and sayings must become regularly performed by you, for you, with you or in relation to you. For example, going on family trips for the first couple of times, parents usually realise by watching or interacting with more experienced parents that providing food snacks is a part of performing family trip practices properly. Fourth, consumption activities are entangled in the trajectories and multiple intersections of different social practices for the individual. For example, the provision of food snacks for the family trip might very well have to be timed and carried out in conjunction with working, transporting, parenting, and relationship practices.

A Practice Theoretical Perspective on Analysing Challenged Consumption

In the last two sections of this chapter, I will outline how I use practice theory in analysing consumers' dealings with challenged food consumption in their everyday lives. The first section focuses on the theoretical use, the second on the methodological implications.

In my own use of practice theory, I draw primarily upon the conceptualisations from Warde that are discussed in the previous section. I also combine Warde's concepts with the arguments from both Reckwitz and Schatzki about an equal and mutual interdependence between the different elements that form practices. This combination enables a practice theoretical approach to focus on the recurring performing and accomplishing of social-life acting and the multi-relational configurations in which performing and accomplishing of acting take place.

I see such a practice theoretical approach as a distinct perspective for empirical analysis. Hence, the purpose is *not* to contribute to a development of a coherent theory of practice, but rather to use and discuss the analytical, empirical capacities of this distinct, analytical approach. Due to the relative openness of this analytical perspective, with its point of departure in the multi-relational character of the dynamics and conditions of practices, it is possible to combine the practice theoretical perspective with other field-relevant theoretical concepts and knowledges as long as they are coherent with the main practice theoretical assumptions.

Everyday Life Analysis without Privileging Phenomenology

With a practice theoretical perspective, it is possible to conduct empirical everyday life analysis without privileging phenomenology. A practice theoretical perspective facilitates a focus in empirical research on the doing and carrying out of practical dealings with food activities in everyday life without necessarily privileging intentionality and meaningfulness, which most phenomenologically inspired everyday life studies of food tend to do, including studies of contested food – be that from environmental, risk or nutrition perspectives (e.g. Chaney, 2002; Halkier, 1999; 2001b; Holm and Kildevang, 1996; Lupton, 1996). In these studies, too much importance is placed on the mental dynamics of social life.

From a practice theoretical perspective, the acquisition of food, cooking food and eating food must be carried out, produced and performed through practical food agency in order to be recognised as shopping, cooking and eating. This does not necessarily mean that food practitioners interpret their doings and sayings as subjectively meaningful and intentionally oriented towards particular purposes. For example, a significant part of people's routine doings in shopping and cooking are carried out habitually with no specific intention or meaningfulness other than 'to go on' practically and socially. What this does mean is that it is an empirically open question whether specific food practices are understood as meaningful or can be interpreted as comprising intentionality. The analytical difference is between approaches where intentionality and meaningfulness are treated as firm theoretical assumptions and approaches where intentionality and meaningfulness are open empirical questions for research.

The current discussions in the sociology of food suggest that this empirical openness is required since the empirical research points to a plurality of overlapping practitioner understandings of shopping, eating and cooking with very different levels of engagement. Cooking can, for example, be understood as a necessary chore and eating as something that is merely done to obtain 'fuel' for other activities (Lupton, 1996: 40, 143–44), thus something you do 'to go on'. Shopping and cooking can be seen both as routine work (Beagan et al., 2008), low in meaningfulness, and as skilled practices (Short, 2006), rich in meaningfulness and intentionality. Cooking and eating can be understood as meaningful family integration (Holm, 2004: 22–24; Moisio et al., 2004: 265–67) and as a pleasurable pursuit (Hollows, 2003; Murcott, 2000).

The variety in levels and types of understandings and engagements in food activities discussed in the literature indicates a range of possibilities for how consumers deal with food consumption in areas of challenged consumption. Consuming organic food, for example, can potentially be related to each (or several at the same time) of the above types and levels of engagement, such as necessary routines, skilled activities, connecting the family, and enjoying food. But at the same time, this food activity will be entangled in all the other little understandings, procedures and conditions of food practices and the intersections of food practices with other types of practices. Thus, consuming organic food can very well in some cases be oriented intentionally towards influencing the market situation politically, as the optimistic 'empowering consumers' position (see Chapter 1) on political consumerism would claim. But this is an empirically open question. A practice theoretical perspective implicates analytical openness towards different ways of handling contested consumption processes in a complexity of conditions, rather than privileging particular types of conducts beforehand.

Consumption as Part of Practices or as a Practice in Itself?

Although I agree with Warde's conceptualisation of consumption as an aspect of every type of practice rather than as a practice itself, I believe that this conceptualisation would benefit from being laid open to empirical diversity or exceptions. Based on the wide variety in, for example, levels of engagement in food consumption, one might argue that some ways of handling challenged consumption are very different in their social forms from more ordinary consumption activities. If this is the case, such ways of handling challenged consumption could perhaps be understood as practices in themselves. One of Warde's arguments for not conceptualising consumption as a practice in itself is that most consumption takes place without being noticed as consumption (Warde, 2005: 150). But the whole point of the media discourses that ascribe societal responsibility to consumers is to make consumption routines become noticed as consumption, thereby making them open for revision. So it might make analytical sense to think of some types of consumption as practices in themselves, if the consumption activity is performed and recognised as a specific practice in empirical social life.

When consumption of food becomes challenged – be that on environmental grounds, on food risk grounds or on nutritional grounds or other grounds – it is usually happening interdependently through media discourses in the public sphere and interpersonal communications and negotiations in everyday life situations and settings (see Chapter 1). The media discourses are capable of 'framing' (Benford and Snow, 2000) particular food consumption patterns as practices. In Denmark, for example, 'organic consumption' or 'nutritionally correct consumption' are society-wide circulating associations to particular, socially recognisable bundles of activities (doings and sayings) (Halkier and Holm, 2008; Holm, 2003b). Likewise, certain practical versions of organic consumption or nutritionally correct consumption can for some everyday food practitioners reach a high level of normative engagement (Halkier, 1999: 31–32; Holm and Kildevang, 1996: 8) and become a project in the Schatzkian sense within the performing of the food practices. For example, if organic consumption begins to involve many activities and tasks related to understandings of organic food as superior, related to shopping and cooking procedures using organic food, and related to an explicit engagement in persuading others to taste organic food, then this type of performance of organic food consumption resembles a project.

So although I adhere in general to the conceptualisation of consumption as an aspect of integrated food practices, I would like to reserve an opening for discussing empirically in the chapters to follow whether there are exceptions regarding some types of handlings of challenged food consumption.

Social Constructivism without Privileging Discourse

With a practice theoretical perspective, the researcher is able to work as a social constructivist but without privileging discourse as most social constructivist approaches typically do (e.g. Burr, 1995; Phillips and Jørgensen, 2002; Polkinghorne, 2007; Potter, 2007). Social constructivism directs analysis towards the potential instability and multiplicity of social categories and dynamics. With the tendency to privileging discourse and discursive practices, however, the danger is that food turns into text (see e.g. Ashley et al., 2004: 2–8; Newman and Gibson, 2005; Hollows, 2007).

Eating, cooking and acquiring food are definitely not an established set of activities. It is all the time practically done, re-done and slightly differently done, even in the most habitual ways of tossing vegetables into a pot or preparing lunch bags for the children. But the production and performing of food practices are carried out through tacit procedures involving body, food and tools (Holm, 2004; Martens and Scott, 2006; Murcott, 1983; Short, 2006). Perhaps food activities are even to a larger degree characterised by implicit understandings and procedures than by food practitioners reflecting and talking about food, eating, acquiring and cooking. Hence, it is important to put appropriate emphasis on body and materiality in the empirical analyses in the obviously body-focused field of food consumption, where food is handled with all senses and many body parts and movements, and food becomes directly incorporated into the body by eating (Falk, 1994; Fischler, 1988; Lupton, 1996; Warde, 1997). A practice theoretical perspective integrates bodily procedures and relations with materiality into its social constructivism. At the same time, a practice theoretical approach diverges from approaches that ascribes independent agency to material objects (Schatzki, 2002: 108–11, 191).[2]

So when food practitioners deal with challenged consumption, the diversities and dynamics in their behaviour are linked to both bodily and mental procedures. Likewise, when consumers deal with contested food, they are doing it under material as well as discursive conditions. For example, to include risk challenges to food in the acquiring of apples for a cake could involve both routinely 'checking' the surface of the apples by looking, sniffing and touching and at the same time reflecting upon mediated knowledge about pesticide residues in fruit. This suggests that doings and sayings among food practitioners who deal with contested food consumption cannot easily be categorised; neither as exclusively bodily or mental, nor as exclusively stable or dynamic.

---

2 An influential example of such an approach is the actor-network theory (Latour, 2005). Here, non-human objects are recognised and analysed as equal participants in networks, and the non-human objects are conceptualised as 'actants' in the networks just like human actors.

Agency Processes Instead of Actor Choices

Using a practice theoretical perspective in relation to challenged food practices enables the researcher to focus at the flow of happenings and processes of agency as both conditioned and constituting. Theories of agency and practice are often occupied with handling the apparent contradictions of choice and determination analytically (Wilk, 2009: 147). The practice theoretical perspective enhances the ability of empirical analysis to focus on the complexities of the social flow of practically performed provisioning, cooking and eating, rather than individual consumer choices about shopping, food and meals. This way, the individual consumer actor is not privileged as in the 'consumption as creativity' approach.

Instead, the individual food practitioner is seen as a carrier of practices and a crossing place for a plurality of practices (Reckwitz, 2002: 256), as explained in the earlier section on Warde's 'translation' of practice theory into consumption research. The agency-capacity in being able to deal with issues of challenged food could, for example, be seen as part of the daily manoeuvring between food practices and other practices in the social organisation of time and space, such as parental practices, work practices and transportation practices (Bove and Sobal, 2006; Kristensen and Holm, 2006; Beagan et al., 2008). For example, how can an evening meal for the children in the family be made more nutritious on a weekday, when there is only one parent present, the other parent has the car, the carrots and tomatoes have gone rotten, and the supermarket is beyond walking distance? Often, agency in food practices will be characterised by practical and social 'do-ability',[3] and a practice theoretical perspective allows analysis of the processes and diversities of do-abilities in relation to challenged food consumption.

In the same manner, food practitioner agency is dependent upon the practitioner trajectory in time and across social spaces. For example, a newcomer practitioner of less unhealthy cooking will have less routinised understandings and procedures to fall back on in order to obtain flexibility in activities and tasks. An experienced practitioner usually draws upon a larger and more diverse repertoire of do-abilities.

Furthermore, it should not be overlooked that the agency in food consumption processes is carried out on the conditions of larger institutional dynamics of food consumption, such as how the whole supply-side of food production and retailing is working, how the national and transnational public regulations are organised and implemented, and how these private and public dynamics are interrelated (Kjærnes et al., 2007; Lang and Heasman, 2004; Marsden et al., 2000).

---

3 Do-ability means what it is possible to do and how it is possible to perform in the carrying out of practices. I use the term in an attempt to catch mundane processes of conditioning the performing of practices.

Performing Normativity Instead of Expressing Values

By using a practice theoretical perspective in relation to challenged food practices, the researcher is able to analyse the processes of normativity[4] – the practical morality – in everyday practices, rather than mapping expressions of individual mental moral values and lifestyle attitudes as the cognitivist 'steering consumers' position (see Chapter 1) and the 'consumption as creativity' approaches would do.

The practice theoretical foregrounding of the performative – the processes of carrying out basic activities – in social life enables the empirical analysis to look at the unfolding of acceptability and normative expectations of proper, practical food conduct. When normative doings and sayings in practices are performed, it means that the normative is being constructed in the social processes and thereby not pre-formed by values, rules or structures (Sjørslev, 2007: 14). What does it mean to engage in 'environmentally friendly food shopping', 'safe cooking' or 'healthy eating'? What kind of food is appropriate for which kind of context? How nutritious does a meal have to be if you are serving is as a dinner for other people's children? How homemade does a meal have to be in order to count as being made from scratch? How risky can the food be that you allow yourself to eat in the company of colleagues? In this sense, normative regulation of consumption moments in food practices is a continuous practical and discursive accomplishment among food practitioners as they play out and negotiate normatively acceptable and expectable conduct. This is in contrast to seeing the handling of normatively challenged consumption as a static measure of particular normative intentionalities, expressions and actions, as the 'steering consumers' position (see Chapter 1) tends to assume. At the same time, the performative angle on the normative highlights the need to acknowledge the importance of social interaction in a practice theoretical perspective.

This way of conceptualising the actualisation of normativities in practices parallels the arguments and analyses made from intersectionality approaches (West and Zimmerman, 1987; West and Fenstermaker, 1995), also within the discussions about practice theory (Butler, 1990). In intersectionality approaches, the main theoretical assumption is that social categories are contextual activities and not essential attributes (Moloney and Fenstermaker, 2002: 194). Social categories

---

4 I am using the terms 'normative', 'normativised', 'normatively' and 'normativity' instead of 'moral', 'moralised', 'morally' and 'morality' because 'normative' is related to social norms. Social norms are more specific, practical and flexible ways of regulating human conduct than moral values, which are often more general and abstract and tend to be treated as more rule-bound (Mortensen, 1992). For example, a moralising discourse in the media would claim that consumers have a co-responsibility for helping to solve the climate problems, whereas a normative discourse in everyday life would suggest practical and socially acceptable ways of acting climate-responsibly. In this sense, 'normativity' means practical morality.

– such as gender or consumer – are constantly performed and re-performed through reproductions, adaptations, improvisations and experiments of what, for example, women or consumers do. We cannot know what it is to be female or to be a consumer without analysing how femininity or consumption is carried out in relevant interaction in social practices and contexts. This argumentation is ethnomethodologically inspired, and thus this type of analysis uses the expressions to 'do gender' or to 'do difference'. This way of conceptualising the normative as performative is paraphrased in the headlines of the conclusive sections of the four empirical chapters of this book.

There is a complex theoretical debate about the performative, which is beyond the scope of this book. However, two related issues in the debate are particularly relevant for a practice theoretical perspective on the normative. First, Judith Butler's use of the concept performance is being criticised for making the performance concept too focused on the discursive elements of social acting (Schatzki 2002: 49, 233). Thereby, the embodied elements of processes of acting become underplayed. Second, Butler is also criticised for leaning too much towards a dramaturgic metaphor in her performance concept (Moloney and Fenstermaker, 2002: 203), which gives performance an overly active and extraordinary character for everyday life activities. But Butler and those who build on her concepts claim that what is needed is to distinguish between performance and performativity (Gregson and Rose, 2000: 441; Salih and Butler, 2004: 344–45). Performance is here seen as the concrete doings and sayings of and among individual subjects, while performativity is seen as the enabling and conditioning processes of such social acting. This way of distinguishing between performance and performativity fits other practice theoretical assumptions, e.g. about agency processes. Performance and performativity must be understood as mundane and embodied as well as discursive in order to make sense in the area of food practices.

Summary

In this section, I have outlined the analytical potentials in using a practice theoretical perspective for analysing challenged consumption. First, it enables the researcher to perform everyday analysis without privileging phenomenological assumptions about intentionality of action. Second, a practice theoretical perspective enables the researcher to work with a social constructivist view, but without privileging discourse in relation to performances of practices. Third, the researcher gets to focus on the complex flow of agency processes instead of actor choices. Finally, the researcher is enabled to analyse performings of normativity instead of expressions of values.

Methodological Strategies

In this last section of the theoretical chapter, I will outline a couple of possible methodological consequences of using a practice theoretical perspective in empirical studies of everyday life processes around contested food consumption. I am not suggesting that the following issues are the only methodological implications that could be drawn from using practice theory in empirical social scientific studies. Nor am I claiming that these methodological issues belong to or are unique for working with practice theory. I am merely pointing towards particular connections between theoretical understandings and methodological procedures that are relevant in order to understand the analyses of the empirical data in the four main case studies of the empirical chapters. Finally, I describe the concrete methods of data analysis for the empirical case studies and a motivated structure of the analysis.

Methodological Implications

One methodological implication has to do with the relationship between theoretical assumptions and data design. It is not necessarily only qualitative methods that could be applied using practice theory. But a practice theoretical perspective tends to lead to an interest in detailed observations, descriptions, interpretations and reflections about social processes, and this is where qualitative methods hold their absolute strength (Silverman, 2006). Since practice theory foregrounds the performativity of social processes, research questions will typically focus on how certain processes of acting are embarked upon, carried out, carried through, reproduced, changed and abandoned. My main working research questions in the four empirical case studies have been along the following lines:

- What kinds of specific food practices are carried out by the participants?
- Which understandings, procedures and engagements do participants draw upon in performing food practices?
- Which doings and sayings are related to normatively contested food-consumption issues and in which ways are they related?
- Which understandings, procedures and engagements are employed in performing handlings of normatively contested food consumption?
- Which normatively contested food consumption activities are parts of the food practices and in which ways?
- How are issues of normatively contested food consumption negotiated socially?

An abductive methodological design (Blaikie, 1993) makes analytical sense when using practice theory, because abduction allows the researcher to work with sufficiently flexible relations between the theoretical elements and the empirical elements in the study. Abduction combines openness to empirical complexities with explicit and revisable theoretical concepts.

This combination in abductive research strategies enables the researcher to clarify which analytical elements are theoretical assumptions and which elements must be held open for empirical questioning. In my own empirical case studies, for example, I assume that the participants deal with normatively contested consumption as a part of their mundane performativity, i.e. practices are carried out in enabling and conditioned multi-relational social processes. At the same time, I am open to empirical questioning and description as to whether and how the participants in the case studies express reflection as part of these processes. This is done in data production as well as in data analysis.

Another methodological implication deals with how methods for data production are viewed. The practice theoretical assumption about the performativity of social life parallels some of the attempts to dissolve or sophisticate the firm distinction between interview data and participant observation data (Atkinson and Coffey, 2003) that are going on within the social constructivist or perspectivist (Polkinghorne, 2007) parts of the qualitative methods discussion.

Atkinson and Coffey make a case against the traditional attempts within anthropology and qualitative sociology to privilege one data production method (participant observation) over the other (interviews). The traditional preference for participant observation data rests on the assumption that participant observation somehow gives direct access to action, whereas interview data only give access to accounts about action. Atkinson and Coffey contend that it is not at all straightforward to observe what goes on in social situations and events, and that participant observation data are just as entangled in social interpretations as interview data. They also contend that the interaction and communication that take place in interviewing are expressions of action. This is based on the constructivist assumption that methods of data production are co-constitutive of the knowledge produced. Thus, Atkinson and Coffey argue that participant observation and interviewing both can be seen to generate social action. Finally, they suggest focusing on the ways in which different contexts of data production form different kinds of social actions performed.

Atkinson and Coffey conclude that it becomes possible to see all types of accounts as well as events as 'enactments' (social acting) of social life: both participant observation data and individual interview data can be seen as social practitioners' performances in different contexts. I would add that the same can be said about other types of qualitative data as well, including focus groups, other types of group interviews, diaries, auto-photographs, etc. (Halkier, 2010). In the main empirical case studies, I have used a combination of individual interviews, family interviews, focus groups, participant observation and auto-photography. I have treated the expressions in the different data materials as expressions of social action; however, social action enacted in different social spaces.

A third methodological implication from using a practice theoretical perspective has to do with how to generalise on the basis of qualitative data analyses

(Blaikie, 1993: 176–81; Kvale, 1996: 223–34). In social scientific analytical generalisations on the basis of qualitative data, the researcher makes theorised claims about the patterns of categories and dynamics of the material (Halkier, 2003: 115–16). Due to the small samples in qualitative studies, it does not make analytical sense to try to make theorised claims about patterns of distributions of the individual participants as it is done in statistical generalisation made on the basis of quantitative data.Nevertheless, it is often seen in publications based on qualitative data that a quasi-quantitative language is used in reporting on data patterns, and that methodological individualism forms the basis of, for example, ideal types.

The agency understanding in practice theory enables the researcher to focus on the ways in which social processes are played out in complex contexts, so the importance of the individual is played down relative to the carrying out of practices, while it is still possible to describe and analyse individual conduct. Thus, the methodological generalisation will focus on the patterns in the enacted social processes, rather than the patterns of the individual person (or the patterns of determining structures). None of my own empirical ideal typologies in the four case studies are based on methodological individualism. Each ideal typical way of handling challenged consumption represents patterns across expressions of several participants. Likewise, each participant's doings and sayings may reflect different ideal types of food practices in different contexts and situations of their everyday lives.

To summarise, three methodological strategies are related to my use of a practice theoretical perspective: to work with an abductive empirical design, to acknowledge that all types of qualitative data generate social action ('enactments' or performances), and to avoid methodological individualism in data analysis and analytical generalisations.

Structure of the Empirical Analysis

The specific data analysis for each of the four main case studies consists of a combination and interaction of four elements. First, I have used the working research questions (see outline p. 39) to direct the analysis. Secondly, I have used a range of the more empirically applicable basic concepts from practice theory such as doings, sayings, activities, understandings, procedures, engagements and performances (see definitions pp. 29–31). Third, I have used qualitative coding, categorising and domain analysis (Coffey and Atkinson, 1996) for the content dimensions of the data materials. Fourth, I have used a number of tools for the social dynamics dimensions of the data materials – especially positioning analysis (Harré and Langenhove, 1999) – that deals with how social interaction processes reproduce and change the content of subject-positions in a social field (e.g. a field of normatively challenged food consumption). For the case studies in Chapters 5 and 6, I have also used visual data analysis techniques (Hurdley, 2007), since the data include photos.

The empirical analysis of the Danish case studies is presented in Chapters 3 through 6. The structure and purpose of each analysis are outlined in the following.

First, each analysis describes and categorises the specific types of food practices that are carried out among participants[5] in each of the case studies. These types are constructed by using the applied concepts for the organising elements of performing practices: activities (doings and sayings), understandings, procedures and engagements. The first step is to describe the food practices, because food practices can be characterised as integrative practices. Integrative practices are complex practices, organised through multiple dynamics and grounded in a particular field of the social; in this case, food. The carrying out of such integrative practices is seen theoretically as a basic constitution of social life. The purpose of this first part of the analysis is to understand the basic configuration of which food consumption is already a part (namely, the food practices), in order to be able to qualify inferences later in the analysis about the ways in which people react to getting their food consumption questioned.

Second, the analysis describes and categorises the different ways of handling normatively challenged food consumption in an ideal typology. The typology is constructed by analytically treating the activities (doings and sayings) enacted in relation to handling contested food consumption *as if* they were potentially activities in performing a practice, using again the applied concepts for the organising elements: activities, understandings, procedures and engagements. Hence, the significant differences in the participant expressions of the practice organising elements are used to distinguish the types in the ideal typology. For example, which engagements seem to go together with which procedures? However, it is an open empirical question whether a type of handling normatively challenged consumption can be understood as constituting a practice in itself, or whether such a handling type should be seen as a more partial kind of performance. The purpose of this second part of the analysis is twofold: first, to demonstrate the variety in reactions to the medialised contesting of consumption. The second purpose is to discuss when everyday life performing constitutes integrative practices and when it does not. If practices are seen as the most basic ways that social life unfolds, then performing that constitutes integrative practices will probably have priority in people's busy daily lives. The result of such discussions could influence the social scientific debate about consumer agency in society and its potentials for stability and change.

Third, the analysis 'zooms in' on the details of how contested consumption activities are performed by focusing on the practical procedures. For each of the empirical case studies of contested food consumption, one relevant field-specific procedure discussion is chosen on the basis of the unique empirical data, as well as in the context of current international literature in the field. The applied concepts

5 The participants in each of the four Danish case studies have been given pseudonyms in order to preserve their anonymity.

from practice theory (practices, activities, doings and sayings, understandings, procedures, engagements and performances) are used in connection with each of the field-specific procedure analyses. The purpose of this third part of the analysis is to highlight the significance and complexities of the practical do-ability involved in everyday reactions to challenged food consumption. This analysis can be used to question assumptions about the primacy of normative engagement in handling normatively contested consumption, whether this engagement is seen as coming from some individual mental capacity or from collectively structured discourses.

Fourth, the analysis gives examples of negotiations of the normative engagement in contested food consumption and how the negotiations reproduce, adapt, change, improvise and experiment with the normative content of three kinds of normative issues. The first issue is agency of ordinary consumers, the second is construction of an important category of the field (e.g. 'organic food' for environmentalised consumption), and the third issue is conditions for exceptions to normatively appropriate conduct. The examples are analysed using the concept of the normative as performative and the methodological tool of positioning analysis.[6] The purpose of this analysis is to show how social interaction is part and parcel of everyday life reactions to contestations of routines. Another purpose of this analysis is, therefore, to discuss the balance between an individual life-world focus and a focus on social processes in other kinds of empirical everyday life analysis in consumption research.

6 Positioning theory works with a concept of agency fairly similar to a practice theoretical one (Davies and Harré, 1999: 35). Positioning is a particular kind of social construction in interaction whereby subject-positions are reproduced or changed. Also, the content of these social constructions cover identification and normativity at the same time (Langenhove and Harré, 1999: 17). Positionings can be e.g. self-positionings, other-positionings and positionings of specific social categories.

Chapter 3
Dealing with Environmental Challenges

Supporting Sustainability?

In this chapter, the first empirical case study of challenged ordinary food consumption is discussed. This particular type of challenge comes from the planned communication initiatives and medialised discourses that frame ordinary consumers as co-responsible for the environmental problems inherent in the modern systems of production and consumption of food (Binkley, 2003; Boström and Klintman, 2008; Dobson, 2003; Goodman and Redclift, 1991; Kolandai-Matchett, 2009; Macnaghten and Urry, 1998; Spaargaren, 2000). Since the end of the 1980s, the mainstream environmental political agenda has changed in a number of European countries in the wake of the UN Brundtland Report and the 1992 UN Rio Summit (Boström and Klintman, 2008: 22–24; Christensen et al., 2007: 94; Niva and Timonen, 2001; Seyfang, 2006: 384; Tukker et al., 2008: 1143). The environmental agendas moved away from seeing environmental problems as pollution problems with technical solutions for which producers and public authorities were responsible, towards seeing environmental problems as complex global problems in need of multiple types of strategies, and for which everybody is potentially responsible, including the ordinary citizen-consumers (Spaargaren, 2000).

The more focused discursive expressions of this were public campaigns and environmental labelling that were launched to inform and encourage the ordinary citizen-consumer to engage in environmentally friendly consumption, at first primarily in the areas of energy saving and recycling (Christensen et al., 2007: 94–95). At the same time, handbooks for consumers were also published, such as the British book *The Green Consumer Guide* (Elkington and Hailes, 1988).

The Danish Context

In Denmark, a Danish version of the green consumer guide was published in 1992, *The Little Green One* (Hansen, 1992), alongside other handbooks on how to live in a more environmentally friendly way such as *The Environmentally Friendly Household – What Shall I Choose?* (Danmarks Naturfredningsforening, 1989), *Against Poison* (Grøn Information, 1995) and *Protect the Environment – and Save 23.600 kr. Every Year* (Lund and Grandjean, 1997). During the 1990s, environmental labels on food and non-food staples were implemented along with other initiatives to enable consumers to act in more environmentally friendly ways. In Denmark, a state-controlled label for organic goods was established in

1991, and the Nordic environmental label for non-food staples ('The Swan') and the European equivalent ('The Flower') were adopted in the 1990s along with mandatory energy labelling on electrical appliances and homes (Christensen et al., 2007: 95). Furthermore, several publicly funded but independent information centres for consumers on environmental issues in relation to their everyday lives were established.

The mainstream retail sector has integrated environmentally labelled goods since the 1990s. For example, Coop-Denmark was the first supermarket in Denmark to sell organic food in 1993. In the food area, but also in other consumption areas, there are many more organic and other types of environmentally labelled goods in different product groups to choose from in mainstream retail outlets today compared to ten years ago (Jensen et al., 2001; www.ecolabel.dk). This, of course, changes conditions for handling environmental issues in food consumption, providing more access and more complexity for ordinary food consumers. On Coop-Denmark's current (January 2010) website, they frame themselves as environmentally responsible through several means. For example, the website has a whole menu on societal responsibilities (including environment and ecology, climate, health, ethics and quality), where the individual consumer is invited to join under the slogan: 'We do what we can. Do you want to join us?' (www.coop.dk).

Environmentally friendly consumption has also become an integral part of official Danish policies (Christensen et al., 2007: 96). Environmentally friendly consumption is now called 'sustainable consumption', which reflects the development in international organisations such as the OECD (Seyfang, 2006, 384), UN (Tukker et al., 2008: 1143) and EU (Nash, 2009). The latest example of this in Denmark is the webpage of the Consumer Agency under the Ministry of Economics and Business. One of the main menu entries is 'sustainability', and here the ordinary citizen-consumers can click their way into practical 'how-to-do' advice on sustainable consumption activities in relation to all the major consumption areas of everyday life, including food (www.Forbrug.dk/baeredygtig). Recent research results from a comparative study of the discursive construction of the food consumer in different European countries (Halkier et al., 2007: 389) suggest that in relation to environmental issues, there seems to be consensus among different organised actors in the Danish food sector that ordinary consumers are co-responsible for solving environmental problems. So the societal legitimacy of constructing ordinary consumers as having environmental agency seems to be broader than ten years ago. This changes the conditions for social interaction involved in handling environmental issues in consumption by constructing 'to do sustainable consumption' as fairly common.

The most recent representative data on Danish consumers' handling of environmental challenges in their everyday lives indicate that 6 out of 10 Danish consumers buy environmentally labelled goods, and that the national consumption of organic food has increased by 77 per cent from 2004 to 2007 (Forbrugerstyrelsen, 2008). Compared to figures from other European countries, Danish consumers claim one of the highest frequencies of buying eco-labelled goods (Eurobarometer, 2008: 33).

Current Studies

The current social scientific literature about the role of the consumers in green consumerism and sustainable consumption roughly falls into three categories. First, there is a group of publications that tend to assume that ordinary food consumers acquire, cook and eat food on the basis of more or less rational reflections and decision-making. Therefore, enhanced levels of knowledge about the global connections of sustainability and positive attitudes towards eco-labelling, organic food, food miles etc. should lead to lower levels of unsustainable food use and larger levels of more sustainable food use. Some of these studies claim to show such connections empirically, e.g. a Spanish quantitative study of how environmentally friendly attitudes are connected to buying organic food and food in recyclable containers (Fraj and Martinez, 2007).

However, a majority of these studies report and lament a lack of cognitive behavioural connections (e.g. Aarset et al., 2004; Kilbourne et al., 2002; McDonald et al., 2009; Thøgersen, 2006; Thøgersen and Ölander, 2003). A French qualitative study reports that the participant consumers ignore information on food miles in relation to their food consumption (Sirieix et al., 2008). A Scottish quantitative study concludes that broader groups of consumers must be educated about the societal benefits of organic food, since they are buying it out of self-interest and not to improve the environmental conditions (McEachern and McClean, 2002). A Swedish quantitative study also finds a larger representation of so-called egotistical motives in eating organic food (Magnusson et al., 2003), and a Polish empirical study of the Integrated Product Policy in the EU[1] argues that consumption patterns ought to be guided by 'reason' (Kronenberg, 2007: 565). Analytically these types of publications have a lot in common with the literature that was grouped under 'steering consumers' in Chapter 1.

Another group of studies build on less cognitivistic and more social relational assumptions about food consumption and environmentally friendly activities. This research tends to focus on how to group and categorise food consumers in relation to how environmentally friendly or sustainable their lifestyles and consumption activities are. Thus, segmentation of populations of consumers is at the heart of this group of research, and there are parallels to and roots in the second wave of researching consumer culture (see Chapter 2), where social structures and social distinctions are seen as the most important shapers of consumption activities. Examples are a study that analyses which segments of consumers in Spain are willing to pay more for organic food (Sanjuan et al., 2003), a study describing consumer segments in France that value organic food above fair trade food (Didier

1 The Integrated Product Policy is an emerging policy framework in the EU that is based on a life cycle approach and thus includes consumption as well as production.

and Sirieix, 2008), and a Finnish study that identifies a large segment of the food consumer population as favouring environmentally labelled packaging (Rokka and Uusitalo, 2008). There is also research where already established categories of social groups are used for segmenting consumers in relation to environmentally friendly consumption activities such as demographics in Australia (D'Souza et al., 2006), lifestyles in Finland (Hanpää, 2007) and gender in Spain (Ureña et al., 2007).

The last type of current studies is a broad group of empirical studies which assume that food consumption activities are embedded in social relations and societal conditions; therefore, how consumers relate to sustainable consumption activities is characterised by ambivalences, mixed multiple conditionings and social interactions. Some of the studies explicitly discuss issues of environmental consumer agency and are thus related to the 'empowering consumers' position in Chapter 1. Other studies focus on demonstrating the complexities of the everyday life dynamics involved in trying to consume more sustainably. They have this research focus in common with the sociology of consumption approaches that are grouped under the heading of 'consumption as everyday practices' (see Chapter 2).

In their book about environmental labelling and green consumerism, Boström and Klintman (2008) discuss qualitative case studies of green consumerism, including a comparison of labelling and consumption of organic food in Sweden and USA. The authors emphasise the complexities and ambivalences of the ways in which food consumers handle environmental issues in their daily lives, and they admonish researchers and policy makers not to underestimate these complexities through a simplistic view on consumers and consumption when including consumer agency into environmental policies. One of their main conclusions about environmental consumer agency is: *'All our research behind this book has led to our final claim: that the production of tools for green political consumerism does not adequately correspond to the hopes, thoughts, uncertainties, ambivalence and reflective capacity of the "typical" concerned consumer'* (Boström and Klintman, 2008: 194). A parallel argumentation is made on the basis of a British qualitative study of consumers' sense-making of organic labelling (Eden, 2009). Here it is suggested that food labels be seen as boundary objects that work as an interaction tool between producers and consumers in order to avoid framing consumers as lacking knowledge and resources in consumer information.

In a similar vein, other researchers warn against underestimating the complexity of consumption and overestimating the potentials of individualised green consumer activities in relation to influencing the outcomes of environmental policies. Based on a case study of the community-based strategy for sustainable consumption, LETS (Local Exchange Trading Systems), in the UK, Briceno and Stagl contend that *'The disregard for social processes in research and policy effects jeopardises the achievements that can be made in the direction of sustainable consumption'* (Briceno and Stagl, 2006: 1541). Likewise, Pedersen warns against over-individualising environmental responsibility, based on her study of Danish consumers' involvement in a range of different environmentally friendly consumption activities, including the use of organic food (Pedersen, 2000: 208). Also in the area of marketing, the number of such admonitions is growing (Moisander, 2007).

The studies that focus on the complexities in everyday life dynamics of green consumption activities tend to emphasise how the social embeddedness of food and other ordinary practices creates ambivalences in relation to the environmentalisation of consumption, but also how the same social relations are part of learning how to live with such ambivalences. A Belgian qualitative and quantitative study of residential energy consumption concludes that consumers normalise ambivalences between environmentalised understandings of their energy consumption and unsustainable energy practices by compartmentalising (separating) them in the practical and social flow of daily life (Bartiaux, 2008). Likewise, a qualitative Irish study of green consumption, focusing on recycling and food, argues that ambivalences and dilemmas arise in everyday life as environmentally friendly consumption activities are embedded in important social relations that carry other priorities than improving the environment (Connolly and Prothero, 2008: 125–29). Similarly, a British study of people living a 'voluntary simplicity' lifestyle, which involves cutting down on material consumption, concludes that the practical carrying out of voluntary simplicity is complicated and multi-relational (Shaw and Moraes, 2009).

The Danish case study of environmentally challenged food consumption that is the focus of this chapter falls in to the category of this third group of studies.

The Danish Case Study: Environmental Challenges to Food Consumption

The empirical project on which this chapter is based is called 'Environmental consideration among young food consumers' (Halkier, 1999).[2] The research is a qualitative in-depth study of how young Danes experience and negotiate environmental considerations in relation to food consumption. The sample of nine young people aged 18 to 21 displays a variety of gender, social background, educational level and geography. One part of the qualitative data in the study was produced through individual interviewing and re-interviewing (Spradley, 1979) about the young participants' life stories, their everyday lives, their food, and their attitudes to environmental issues. Another part of the data was produced through focus group discussions (Morgan, 1997) on what consumers should do about environmental problems, and whether the individual consumer should care about the environment. The participants of each focus groups consisted of the young person already individually interviewed and members of her or his social network. The data analysis reported in this book is based on a combination of qualitative coding, categorising and domain analysis (Coffey and Atkinson, 1996),

2 The study was financed by a Ph.D. scholarship from Department of Environment, Technology and Society, Roskilde University.

and methods for analysing interaction, mainly positioning analysis (Harré and Langenhove, 1999).[3]

There is, of course, a question of historical contextualisation when re-analysing data that are 10 years old. This is one reason the introductory section of this chapter contains a brief sketch of some relevant developments in the Danish environmentalisation of consumption. The two main relevant changes that have occurred since the data were produced are the mainstreaming of organic food in the retail sector and the normalisation of the consumer agency issue in public policies and debates.

The presentation and discussion of the Danish case study on environmentalised consumption follows the form for all four empirical chapters, outlined in more detail in the general methodology section (see last section, Chapter 2). The following briefly summarises this outline.

First, the analysis describes and categorises the specific kinds of food practices that are carried out among the young Danes. This is done in order to understand the basic configuration of which food consumption is already a part; namely, the food practices. This lays the groundwork for inferences later in the analysis about the ways in which people respond to having their food consumption questioned.

Second, the analysis describes and categorises the different ways of handling environmentalised food consumption in an ideal typology. The purpose of this second part of the analysis is twofold: first, to demonstrate the variety in reactions to environmentalisation of consumption; second, to discuss when everyday life performing constitutes a practice in itself and when it does not, in order to contribute to the discussions about societal consumer agency.

Third, the analysis 'zooms in' on the details of how environmentalised consumption activities are performed by focusing on the practical procedures. The purpose of this third part of the analysis is to highlight the significance and complexities of the practical do-ability involved in everyday reactions to challenged food consumption.

Fourth, the analysis gives examples of negotiations of the normative engagement in environmentalised food consumption and how the negotiations reproduce, adapt, change, improvise and experiment with the normative content of three issues: agency of ordinary consumers, the category of 'organic consumption', and exceptions to appropriate 'green' conduct. The purpose of this analysis is to question the balance in current everyday life analytical research of challenged consumption between an individual life-world focus and a focus on social processes.

3 Part of the data in this chapter was originally analysed and presented 'differently' in B. Halkier (1999). Consequences of the politicization of consumption: The example of environmentally friendly consumption practices, *Journal of Environmental Policy and Planning*, 1, 25–41.

Food Practices

One of the basic assumptions in Alan Warde's practice theoretical approach to sociology of consumption is that consumption cannot be seen as an integrated practice in itself, but that practices – such as food practices – inevitably entail getting involved in consumption activities. If this assumption is accepted, then it is necessary to begin the analysis of how young Danes handle environmentalised consumption by describing the food practices that become potentially challenged by this environmentalisation. Thus, this first section describes the variation in food practices among the young participants in the Danish case study.

Food Practices as Necessity

This type of food practice is mainly coordinated by necessities. The main understanding is that it is necessary for the person or the household to get something to eat, and thus it is necessary that somebody provides these meals. Providing and eating food have to be manageable, and the activities are manoeuvred in relation to all the other practices of a busy everyday life, such as (particularly for this age group) work practices, socialising practices and leisure practices such as sports. Here is a quote from a young woman about cooking and eating when she is very engaged in sports practices: *'I am a bit like my mum, it has to be a bit quick, we just have to get something to eat'* (Anne, female clerk apprentice). Only major shopping is planned, and often cooking is done on the basis of experimenting with what is already in fridge, freezer and cupboards. Food and eating is mainly understood as fuel (Lupton, 1996: 143–44) that keeps you going in order to do all the other things in your life, and how this eating takes place is less important. One of the participants puts it this way:

> When I come home I make something … I do a lot of potatoes and gravy, and some kind of meat. But I eat rice, noodles and spaghetti as well, that depends on what I feel like and how tired I am, whether I can take the trouble to do it. It depends very much on that. (Nis, male unskilled worker)

Shopping and cooking are primarily understood as necessary everyday chores just like other everyday routine chores. The engagement in this type of food practices is thus primarily linked to practical do-ability, which is here voiced by one of the young women: *'Not particularly varied and not particularly healthy, it's mostly just something to be done with, we don't think especially about what we eat, it's more determined by the price and how long a time it takes to make'* (Lena, female home care).

Food Practices as Pleasure

For this kind of food practice, pleasure is a crucial aspect of the coordinating elements of the practice: the understandings of food, the procedures for handling food and the engagements in food. Cooking is mostly done on the basis of what the practitioner feels like eating on that particular day and which food is found in cupboards, fridge and freezer, including leftovers. Shopping is done without a plan for specific meals but in order to have storage of food with which to improvise cooking and eating (Moisio et al., 2004: 374–75). One of the participants describes it in this manner:

> Yesterday, we had our old favourite meal, hotch-potch … it's an easy meal. Because you mix everything, and it has no character of its own, because you stuff it with spices, so you cannot tell the difference between a celery and a carrot, but you know … it was a good meal. (Helga, female unemployed worker)

Eating is understood as a pleasurable and cosy activity that can also be exciting when new food and meals are tried out and tasted. One of the young women expresses this understanding here: *'Yes, I think its cosy if I have guests to go about cooking some delicious meal and serving it nicely, or if I am visiting someone who likes to eat and cooks food made with feeling, I like that'* (Sonja, female postwoman).

Sharing meals with a partner, family and friends is attempted as much as possible in the intersections with other practices, and this relates to the understanding of cooking as a fun activity that is done together with family and friends. Engagement in this type of food practice seems to be linked to obtaining flows of pleasant experiences through food activities, whether these are performed together with members of the social network or not, as in this last quote:

> I try to make it a good experience every time I eat, if that doesn't sound too rosy, but again to vary things a bit and to get some … things on top that taste good. Instead of butter under the cold cut on rye bread,[4] I try this fat you can get, and I know that sounds terrible in the ears of a health-fanatic, but anyway it gives a different flavour under the 'rullepølse' [5] with raw onion and jelly … so I think you might as well make it taste nice and enjoy it instead of just quickly swallowing it. (Jens, male agricultural student)

4 Rye bread with cold cuts and spreads is the traditional and most common Danish lunch.

5 Rullepølse is a type of rolled sausage made from pork belly meat.

Food Practices as Health

This kind of food practice revolves around 'doing healthy' by using procedures and products that are constructed as healthy, such as, for example, low-fat products, organic products, and cooking your own meals from scratch:

> Everything must be rinsed very thoroughly before I eat it, because I don't know what they have sprayed it with. From oranges to carrots to apples, everything must be rinsed, because you can't count on anything. You don't know what's genetically manipulated and what's not. I take care to rinse what I buy and try as far as possible to buy organic, so I can count on the animals to have had a good time or the vegetables to have grown in earth that's not too pervaded. (Sonja, female postwoman)

Shopping is done every other day, but a supply is kept from which to graze on snacks or compose meals that are considered relatively healthy. Here, one of the young women talks about food that she and her flatmate always make sure to have:

> We both like – now that sounds oh so sensible – but we both like, you know, healthy food. Of course we also like to run amuck now and then and buy candy, and we always have thin slices of chocolate for sandwiches, right? But we like that there is fruit in a basket that you can go and pick from. And we like that there are vegetables in the fridge and cheese and cold cuts and such things. And we also like to pay more for something with less fat in it. (Signe, female high school student)

Food and eating is viewed as contributing to the protection and well-being of the body (Holm and Kildevang, 1996: 8). Cooking is viewed as an activity that results in well-being, both in terms of the procedures as well as in terms of the results. The engagements of this type of food practice thus revolve around variations over doing good for yourself and others as eaters. One of the young men puts it like this:

> I need fibre. Like those in pasta and potatoes. You have to eat lots of those if you look at dietary advice. And I do eat a lot of this through pasta. And then rye bread, there are many fibres in that, and that's also healthy for the body, it takes a lot of waste products from everything else and washes it out. (Anders, male university student)

Food Practices as a Project for Changing the World

All the coordinating elements of this type of food practice – understandings, procedures and engagements – seem to include conscious and socially proactive reflexivity in relation to food activities. The main understanding is that food activities and the consumption implied in these can be used to improve the world in different (but to the practitioners relevant) ways. Eating, cooking and providing food is performed in various manners, but the doings of the food activities are typically reflexively restricted by particular sayings that link them across different everyday contexts of social space and time. Thus, food activities are restricted by understandings of and reflections upon what is better food – such as, for example, nutritionally correct food, animal welfare ethical food, organic food and high-quality food. Food activities are also restricted by what is constructed as better ways of providing food and meals – such as, for example, shopping in small, local shops, shopping as little as possible, and eating out at small, ethnic restaurants. One of the young men puts it like this:

> It's not very fashionable to say that you are materialistic. I think you spend a lot of time thinking about that, right, your image, that you must not be that consumer-pig you have seen images of with a giant shopping trolley, crammed with goods. (Morten, male employed in supermarket)

Food, eating, shopping and cooking are all understood as means of signalling engagement in changing the world, and the engagement of this type of food practice revolves around politicising food. In practical terms, this is done through the specific food activities of the practitioners themselves. But it is also done through using opportunities in social interaction with friends, family and colleagues in every day life to involve them in discussions about how to change their own food consumption patterns: *'Yeah, at least they always get a kick, for example if they have bought milk that's not organic, with such things that are so easy to get hold of. So in that way, we talk about it ... '* (Morten, male employed in supermarket).

Connections Between Food Practices and Handling of Environmentalised Food Consumption

Perhaps it seems simple to hypothesise about which types of food practices among the young Danish consumers open up for particular types of handling of environmental issues in consumption. Some types of handling are already described as groups or segments of consumers in the international literature, e.g. as proactive versus passive consumers, green consumers versus grey consumers, or consciously green versus action-green consumers (e.g. Didier and Sirieix, 2008; Hanpää, 2007; Pepper et al., 2009; Rokka and Uusitalo, 2008; Sanjuan et al., 2003). However, in this Danish empirical case study, it is the different ways of handling consumption that are analysed and not different groups of consumers. Furthermore, simple relationships cannot be established between the kinds of food practices among the young Danes and the different ways in which environmentally contested food consumption is dealt with in the everyday lives of the young consumers.

The next part of the analysis aims to show the variety and complexity in the ways of handling environmentalised food consumption among the young Danes. Hence, the next section of this chapter discusses a typology of performances of environmentalised food consumption and the complexities in and across these types. The analytical purpose of doing this is to discuss when and how a way of performing environmentalised consumption amounts to an integrative practice.

Ways of Handling Environmentalised Food Consumption

In this section, some of the complexities in conceptualising handlings of environmentally contested food consumption become apparent through the use of some of the more applied concepts from a practice theoretical perspective to construct an ideal typology. Hence, this section also experiments with what happens if we try to look at handlings of environmentally contested food consumption as a kind of practice in itself. Such an experiment requires sufficient occurrence of handlings – of doings and sayings in handling environmentalised consumption. Therefore, this part of the analysis begins with the 'simplest' type in the typology, where clear bundles of doings and sayings are expressed among the young participants.

Identifying

This way of handling environmentally challenged food consumption is characterised by the young practitioners explicitly having turned environmentalised food consumption into activities (doings and sayings) that form a central part of their practical and social everyday lives. I will argue that this type, 'identifying', can potentially be understood as a practice. The argument is exemplified by analysing the 'enactments' with two of the young participants; namely, Sonja (the female postwoman) and Morten (the male employed in a supermarket). From a practice theoretical perspective, there are two arguments for seeing the type 'identifying' as an integrative practice.

The first argument is that it is possible to see a range of activities, understandings, procedures and engagements within an environmentally friendly food consumption practice in the doings and sayings expressed by the two young consumers. This is both according to their own constructions but also according to public discourses about what more sustainable consumption patterns may contain (www.Forbrug.dk/bæredygtig). It is even possible to see groups of activities within environmentally friendly food consumption that form a project (combination of tasks) in the Schatzkian sense (Schatzki, 2002: 73–74). This means that specific, recurrent food doings and sayings can be grouped into tasks such as 'eating less meat'. Eating less meat as a task can be combined with other tasks, such as using as much organic food as possible; thus, it becomes a normative project of trying to consume in more environmentally friendly ways.

Activities performed by the young participants include, for example, consuming organic goods, consuming local food, using fewer resources and eating more vegetarian meals. The understandings include having to be conscious about what they use and eat; that food has to be consumed in good conscience; and that organic, local and free-range food provide this, because they are seen as improving environmental conditions. The procedures include cooking meals from scratch in order to keep control of the food, shopping in particular places such as local shops and the coop supermarkets, and restricting eating to particular genres of food and meals such as vegetarian ones. The engagements revolve around using consumption activities to perform societal agency and using these activities in interactions within their social networks to recruit new environmentalised food consumption practitioners. The engagement in consumption activities can be illustrated with this quote:

> I think it's worrysome that so many different materials are used to grow this, that's why I'd rather go for the organic things. As far as possible try to get it stopped, because that's the only small way in which we as consumers are able to put our foot down. (Sonja, female postwoman)

This engagement element of identifying with more sustainable consumption parallels the analysis about identifying with doing politics through consumption in Connolly and Prothero's study of Irish green consumption (Connolly and Prothero, 2008: 129–33), where the primary everyday life engagement for these consumers is to regulate their own – especially food – consumption. Another parallel can be found in Cherriers's qualitative analysis of identities in anti-consumption discourses in Australia (Cherrier, 2009: 189). Cherrier analyses two identity positions in Australian consumers' expressions of resistance against excessive material consumption: a hero identity where the consumer fights against the dominant societal system of material growth in order to change society, and a project identity where the consumer frees herself personally from materialism by engaging in alternative ways of consuming. The identifying way of handling environmentalised food consumption seems to be drawing upon both types of identities. A third, comparable study is Horton's fieldwork on identity work among English environmental activists (Horton, 2003), which includes everyday life practices of the activists such as food and transportation. Among the English environmental activists, social norms of appropriate green everyday life conduct are identified, and the proper performance of these principles is an important element in belonging to and signalling a green identity – or rather, one out of several possible elements (Horton, 2003: 67–70).

The second argument for understanding the 'identifying' handling type as a practice is that the environmentalised food consumption activities are clearly noticed as connected bundles of doings and sayings and recognised as 'green consumption' of some sort. This is expressed by Sonja and Morten themselves in their descriptions of the food activities of people in their social network, where they identify some as doing green consumption and others as not. But it is also expressed by members of the social networks of the two young people. The social recognisability of performance of practices is one of Schatzki and Warde's criteria that help define something as an integrative social practice. Here is how an individual from Sonja's network describes this recognisability: *'I suppose I think too little about it. Whereas somebody like Sonja, already when she still lived at home, then she wondered a lot about what vegetables are sprayed with, and you have to rinse them properly'* (Signe, high school student). Another example comes from the focus group with Morten and two people from his network:

> Rune: I think you have to be careful – people like you two are such people that can make others go to the opposite extreme and not be bothered at all. These people who jump into your fridge and check whether everything is organic … (Group laughter) (Morten: 'Come on, give us a break!')

In Horton's study of performances of green identities among English environmental activists, he argues that norms (which he calls cultural codes) become most noticeable either when they are broken or when they become 'overperformed' (Horton, 2003: 68). In the example with Morten, his friend Rune apparently identifies Morten's everyday activities with a socially recognisable 'overperforming' type of green consumer.

This recognition of a social category of green consumption or green consumers can be found in other qualitative studies of handling environmentalisation of food consumption. Here is an example from an Australian focus group study of organic food consumption, where some of the participants categorise organic consumers as 'greenies' and 'health nuts', and one of them goes on to say:

> They are not very welcoming, you don't feel very welcome. There is a sort of a clique and it's like, well, to be in that clique you have to look a certain way. Yeah, you have to look like a feral and you have to be so-called cool with it. (Lockie et al., 2002: 33)

The English study of everyday life practices of environmental activists argue that it has recently become much easier to perform green identity through ordinary food practices, since the market supply of more sustainable food has expanded noticeably. Thus, particular, ordinary food activities are socially recognised as belonging to a 'package' of green identity, such as shopping for food at the whole-food coop and sharing vegetarian meals made by organic and home-grown ingredients (Horton, 2003: 70–71).

However, suggesting that we see the 'identifying' handling of environmentally contested food consumption among Danish young people as a practice in itself does not imply that such practices are unified and systematic entities. The varieties and differences in performing 'identifying' with environmentalised food consumption are related to the complexities and conditions of the flow of acting of the young food practitioners. The two young practitioners discussed above have, for example, embarked upon this type of practice through different social life trajectories. They have both been exposed to environmental issues through the media. But Sonja grew up in a family with a father who was a vegetarian and where environmental risks and food quality was discussed over the dinner table. Morten, on the other hand, grew up with traditional Danish food [6] in his family, and he did not encounter environmental issues or food issues in his family, but at school.

Furthermore, Morten can fairly clearly be categorised as mainly enacting food practices called 'food as a project for changing the world', which tends to overlap and intersect with doings and sayings in the 'identifying' type for handling environmentalised consumption. But Sonja enacts a mixture of two other types of food practices; namely, 'food as pleasure' and 'food as health'. This suggests that there is a complex relationship between the food practices of the young Danes and the types of handling environmentalisation of food consumption.

Both of these young practitioners reflect upon contradictions and ambivalences in their environmental food performances, which supports the argument made by other researchers in the field about the ambivalences and reflexivities among environmentally concerned consumers (Boström and Klintman, 2008: 36–38; Connolly and Prothero, 2008: 127–29; Horton, 2003: 67–70). But again, the two Danish food practitioners deal with ambivalences in slightly but importantly different ways. In reflecting upon her identification with her environmentally friendly food activities, Sonja stresses that nobody can perform consistently; thus, her own dilemmas, conflicts and what she sees as her own 'under-performing' are constructed as socially normal: *'I don't think anybody honestly can say that they don't pollute just a little bit.'* This can be compared to one of the English environmental activists in Horton's study, who tries to legitimise her environmental 'under-performing' (having a car) by explaining how she can make other environmental trade-offs such as wash the laundry less frequently (Horton, 2003: 73). Both women perform less environmentally benignly in everyday life than they want to, and both understand this under-performance as tied to material structural conditions, but they construct their social distinctions differently. The young Danish woman places herself together with a majority of mainstream consumers, whereas the English activist places herself together with others who follow an acceptable green way of dealing with dilemmas. This difference could reflect the difference in the ways the environmental issue is institutionalised in the two national settings. In Denmark, taking environmental responsibility through individual private consumer activities is fairly normalised as a discourse, assumed by mainstream supermarkets and institutionalised as policy instrument

6 Lots of pork, potatoes and gravy.

in environmental policies (Christensen et al., 2007: 96; Halkier et al., 2007: 389). Perhaps the environmental issue tends to be politicised in more polarised ways in the English setting.

In a similar reflection, Morten shows he is aware of other practitioners seeing him as 'the green consumer', and he highlights his own under-performance in order to construct his identification as more compound and hence normal: *'But I won't call myself an over-organic consumer. Because I do buy ordinary clothes. I for sure don't want to walk around in those puke-white coloured clothes.'*

So proposing to see 'identifying' with environmentally friendly food consumption as a practice in itself does not lead to finding simple, unified ideal types. But neither does it necessarily imply that the two other types of handlings of enviromentalised food consumption found among the Danish young people can be seen as practices in themselves.

Appropriating

This kind of handling environmentalised food consumption revolves around practical and social do-abilities. 'Appropriating' refers to the processes whereby practitioners make things, experiences, texts, representations, etc. their own in their own contextually adapted and negotiated ways, which are not necessarily related to identifications (Thompson, 1995: 42–43). This section illustrates the diversity in appropriating the environmental contestation of food among four of the young practitioners. This type of handling, however, does not contain enough of the organising elements of integrated practices to be viewed as a practice in itself. Patterns of doings and sayings cannot be seen as parts of a practice, unless the doings and sayings systematically express the elements that organise a practice (Schatzki, 2002: 87); i.e. understandings, procedures and engagements. Rather, 'appropriating' could be seen as a particular kind of environmentalised mundane performance among the young food practitioners.

Appropriating environmentalised food consumption is characterised by processes of practical and social negotiation. Environmental problems are seen as important, and especially organic food is understood as part of a strategy towards sustainability, and as food of a better quality. Consumer agency, though, is done quite ambivalently. On the one hand, consumer responsibility for environmentalised food issues is normatively accepted, but on the other hand, consumer activities are regarded as carrying limited or no effects as societal agency. One of the young women expresses this ambivalence about consumer agency:

> Then you can say, you can do it and then tell people, I do it, and I know it doesn't help shit, because I am nearly the only one doing it, but then on the other hand you can feel good about actually doing something. (Helga, female unemployed worker)

Linked with this ambivalence about consumer agency, appropriating environmentalised food consumption can imply very different activities and ranges of activities, because doing environmentalised consumption here consists in subtle 'fitting-in' processes in established and reproduced patterns of food practices and the intersections of these with the other practices and conditions of everyday life. This also means that even when environmental problems or solutions are in the proxies of everyday life as very visible or very tactile materialities, environmentally friendly activities are not necessarily performed (Feagan and Moris, 2009; Petersen, 2008), as it is otherwise argued in parts of the field literature (Bartiaux, 2008: 1177–78; Cole et al., 2009: 166; Macnaghten, 2003: 73–74; Pedersen, 2000: 208). Seen from a practice theoretical perspective, there is never just one visible or tactile materiality that could urge food practitioners in an environmentalised direction with their activities. Rather, everyday life holds a multiplicity of materialities, entangled in and intersected by numerous social practices and relations.

Anders (student), Lena (home care) and Helga (unemployed) have as food practitioners had parallel trajectories in relation to the environmentalisation of food, since each of them grew up with parents who practised environmentally friendly food consumption; thus, they have not just encountered the environmentalisation of food consumption through mediated communication. Their own doings and sayings, however, seem quite diverse. Lena buys organic eggs, Helga uses several types of organic food, and Anders routinely negotiates whether it makes sense to buy particular organic goods, based on his evaluation of price, quality, and effect on environmental problems.

In Lena's everyday life, socialising with friends is a dominant practice with which the practical and social do-abilities of all other practices (including food practices, oscillating between food as necessity and food as pleasure) and performances are negotiated and adapted:

> But certainly, I think it's something you ought to think about, but it demands that you change your habits totally, and that requires some time. And I don't have time now, and I don't think very many young people have that. (Lena, female home care)

In Helga's everyday life, the social do-ability of environmentalised food performances is supported by a social network of friends sharing norms and everyday reflections about consumer agency. That sharing and talking about green norms in social networks support environmentally friendly consumption activities is shown in qualitative studies from Norway (Vittersø, 2003), Belgium (Bartiaux, 2007) and other studies from Denmark (Pedersen, 2000). These network-supported environmental reflections seem to help in overcoming some of the dilemmas reflected upon in relation to the practical do-abilities:

> Because when I sit here and describe all the things I do, I can hear that there is something not at all in accordance between what I do and what I say, and this

> way I think that I ... if I am to be able to defend what I'm saying towards myself, I ought to, as the conscientious person I am, hurry up and do something about it. Because you sit and smear the discount culture, and then you ... live in it perfectly well. (Helga, female unemployed worker)

In Anders' everyday life, the social do-ability of environmentalised food consumption is taken for granted, whereas the practical do-abilities become constantly negotiated with understandings and procedures in his food practices: *'With daily goods, you ought to do something, if you can afford it'* (Anders, male university student).

Appropriating as type of environmentalised mundane performance is not necessarily connected to a life-long trajectory of the practitioner. Nis, unskilled worker, only encountered the environmentalisation of food consumption through media until some of his friends recently served organic milk for him, and the bodily experience of the taste reminded him of his childhood milk. After that, he began to try out and to use several types of organic food, but this performance is tightly negotiated with the practical do-ability implied in one dominant practice in his everyday life, his work: *'... as far as I am able to and can afford it, I buy organic, it's a way to begin to think about not getting all that artificial shitty stuff that they put in the food and sort of trying to get things raw from the nature'* (Nis, male unskilled worker).

Just like 'identifying' as type, 'appropriating' as type shows no simple relationship with the food practices among the young people. Lena enacts elements from both food as necessity and food as pleasure, Helga expresses mostly food as pleasure, Anders primarily enacts food as health, and Nis enacts food as necessity, but also food as health.

Appropriating as environmentalised performance type involves acceptance of consumer agency. This is not the case for the last type of environmentalised performance type to which we now turn.

Distancing

The flip side of the social coin of identification processes and elements are the processes and elements of distanciation (Bourdieu, 1984; Warde, 1997). The distancing type of handling environmentalised food consumption revolves around an understanding where consumer agency is rejected. Environmentally friendly consumption does not form part of the food practices, and neither is it included in the doings of other practices in everyday life, whereas it can be included in the sayings. Everyday life is crammed with different, intersecting practices of work, study, partnership, leisure activities and socialising, and when ordinary consumer agency at the same time is rejected, the practical do-abilities of environmentally friendly consumption don't arrive at any point of negotiation – as it does in the type 'appropriating'. Still, this type of handling environmentalised food consumption also covers social diversities, which is exemplified by the expressions from three of the young Danish participants.

Environmentally friendly food consumption is not an element of the activities of the everyday food practices of Anne (clerk apprentice), Signe (high school student) and Jens (agriculture student), and they share the understanding of rejecting consumer agency. Instead, responsibility for dealing with environmental problems in food is placed with public institutions, experts and producers. Signe expresses this here: '*... and when I take a glass of water from the tap, I don't think about how dead polluted our ground water has gradually become, because I think if it was that polluted, they would do something about it.*' In the quote, 'they' are public institutions and experts.

Arriving at distancing from environmentalised food consumption, however, has happened through different trajectories, and it is being performed in different network contexts. Anne has only encountered environmentalisation of food consumption through media and in school, and such activities are not being recognised in her social network. '*We would never have had such discussions on our own accord*', Anne comments after the focus group with her and members of her social network. Signe grew up with a mum working as an environmental consultant, so she refers to specific episodes she remembers about her mum pointing out what not to do in order not to pollute, and Signe explicitly mentions members of her social network, who practise environmentally friendly food consumption. Jens grew up on a farm with parents who expressed lack of trust in relation to, for example, organic food, and he disagrees and discusses with members of his social network who use the consumer strategy in relation to sustainability: '*So when you meet someone who is ecological to the fingertips, then I feel like this, I take a counter position, so you can run up hard fronts and have a bit of a talk about it*' (Jens, male agricultural student). Jens distances himself as food consumer from those he sees as 'ecological to the fingertips', which is parallel to some of the expressions among Australian food consumers about organic consumers (Lockie et al., 2002: 33).

Also with regard to this type of environmentalised performance, there are no clear relations to the food practices. Anne mainly enacts food as necessity, Signe enacts both food as health and food as pleasure, and Jens mainly enacts food as pleasure.

Environmentalised Consumption Performances as Practices?

When comparing the three types of environmentalised consumption performances, it seems clear that only the first type – 'identifying' – qualifies as an integrative practice. In 'appropriating' and 'distancing' there are not enough of the elements that organise practices (understandings, procedures and engagements) present in the practitioner expressions about environmentalised food for the performances to be seen as socially recognisable bundles of doings and sayings. The type 'identifying' works as a marker of social distinction (Bourdieu, 1984; Horton, 2003), precisely with reference to a socially recognisable category. 'Distancing' also seems to work as a marker of social distinction but lacks the other elements of a coordinated practice. Both 'appropriating' and 'distancing' denote performances of food consumption that form parts of other practices, including the food practices of the young participants. However, it is not possible to substantiate any straightforward analytical relationships between the food practices among the young people and their environmental consumption performances.

A specific diversity of constellations seems to be involved in the making of environmentalised food consumption performances and their conditionings. Therefore, the next section of this chapter zooms in on the details of the practical procedures of handling environmentalised food consumption. The aim is to emphasise the significance and complexities of practical do-ability in performing environmentalised consumption in order to question assumptions about the primacy of engagement-like factors such as moral values, attitudes, lifestyle identities, etc. that appear in the debate.

Complexities of Practical Procedures

This part of the analysis focuses on procedures (principles and rules of how to do) in handling environmentalised food consumption. Across the current literature on environmental issues and consumption, a lot of attention is given to the importance of consumers' relations with different types of knowledge. In particular, the model of seeing consumers as lacking in knowledge and being passive recipients of information from experts – the so-called deficit model of communication – is being criticised on the basis of empirical studies that show how consumers reactions are more complex and contextually bound (Eden, 2009: 2–3) but also more characterised by reflexivity (Boström and Klintman, 2008: 194). Therefore, procedures in relation to uses of knowledge are relevant for the analysis of the environmental challenge of consumption. As a consequence of the practice theoretical perspective, where procedures are seen as bodily/mental, the analysis looks at the procedural relations between the uses of more embodied (routinised) and more discursive (reflexive) knowledges.

Routinisation occurs when understandings and engagements in practices and performances are based on tacit knowledge through practical consciousness, and when procedures in practices and performances are taken for granted. Reflexivity occurs when understandings, procedures and engagements in practices and performances are explicit and reflected upon through discursive consciousness (Giddens, 1984: 5–14). The main argument in this section is that environmentalised food consumption performances are neither exclusively reflected nor just routines. Rather, the two bodily/mental procedures are always to some degree intertwined with each other. This resembles the findings in studies of how consumers manage environmentally friendly concerns in Belgium (Bartiaux, 2007), Denmark (Gram-Hanssen, 2007; Pedersen, 2000) and Italy (Miele, 2006).

Routinisation of Reflexivity

In this specific procedural blend, reflections upon consequences of food consumption and active environmentally friendly choices have become routinely integrated and incorporated into the practical food consumption moments. This particular bodily/mental procedure is part of the organisation of the food practices to such a degree that it is taken for granted as an integral part of performing food practices. This way, a positive normative engagement in doing good for the environment has become routinised.

Here, one of the young people talk about his food shopping, where he routinely buys organic products and Danish vegetables in the season:

> I just think … then it's just become such a natural part of my day … think about it, really it's just … ok, you think about it, but it's just become natural, it doesn't occur to me to buy the other goods. (Morten, male employed in supermarket)

So, reflexivity is present at this mundane level of briefly becoming reminded of environmental problems and solutions while going about providing for food. But at the same time, which products to choose or not to choose are taken for granted and worked into the bodily movements and trajectories in the store. This way, environmentally friendly food consumption becomes a practical social accomplishment.

Routinisation as Release from Reflexivity

In this procedural blend, environmental reflexivity is facilitated by routinised food consumption doings. Normative engagement in environmentally friendly food consumption is neither necessarily expressed, nor seen as appropriately directed towards ordinary consumers. In 'routinisation as release from reflexivity', routinisation keeps environmental doubts and reflections at bay, thus getting away from the practical and socially difficult do-abilities of conscious consumer agency. Thus, these bodily/mental procedures are different from the procedures in the first example, routinisation of reflexivity, where routinisation as procedural element includes environmental reflexivity.

One of the young women explains how the larger regulatory systems of society – such as public authorities – ensure that she can carry on in her own everyday life routines without having to show engagement in environmental reflexivity:

> I think waste-sorting ought to be everywhere. It really isn't troublesome. When you had finished eating, food waste went into one bucket and napkins and other things went into another one. It takes no time. I think you could introduce that country-wide. Absolutely. (Anne, female clerk apprentice).

Here, it is *not* a question of having incorporated a normative engagement into everyday agency such that it has become routinised, which was the case in the first example. Rather, agency is placed with other actors in society (such as the state or the local communities), presumably more powerful and responsible. This is a well-known finding from the field of consumer trust (Halkier and Holm, 2004).

Another example of how routinisation can produce relief from reflexivity is when responsibility for environmental solutions is not placed with other actors but rather with the conditions and the routine character of everyday food procedures themselves:

> Of course I have been thinking that it would be nice if you could buy organic food, but it's simply the money that determines it. But I admire those who do it. It also takes time to think that way all the time, it takes a long time to go shopping when you have to look at all the goods to see which substances are in them. For example, families with allergic children have to do that. I don't have time for that. I just go out and buy the goods I need and look at what it costs (Signe, female high school student)

Hence, actively using the environmental reflexivity does not only require better economic conditions, but also a different organisation of routine time use (Southerton, 2006). Thus, this kind of mixing of routines and reflections come close to typical rationalisations explaining low involvement in environmentally friendly activities, e.g. cost, convenience and competing priorities around food (Lockie, 2002: 285).

Ambivalence Between Routinisation and Reflexivity

In this procedural blend, manoeuvring in relation to environmentalised food consumption entails a potential conflict in the food consumption practices, because the bodily/mental procedures of shopping, cooking and eating are experienced as being contested by environmental challenges. Ambivalence does not necessarily have to be understood as tension, as there are several other ways for food consumers to deal with ambivalence (Bartiaux, 2007: 1179; Halkier, 2001a; Walker and Shove, 2007: 223); however, this analysis focuses on the expression of ambivalence as tension.

Ambivalence as tensions between environmental reflexivity and routinised food practices is clearly narrated by one of the young women:

> And when I went to school and had a roll with something in the lunch packet, I had to bring back home the tinfoil and it had to go to recycling, and I can see that it's enormously important, and really, it would be, if everybody did it, but I think it's ridiculous when so few are doing it. Even though it's really important, and I am relatively environmentally conscious, due to my mother, of course I think

> about it, and I think about now there is salmonella in pork meat, and in chicken and eggs, and I think that there are so many things that are wrapped in PVC and that's bad for the environment, and I also think that I ought not to buy that Dutch cucumber because it's probably filled with pesticides, but it's not something I think about in daily life. (Lena, female home care)

The trajectory of this young food practitioner with a mother who practised environmentally friendly consumption has helped form the reflections of the practitioner today at the level of general understandings, in Schatzki's terms. The level of more mundane environmental reflexivity in relation to the understandings, procedures and engagements of her food practices is not activated.

One of the other young women explains the ambivalence in terms of the distinction between natural and unnatural:

> But it's also easy, for example, in a way to put away responsibility and say, but I can't help that they pack their goods in all that stuff, you know, in a way that's to get around it. That … but it's also difficult to put a finger on, because … there are so many … things that are just natural, that you don't think about … whereas you probably ought to have moral scruples, right, but suddenly there are some things that have become so integrated in our daily lives that … to do otherwise would be unnatural. (Helga, female unemployed worker)

When shopping for food, a large part of the doings are characterised by routine bodily movements and implicit understandings of what to do with the concrete products and other material conditions, and environmental reflexivity disrupts this routine flow and helps create ambivalence.

Routinisation/Reflexivity and Engagement

The combinations of the procedural elements of routinisation and reflexivity are acted out in all of the three ideal typical ways of handling environmentalised food consumption – identifying, appropriating and distancing. This points to the significance of such procedural processes and their complex forms in relation to what can be expected of everyday consumption agency for environmental change. In other words, a high engagement in consuming organic food (as in the 'identifying with environmentalised food' type) is not sufficient to produce a noticeable amount of changes in relation to society. Such agency has to be do-able in fairly specific, practical manners. Thus, complex bodily/mental procedures seem to be just as important as engagements in the ongoing accomplishment of dealing with the normative environmental challenge in food practices.

That engagement, however, does matter, is shown in the analysis of procedural blends. Levels of engagement in each of the procedural mixes vary systematically with the types in the ideal typology of ways of handling environmentalisation. Identifying tends to include the routinisation of reflexivity mix, appropriating tends to include the ambivalence between routinisation and reflexivity mix, and distancing tends to include the routinisation as release from reflexivity mix. It is not surprising that engagements matter when ordinary food practices have become normatively challenged by environmentalising discourses, since the concept of engagement covers emotional and normative orientations towards what and how to do in social practices (Warde, 2005: 134). What is unique about a practice theory-informed analysis of environmental normative engagements is, however, that it shows how the normative becomes unfolded and reconstructed in the mundane performing that takes place in everyday life acting and interacting.

This is the focus of the last empirical section of this chapter, with a special emphasis on the negotiations of the content of environmental normative categories in social interaction. The analysis aims to show how social interactions are influential in shaping the normative content of categories such as 'doing green consumption', thus questioning the individual life-world focus that is apparent in many everyday life analytical approaches to consumption research.

Normative Negotiations of Environmentalised Consumption

It is clear from the empirical quotes presented earlier in this chapter that quite of lot of normative negotiation is taking place. In this section, some of the negotiations that took place in the focus group discussions are presented as particularly explicit examples of three types of normative negotiations about environmentalised food consumption: negotiations about the agency position of the ordinary food consumer in relation to environmental responsiblity; negotiations about an important normative category (organic food); and negotiations about exceptions to expected normative performance. These three types of normative negotiations can also be observed in the empirical material of the three other Danish case studies that are included in this book (see Chapters 4, 5 and 6, the sections on normative negotiations or normative positionings).

Negotiating the Agency Position of Ordinary Food Consumers

The first normative negotiation is an example of a negotiation about what consumers can expect of and demand from each other when it comes to doing something about environmental problems through everyday acting. The negotiation revolves around what it is possible to do in everyday life as a consumer (do-ability) and how these possibilities are related to normative responsibility.

The following sequence of negotiations comes from a group of members of the social network of Morten, the male supermarket employee. The negotiation is a distinct example of disagreement over how to perform normatively in daily life, and the participants are constantly positioning each other actively during this sequence. The sequence is from the last part of the focus group, where the participants are trying to conclude some of their discussions.

> Rune: 'So … you just think organics is cool, and I have a resistance against it?'
> Morten: 'No-o!'
> Svend: 'I think we have met in some places, but it doesn't hold water to say, I can't be bothered, I don't want to feel like a lemming in a fashion craze, I consciously choose away from it, I become obstinate …'
> Rune (interrupts): 'It's not just that, I have given other reasons too, among others the economic [Svend: 'That's even more embarrasing.'] … I really don't think so.'
> Morten: 'What is it per month, Rune? 200–250 kr.?'
> Rune: 'I really don't have a clue.'
> Svend: 'I can understand if you had something ideological against it, but that's a really bad argument. [Rune: 'Why?'] [Morten: 'Arh, Rune!'] You can buy fewer clothes or go less out. Of course it's a question of prioritising, don't buy a flat, what do I know.'
> Rune: 'It's a question of prioritising – then I just do it a bit earlier than you do. Because then you buy some organic food, but you don't take it further in that sort of lifestyle. What you really mean is …'
> Morten (interrupts): 'Yep, you think about it when you shower, and you don't switch the lights on when walking down the staircase and such little things. And if you see a man standing on the street, washing his car, you scold him for wasting water.'
> Rune: 'You know that Svend works at McDonalds …'
> Svend: 'Yeah, that does not hold water. It's a direct contradiction of what I'm saying.'
> Rune: 'Yep, that's what I mean, you have just put … [Morten: 'It's to fight the system from within!'] … it's not at all … [common laughter] … [Svend: 'No, it isn't.'] … you work at McDonalds, and you would probably buy a car if you could afford it.' [common laughter].
> Svend: 'I would not, in fact. I got to get rid of that McD job, it doesn't hold water.'
> Rune: 'My point is just that you are also self-contradictory!'

The specific normative issue negotiated here is how much 'doing green consumer' you can demand of each other, so among other things it is the social do-abilities of environmentalised food consumption activities that are in the process of making. One normative position here taken by Svend and Morten is that people should demand as much coherence as possible in doings and sayings in relation to environmentalised food consumption of themselves and each other. The other normative position, taken by Rune, is that everyday life is incoherent, so everybody has to prioritise; thus, it's not legitimate to blame other people for prioritising. The interaction reaches a turning point when Rune introduces an element that could be considered a major self-contradiction in the normative position of his two friends; namely, that Svend works at McDonalds.[7] Working at McDonalds seems to constitute what Horton in his study of English environmental activists calls 'a breach of green cultural codes' (Horton, 2003: 68), which is why such an activity can be used in a normative conflict. This apparent breaching of the cultural codes of 'green' food consumption by Svend enables Rune to conclude normatively on behalf of the group: namely that everyday life is incoherent and thus leads to inconsistency in performing environmentalised consumption. Analytically, this shows how normative engagements in 'doing environmentally friendly consumption' are dependent upon the messy configurations of everyday life do-abilities. The limits to consumer agency do not necessarily come from lack of engagement.

Negotiations about the Category Organic Consumption

In the next set of negotiations, one of the key potential solutions in the discursive environmentalisation of food consumption is being discussed; namely, the consumption of organic food. In the following examples from two different focus groups, there is a shared understanding of negotiations about what might constitute the difficult everyday conditions in relation to 'doing organic food consumption'; however, the two groups end up with very different practical normative conclusions, due to, among other things, the social processes involved in the negotiations.

The first example comes from a social network group of Sonja, the female postwoman. In this sequence, the group reaches an explicit consensus in favour of prescribing organic consumption as the right thing people ought to do in their everyday food practices. This sequence is from the second half of the focus group, where the group tries to conclude some of their discussions.

> Lena: 'Begin with yourself, right?'
> Signe: 'They ought to go for organic goods.'
> Sonja: 'That's the only thing we can do.'
> Lena: 'But I can understand if some single mum cannot afford organic goods. That's quite understandable.'
> Signe: 'I think that everybody – if they could afford it and it was possible – would go for the organic goods [Anders and Lena: Mmm …] … because we know … attention has been drawn a little to the difference.'
> Lena: 'If the price was the same, everybody would do it, no doubts. But then again, it's a question of prioritising.'
> Anders: 'Otherwise, you must vote politically. But you can't really trust that completely.' [Sonja, Lena and Signe: 'Mmm …']
> Moderator: 'Is it clear to you where you disagree?'

7 In a Danish context, McDonalds is often seen as a major symbol of the worst of late-industrial society and its mass-produced low-quality food and environmental problems.

Lena: 'I just simply think it seems so ridiculous. You know, my parents have always had a compost bin and taken bottle caps and tinfoil for recycling and all such things, right. And it's really fine to do such things. But I've always seen it as completely ridiculous … [Signe: 'Hopeless.'] … because it … [Signe: 'It doesn't help when one person is doing it.'] … of course you have to begin with yourself, but maybe there is one out of thousand people in Denmark who does it.'
Anders: 'But that's exactly what you are not allowed to say, isn't it?'
Lena: 'When I think about it, it seems hopeless.'
Anders: 'But look what happened with the French wine.'[8]
Sonja: 'That's hopeless too, but you do it anyway.'

In the first half of the sequence, the group constructs a consensus around the engagement in the normative position that consumers ought to buy organic food. The sequence becomes more questioning after Lena introduces her personal narrative about her life trajectory into environmentalised consumption activities. Her conclusion is to question whether performing environmentally friendly actions as an individual consumer changes anything if you are part of a minority. Anders expresses how Lena's conclusion to her story can be understood as normatively inappropriate. He suggests that it is not acceptable to say that the activities of the individual consumer are of no societal consequence. Here, the normative consensus of the group becomes threatened, and Sonja quickly concludes for them all that consumers ought to do the appropriate green thing anyway.

In the process of producing consensus about the normativity that prescribes organic consumption, the group reflects upon the normative procedure of 'beginning with yourself', negotiated with their understandings of the conditions of everyday life and their doubts about the effects of organic food consumption. Hence, the group does not question organic food as normatively better goods, they question the extent to which change of routines in everyday life is possible and worth the effort. This parallels discussions in the focus groups from Lockie's Australian study of consumption of organic food:

> I guess the thing that really hits home for me at the moment, is okay, we've got a choice, to choose organic foods possibly from some products that we buy, but certainly not all. So no matter what you buy, you are only going part of the way in achieving a healthy lifestyle for yourself, achieving good land use and other planetary global issues. (Lockie et al., 2002: 28)

The next example constitutes the opposite of the first; namely, a consensus against a normatively prescribed organic consumption. The negotiations take place in a

8 This focus group was conducted in the wake of the boycotts of French products after the revival of French nuclear tests in the Pacific.

group from the social network of Anne, the clerk apprentice, and the sequence comes from the beginning of the focus group discussion.

> Tilde: 'Oh, what you ought to do.'
> Anne: 'We haven't talked at all about what we ourselves ought to do.'
> Yamani: 'But as a consumer, you can't do very much, you can't just go out and change …'
> Tilde: 'Otherwise, we must all buy organic.'
> Yamani: 'Yep, and that's mega-expensive!' [everyone giggles]
> Tilde: 'So none of us do that.'
> Yamani: 'Then it's just too bad with the environment [Anne: 'Aha-aha!'] … well, yeah, you know that's how most people think. That's fair enough.'
> Anne: 'And you don't think like that?'
> Yamani: 'You don't think differently when you are out shopping, ha, ha, that much I do know. How do you shop, Tilde?'
> Tilde: 'Like you two, I think. Cheap. [Yamani: 'Really?'] … yeah.'

The normative performance of consuming organic food is here constructed as the 'right thing to do', but also constructed as unrealistic engagement under the conditions of other practices and conditions of everyday life. This normative position on organic food consumption is also found in Lockie's focus groups in Australia (Lockie et al., 2002: 28). The Danish group quickly forms their consensus against normatively prescribed organic consumption, although Anne tries to question the legitimacy of not taking environmental responsibility. Yamani refers to his knowledge of Anne's everyday routines to argue that her doings and sayings are no different from those of the rest of the group, as she is also not performing environmentally friendly actions. This way, the content of the normative conclusion becomes a rejection of performing organic consumption. In a way, this negotiation builds on a normative assumption that it is not legitimate to demand environmentalised performance of each other if one is not prepared to do it oneself. This resembles the normative content of 'beginning with yourself' in the first negotiation about the category of organic food, but the practical conclusions are very different.

Negotiations about Exceptions from Norms

Normativity is a broader concept than norms. Normativity includes not just the concrete rules for normative procedures – the norms – but also the multifaceted processes of accomplishing the normative (see Chapter 2). Thus, in a practice theoretical perspective it is not expected that norms are necessarily consistent across practices, contexts, relations and situations, whereas this appears to be expected in more cognitive approaches to social norms in relation to environmentally friendly consumption (e.g. Thøgersen, 2006). An important part of these processes is usually related to how practitioners define, negotiate and justify exceptions to the rules for the normative procedures. What follows is an example of a negotiation that involves a social construction that is typically used to justify exceptions from a norm about 'doing green consumer'.

This sequence is from the social network group of Helga, the unemployed female, and the group is producing consensus about how evaluations of quality and price are legitimate procedures to establish exceptions from the norm of using organic goods.

> Malene: 'But really I don't think that … I think it takes a long time before … I don't think I will ever become totally converted. Like you said before. It's a minority that completely buys organic … [Helga: 'That depends on the supply.'] … but right now at least it seems pretty hopeless.'
>
> Helga: 'Now that I've said that I want to try, it's a bit as if … then I can come home from the supermarket and be half depressed, because then there are some things that I haven't bought as organic although they were there … where it has been something about how the goods looked compared with the price … you know, one thing is that it has to be organic, but it depends on quality as well. You don't want to by some e-ehm [Malene: 'Just to buy it.'] tomatoes or something, you know, just because …'
>
> Lars (interrupts): 'Just for the cause.'

Such discussions about exceptions from 'green' norms are found in other qualitative studies as well; for example, in Connolly and Prothero's Irish study: *'You compromise every day. You have to. I don't think anyone could live a completely green life. I suppose you could wear all natural fibres, but even natural fibres are not fully green'* (Connolly and Prothero, 2008: 127). In the Danish sequence of negotiation quoted above, the young participants support each other in their practical exceptions from an otherwise shared convention of buying organic, and they do it by talking about practical procedural conditions to their consumer agency that they clearly expect to be acceptable exceptions, since their co-construction is so tight-knit that they finish each others' sentences! This way, social interaction and practical procedure tend to change the normative engagement in practice.

Environmental Normative Do-ability

The examples of normative negotiations illustrate how the practical and social accomplishment of appropriate environmental consumption conduct is dependent upon the messy webs of everyday life do-abilities, and how social interaction and practical procedures tend to change normative engagement in practice. It is into such complex processes that the calls for environmental consumer agency become embedded, and not necessarily into neat, individual, meaningful life-world engagements.

Doing Political Consumption?

What happens in everyday life when ordinary food consumption becomes challenged by requests to help solve environmental problems in society? There is, of course, no simple answer to that, but on the basis of the analyses in this chapter, discussed in relation to the current international literature, it is possible to provide some suggestions about the range of possibilities.

In this chapter, a practice theoretical perspective provided several insights into the diversity of consequences in everyday life. First, three types of handling environmentalisation of food consumption were established on the basis of the data-material with the young people in the Danish case study; namely, identifying, appropriating, and distancing. The type identifying with environmentally friendly food consumption can be viewed as an integrated practice, whereas the other two types can be viewed as specific environmentalised mundane performances that are part of the existing food practices of the young practitioners. Thus, not all consumption is necessarily just an aspect of social practices, contrary to one of Alan Warde's central arguments in his article about practice theory and sociology of consumption (Warde, 2005: 137). Some types of consumption seem to exhibit the social forms of integrated practices in everyday life, and current research on the everyday 'greening' of ordinary consumption types such as food supports this claim (Connolly and Prothero, 2008; Evans and Jackson, 2008; Horton, 2003; Lockie et al., 2002). The reason why this is important is that activities and performances that can be understood as 'whole packages' of integrative practices probably are given priority in people's daily lives. The changes in the Danish context since the data production took place seem to support this suggestion of seeing the identifying type of consumption performance as a practice in itself. Organic products have become widely available in mainstream supermarkets and across many food categories, and the discourse of ascribing environmental responsibility to the individual consumer has become part of mainstream policy making.

However, within both the environmentalised consumption practice identifying and within the two environmentalised performances appropriation and distancing, important differences are expressed in the specific combinations of understandings, procedures and engagements. Furthermore, the young Danes deal with environmentalised consumption within a context of complex bodily/mental procedures. Routinisation and reflexivity are always combined in practical handlings of environmentalised food. One of the problems in the current research on environment and consumption is that a large proportion of segmented consumer types in the field of challenged consumption is constructed on the basis of an assumption that routines and reflections can be kept apart. Likewise, the analysis of normative negotiations points to the importance of social interaction as well as practical do-ability in dealing with the normative environmental challenge in food practices. It is not just meaningful, individual life-world engagements that drive the normativised performing. Normative engagements are subjected to practical adaptations and social negotiation.

These diversities and complexities suggest that researchers ought to be more careful when they attempt to establish new, segmented types for consumers, regardless of how well researched and analytically reasonable such types might be (e.g. Boström and Klintman, 2008: 37–45). Maybe it is necessary to go further than merely discarding the analytical construct of a 'generic active citizen-consumer' as Jacobsen and Dulsrud suggest (Jacobsen and Dulsrud, 2007: 472). The diversities not just between but also within the types of handling environmentally challenged food consumption suggest that research should discuss do-able environmental food performances and practices and their conditionings. In his analysis of everyday practices among English environmental activists, Horton puts it like this: *'Rather than aiming to produce "sustainable citizens", therefore, it is perhaps the making of "sustainable performances" which should take centre-stage'* (Horton, 2003: 75).

The question is whether such an analytical suggestion is fruitful in the discussion of agency and political consumption (Boström et al., 2005; Micheletti, 2003; Pattie et al., 2003), or whether this focus on the 'accomplishment of environmental performances' is too much of a process concept to be of use outside of academic discussions.

It could be argued that at least the identifying type of dealing with environmentally challenged food consumption can be understood as a kind of political consumption, since as a type of practice, it fulfills the criteria for political everyday agency; namely, intentionality and autonomy (Halkier and Holm, 2008: 669). In identifying with environmentally friendly food consumption, practitioners express understandings in their sayings oriented towards specific tasks (such as using organic food), and practitioners express engagements in their doings that amount to practice projects (such as experiencing enough autonomy to make changes to environmental problems). This can be seen as performing political consumption practices (ibid.: 672).

On the other hand, this analysis and other studies (e.g. Cole et al., 2009; Collins, 2004; Connolly and Prothero, 2008; Horton, 2003) show that boycotts and supportive buying (such as buying organic food) are entangled with other everyday practices, social conditionings, and negotiations of how to do normative to a degree that makes it difficult to distill political consumption from everyday life – even when focusing on the activities and performances rather than on the consumer.

Chapter 4
Dealing with Food Risk Challenges

Putting your Family at Risk?

The challenge to ordinary food consumption discussed in this chapter comes from the changed food safety policies and medialised discourses about risk, safety and food in Europe. In the 1990s, European societies, including Denmark, witnessed several so-called food scandals and public debates in the media about food risk and food safety, which have resulted in shifting levels of trust and distrust in relation to ordinary food (Millstone and Zwanenberg, 2007). The most spectacular of these was, of course, the BSE outbreak, but other issues include hygiene problems with bacteria such as salmonella and campylobacter, risk issues associated with genetically modified foods (GMO), chemical residues of different kinds such as pesticides and dioxin, surface-treatment of fruit, and the multiplicity of artificial additives in some types of modern food. All of these food safety issues are connected to the industrialisation and supermarketisation of food provisioning, whereby the distance from farm to fork has increased (Ansell and Vogel, 2006: 4–6; Kjærnes et al., 2007: 1–4; Marsden, Flynn and Harrison, 2000: 2–4).

In response to these food safety issues, public institutions and societal regulations were changed both at European level and in national political systems in the different European countries during the end of the 1990s and beginning of the 2000s (Holm and Halkier, 2009). One of the distinctive features of this new set of policies is the new framing of consumers as active agents for change (Halkier et al., 2007: 380–81). Consumers are recognised as stakeholders and included in a dialogue about food safety, and ordinary, individual consumers are ascribed with responsibility to make informed choices via their food shopping and food handling in their homes (EU Commission, 2000; 2005).

The Danish Context

In Denmark, the institutional reforms have been most extensive regarding the position of the individual consumer. The reforms included incorporating the ordinary food consumption choices of individual consumers directly into the public regulation of food safety (Kjærnes et al., 2007: 188). An example of this is the 'Smiley system' (Nielsen, 2006: 148–49). Danish restaurants and retailers have to publish the results of public inspection of their food hygiene standards etc. in a visible place. The four categories of inspection results are visualised by four different Smileys, smiling more or less. It is then assumed that consumers can use this simplified information to act upon and to decide whether to eat or shop at the premises or not.

In the latter half of the 1990s, a number of food labelling initiatives from food producers began to appear on the supermarket food shelves, fridges and freezers in at least some European countries, including Denmark (Kjærnes et al., 2007: 173–77). In Denmark, 'salmonella-free chicken' was one of the most used labels, but 'bread baked without straw shortener', 'Danish beef' and 'GMO free' were others. Furthermore, the public Danish label for organic goods was linked with a 'GMO free' claim by some producers, in the wake of the international debate about whether to work with absolute or relative rules for GMO in organic food (Klintman, 2006).

At the same time, the public Danish Food and Veterinary Agency ran several information campaigns addressing a number of food safety issues, which were communicated to consumers through various means, including leaflets distributed to supermarkets where they were placed on the shelves next to the food. The leaflets had titles such as 'Organic food from the southern hemispheres', 'Additives – why?', and 'Some bacteria are worse than others'. Currently, food safety information for ordinary food consumers can be found on various public websites, such as the Consumer Agency under the Ministry of Economics and Business, which has a menu entry called 'dangerous?' where the consumer can click, for example, on a link to information about risky food (www.forbrug.dk/erdetfarligt). Similarly, the websites of the two largest supermarket chains in Denmark both have menu entries with the heading of 'responsibility', providing information about the Smiley system and food safety for individual consumers (see www.coop.dk and www.dsg.dk).

A recent comparative analysis[1] of how the position of the individual food consumer is constructed in Denmark shows a pattern in the Danish context that should be included in analysing how the risk challenging of food consumption is handled. Across the variety of organised actors in the food sector (e.g. producers, manufacturers, retailers, public authorities and NGOs), a consensus is expressed that ordinary food consumers are complex, in the sense that they are both seen as trusting and at the same time seen as active choosers in relation to food risks. Here is a quote from an interview with a representative from a consumer organisation:

> I believe the consumers, too, carry a responsibility. They shouldn't buy the worst products, because if nobody buys them, there would not be any reason to produce them, right? But it is difficult because so much is tied to knowledge

1 The analysis is based on data from a comparative European research project, 'Consumer trust in food: A European study of the social and institutional conditions for the production of trust', funded by the EU. The data are comprised of nationally representative surveys with food consumers in six countries, and qualitative case studies of the food sectors in each of the countries and at EU-level, building on interviews with organised actors as well as textual analysis (see Kjærnes et al., 2007).

> and attitudes and to what you want to spend your money on etc. etc. There is a lot of what you would probably call 'socio-economic factors' influencing what people consume.

Furthermore, consensus is expressed about the public sector having the primary responsibility for food safety (Halkier et al., 2007: 387–89). In a representative survey with Danish food consumers, the consumers constructed themselves in a complex way. On the one hand, Danish consumers did not see their own voice in society as particularly important, compared to how consumers thought of themselves in other countries. On the other hand, Danish consumers reported a comparatively high level of participation in using the consumer strategy to perform politics (ibid.: 396).

Current Studies

In other words, some of the current research (both quantitative and qualitative) on consumers in relation to risk and food safety point towards paying attention to risk-handling as a compound. Being aware of the conditions of this complexity seems, however, to be a problem in some of the current empirical research in the area of food consumption and risk.

In her much-quoted book on risk, Deborah Lupton presents a mapping of the field of theoretical approaches to risk in the social sciences (Lupton, 1999: 35). One of the three approaches on a continuum that she outlines is the so-called 'realist epistemological position', where risk is understood as objectively measurable threats and dangers, and where the associated theories are usually cognitive science theories. An overview of current empirical research on risk in relation to food consumption confirms the relevance of such an approach (Kjærnes, 2006: 918–19). Studies of food consumption and risk within this approach often build on the knowledge deficit model (Hansen et al., 2003), where food consumers are seen as lacking sufficient knowledge about risk in food to assess and act upon such risks as experts advise them to do (Frewer et al., 2002; Hagemann and Scholderer, 2007; Lin et al., 2005; Qin and Brown, 2007; Roe and Teisl, 2007). A typical example is Hughner et al.'s (2009) quantitative study of American consumers' awareness of warning disclosures on cans of tuna fish (and related species such as swordfish) about higher levels of mercury than in other types of fish. They conclude that consumers only pay brief attention to the warnings, and that the warnings did not have a significant impact on the consumers' tuna-buying behaviour.

Other studies acknowledge that consumers' risk definitions can be subjectively and culturally influenced; therefore, consumers should be involved in public risk discussions, in order for experts, public authorities and businesses to better communicate with them (Devcich et al., 2007; Lofstedt, 2006; Renn, 2006; Slovic, 1999). But the ways in which consumers are understood to be handling food risks still build on cognitivist assumptions about attitudes as individual attributes and attitudes leading to behaviour. An example of this is Michaelidou and Hassan's

(2008) quantitative study of Scottish consumers and how their purchase intentions toward organic food are predicted from their concern for food safety, measured as individual attitudes, thus building on the theory of planned behaviour (see Chapter 1 and Chapter 3).

Another part of the current literature on food risk and consumption build on more constructionist assumptions, where risk is mediated through social and cultural processes (Lupton, 1999: 35), and how consumers handle risks is embedded in everyday life relations and interactions, institutionalised in the larger context of society (Kjærnes, 2006: 923). One example is Lupton's (2005) own qualitative study of Australian laypeople's discourses about food risks. She argues that the literature on consumer's handling of food risk is characterised by either general accounts of reflexivity and risk society (Beck, 1992; Giddens, 1991) or by European studies that focus only on particular types of food risk, such as BSE. The study shows that Australians associate dietary fat much more with food risk, and a variety of ways of navigating in relation to such food risks in everyday life practices are analysed and discussed in relation to institutionalised context-dependence of consumer handling of food risk.

Two other typical studies are from the US and from Holland. The American qualitative study of laypeople's understandings of GM foods concludes that consumers enact more complex understandings of, for example, negotiations between risks and benefits of GMOs in food than traditional risk research assumes (Knight, 2009). The Dutch qualitative study analyses consumers' handling of avian influenza in relation to poultry products, building on practice theory, and four different 'rationalities' in relation to food safety governance of avian influenza are outlined (de Krom, 2009).

The Danish case study analysis that is discussed in the remainder of this chapter is closely related to this more constructionist second type of studies about consumption and food risks in everyday life.

The Danish Case Study: Risk Challenges to Food Consumption

The empirical project that is analysed and discussed in this chapter is called 'The risks of consumption. Environmental norms and consumer practices' (Halkier, 2001b).[2] The research consists of a qualitative in-depth study of how parents with young children handle environmentally related (and other) risks in food in everyday life. The sample consisted of 31 parents with children below the age of five who displayed a variance according to gender, social background, educational level and habitat. The data material primarily used in this book consisted of six focus groups (Morgan, 1997) with parents who in each of the focus groups were

2 The study was carried out under the auspices of Centre for Social Scientific Environmental Research (CeSam), and it was financed by the National Danish Strategic Environmental Research Programme, 1998–2000.

part of each others' social network.[3] In the focus groups, the participating parents discussed what concerned them most about food in daily life, what kinds of food they associated with risk, whether and how they experienced environmental issues to be a part of food risk, and what ordinary families can do to handle questions about risk. Data analysis for this book is based upon a combination of qualitative coding, categorising and domain analysis (Coffey and Atkinson, 1996) and methods for analysing interaction, mainly positioning analysis (Harré and Langenhove, 1999).[4]

As in Chapter 3, the analysis in this chapter must take into consideration the changes that have occurred in the Danish context since the data were produced in 1999 and 2000. The biggest change has been the incorporation of the concrete choices of individual food consumers regarding food safety control via the Smiley system.

The presentation and discussion of the Danish case study on risk handling in food consumption follows the form for all four empirical chapters, outlined in more detail in the general methodology section (see the last section of Chapter 2). The following briefly summarises this outline.

First, the analysis describes and categorises one specific kind of food practice that is found among the Danish parents. The other kinds of food practices carried out among the parents are similar to the ones described and categorised in Chapter 3 about young consumers and environmentalisation. Again, food practices are described first in order to understand the basic configuration of which food consumption is already a part; namely, the food practices. This lays the groundwork for inferences later in the analysis about the ways in which people react to having their food consumption questioned.

Second, the analysis describes and categorises the different ways of handling risk in food consumption in an ideal typology. The purpose of this second part of the analysis is twofold: first, demonstrate the variety in reactions to 'riskified' food consumption, second, to discuss whether everyday life performing in relation to food risks constitutes a practice in itself or not, in order to contribute to the discussions about consumer agency.

3 The other part of the data material consisted in a textual analysis of different genres of public texts about the individual consumer and different kinds of food risks. The genres of texts were goods (food products, used in the focus groups), leaflets from public authorities about food risks on display in supermarkets, television shows on risk and food, and the coverage of a particular food risk case in national Danish television news.

4 Some of the data in this chapter was originally analysed and presented 'differently' in B. Halkier. (2001b). Risk and food: Environmental concerns and consumer practices, *International Journal of Food Science and Technology*, 36, 801–12 and in B. Halkier. (2001a). Consuming ambivalences. Consumer handling of environmentally related risks in food, *Journal of Consumer Culture*, 1, 205–24.

Third, the analysis zooms in on the details of how risk challenged consumption activities are performed by focusing on the practical procedures. The purpose of this third part of the analysis is to highlight the significance and complexities of the practical do-ability involved in everyday reactions to risk and food consumption.

Fourth, the analysis gives examples of negotiations of the normative engagement in risk challenged food consumption and how the negotiations reproduce, adapt, change, improvise and experiment with the normative content of agency of ordinary consumers, the category of 'safe food', and exceptions to proper 'safe' conduct. The purpose of this analysis is to suggest less individual life-world focus and more focus on the influence of social processes in research on risk and consumption.

Food Practices?

Before we move on to describe and discuss the diverse ways of dealing with risk challenges to food in everyday life, a practice theory-inspired analysis begins by looking at the patterns of food practices that are becoming contested by risk discourses. What are the food practices into which the consumption contestations enter?

Parents with young children obviously belong to a different life stage than the young food practitioners in Chapter 3. However, the kinds of food practices described in Chapter 3 can be recognised among the parents of young children too: Food as necessity, food as pleasure, food as health and food as project for changing the world. This is not surprising, because these kinds of food practices resonate with the types found in other qualitative sociological and anthropological studies of food routines (Coveney, 2000; Holm and Kildevang, 1996; Lupton, 1996; Murcott, 2000). Hence, rather than describing these four kinds of food practices again, this section describes a fifth kind of practice that is only expressed among the parent food practitioners.

Food as Skill

This type of food practice is coordinated by understandings, procedures and engagement in knowing how to deal with food and food work (Bove and Sobal, 2006; Short, 2006: 103–5). Food is acquired not only through shopping but also by growing one's own vegetables, fruits and berries, having a compost bin in the garden and by keeping hens, or by getting this kind of food as well as meat and fish from members of the social network. Furthermore, most meals and certain foods such as bread are cooked from scratch. The main understanding here is that by producing food yourself or getting it from someone you know personally, you'll know your food thoroughly and you do not have to worry about the quality, the taste or the safety. The following shows how one of the couples in a rural focus group expressed this. Karen (female pharmacy assistant) and Nis-Peter (male farmer) are married; Grete (female childcare assistant) and Lone (female housewife) also participate.

> Karen: 'You know, we eat lots of meat. But we don't have to get out and buy it, we buy whole pigs and butcher them … so it's a bit different, you know, I don't worry about the things I dive into the freezer for [Grete: 'No.'], I assume that the meat is okay [Grete: 'Yep.']. Then there's everything else … [laughter] … that there are problems with.'
> Nis-Peter: 'We are probably not so occupied with this as you are … although … no, we don't, no doubt … That's perfectly all right, but it's probably because we produce a lot of food ourselves, I think. Then I think we … perhaps we feel a bit more that we know how things are made.'
> Karen: 'I do also cook everything from scratch, you know I wouldn't dream of buying a ready-made pizza. [Nis-Peter: 'No.'] So in that sense, I actually believe that the food we get is … it's safe, you know. You can hardly know that if you buy absolutely pre-fabricated food.'
> Lone: 'That's been heated and re-heated and re-heated …'
> Karen: 'Yep.' [laughter]

This main understanding can also be found quantitatively in a survey with a representative sample of Danes, where the majority answered 'agree completely' to the statement, 'The food I or my family or friends grow in the garden is more safe to eat than the food I can buy' (Halkier and Holm, 2004: 22). This understanding of local food as safer food is also found among food consumers in the international literature (e.g. Murdoch and Miele, 1999: 480–81; Day and Truninger, 2007: 24).

The engagement in this type of food practice revolves around a pride in knowing how to provide good food and meals. This could mean, for example, to get a 'good catch' of meat by buying eco-pork from one of your football mates, or to teach the children how peas really taste by letting them pick them in their own garden. Training the children to become skilled food practitioners is a part of this engagement, and a procedure would be to involve the children in daily cooking and food provisioning from an early age. This engagement comes forth in the following quote from the other rural focus group. Helle (female nurse) and Hans (male unskilled worker) are married, and Lisa is their daughter. Johannes (male social worker) and Minna (female preschool teacher) are married.

> Helle: 'It's also a bit this about giving the kids, you know we do give them some food routines, because they [Johannes: 'I think so too, that's important.'] can eat themselves fat in the kitchen garden, right.'
> Hans: 'We haven't bought seeds yet this year, because Lisa, she thinks, now we have to get some …'
> Johannes: 'Yep … that's actually one of the good things about it …'
> Hans: 'Because she began having her own slot in the vegetable garden last year … and this year she has planted some strawberry plants, because she wants to

> have her own strawberry jam toast, right? I think that's important, this way we can give them some baggage.'
> Minna: 'A bit like from farm to fork, right? That's something you … it's a bit important to give your children.'

The parents here are explaining how getting to know food and food practices arise from practising the physical elements of acquiring, preparing and eating food.

Food Practices and Practitioners

Just like the young food practitioners, these parent practitioners express different kinds of food practices across the exchanges and negotiations in the focus groups. This is the first set of variations one must take into account when analysing how the risk challenge of food consumption is handled in everyday food practices. In the practising of food activities, food practitioners rarely stick to one kind. This could be related to the character of food practices as integrated practice. Food practices are something that is done every single day, many times a day, and to practise food is necessary to survive; everyone has to be a practitioner! This is very different from both leisure practices (such as swimming) and other everyday practices (such as laundering) that are not necessarily practised every day or by everyone. Therefore, food practices tend to nearly always be involved when the intersections of the multiple everyday practices tend to clash, which may contribute to the crossover of the different expressions of practising food. If food practice can be so varied even for the individual practitioner, how then can food practices be understood as an integrative practice? This is because each of the ways of practising food is organised through the dynamics of food understandings, food procedures and food engagements, and because practitioners recognise what goes on as practising food.

In other words, food practitioners do not stick to one kind of food practice when practising food. They may perform food as necessity on a Monday evening, food as health in the cafeteria at work, and food as pleasure when friends are visiting on the weekend. This complexity in food practices has, of course, consequences for the connections between everyday food activities and the way in which the risk contestation of food consumption is carried out. The diversity in ways of handling food risk is discussed in the next section of this chapter.

Ways of Handling Food Risk

In this section, some of the complexities in handling food risks through consumption are analysed by using the more applied concepts related to the concept of practice (doing, sayings, activities, understandings, procedures, engagements and performances) to construct an ideal typology. Specifically for the risk-handling analysis, one should be aware that food practitioners do not usually distinguish between different types of food risks in their expressions of their food doings and sayings. Other societal actors – experts, producers and public authorities – would, for example, distinguish between health-related food risks (such as salmonella) and environmental food risks (such as pesticide residues), and they would probably not talk about fat and sugar in food as a risk issue at all, but rather as a nutrition issue. This tendency for consumer-citizens to hold more complex understandings of risk is supported in current research, (Blok et al., 2006: 326; Kjærnes et al., 2007: 190; Knight, 2009: 187; Sellerberg, 1991: 196; Simmons, 1997: 253).

A second purpose – apart from demonstrating the variety in risk-handling reactions – is to discuss whether handlings of risk in consumption can be understood as a practice in itself. Integrative practices probably hold priority in everyday life, so knowing analytically if some activities are performances or practices should influence realistic expectations to societal consumer agency. This is also a reason why the mundane constructions of consumer agency among the participants in the case study form a part of the ideal typology.

When looking at patterns in risk handling from a practice theoretical perspective, it seems less obvious to look at handlings of risk in food as a practice in itself, compared to the discussion in Chapter 3 about environmentalised consumption. This is due to two reasons, which will be discussed for each of the elements of the analysis. First, it is more difficult to see expressions among the parental food practitioners as constructing one way of handling risk as a particular category of socially recognisable consumers or consumption that they either identify with or distance themselves from socially. This is compared with the socially recognisable construction of 'the green consumer' among the young food practitioners. Second, there is no single food consumption activity among the different risk-handling activities that can easily be associated with a potential risk-handling practice and therefore become constructed as such among the parent food practitioners. Among the young food practitioners in Chapter 3, buying organic food was one very clear marker of environmentally friendly food consumption practices. Among the parent practitioners, a variety of more or less equal markers of 'safer food consumption' are represented.

Worried

This first way of handling risk challenges of food consumption is exemplified by the worried type. Dealing explicitly and proactively with risk challenges of daily food consumption is the main characteristic of this type of risk handling. The food practitioners pay attention to the medialised discourses about food risks, and they look for specific knowledge on particular problems, such as, for example, salmonella in pork or artificial additives in wine gums, in order to learn how to use less risky food and food handling procedures.

Activities in dealing with the risk challenges of food are, for example, to seek knowledge, to discuss issues about risk, safety and food in the family and social network, and to provide, cook and eat food and meals that are understood as less risky. A woman in one of the rural focus groups expresses it like this:

> No, no, but a better kind of food in the sense that … well, we can't know that, can we, but it's probably because we hope that, but there are not so many residues of all these strange things, that we don't know how they will react in our bodies, right. That's also why we are willing to pay a little bit more for it, right. (Minna, female preschool teacher)

In de Krom's qualitative study of Dutch consumers' involvement in handling food safety, a very similar expression can be found in one of the quotes: *'Noxious substances that are present in conventional meat enter your body and add up in there, which results in people falling ill, like my wife did … when my wife fell ill, we decided to stop eating rubbish'* (De Krom, 2009: 7).

What is understood as 'not rubbish' or less risky food and meals in the Danish study are, for example, own produce, friends' and neighbours' produce, Danish food products, organic food, meals where the raw ingredients are treated according to public advice on hygiene, and food without straw shortening chemicals, pesticide residues, GMOs and artificial colouring. A typical expression of this is found in this quote from one of the big city focus groups:

> But mostly I become a little angry, really irritated about, it's damn well … too much that food products are made and sold in this way that are so lousy and infested with bacteria and such and sprayed and everything. Um, and it doesn't give the consumer, as a consumer you don't get a real choice I think. Because it's like choosing between the devil and the deep blue sea, right? Yeah, you can choose organic goods and then … send up a quiet prayer that it's okay. (Sara, female unemployed academic)

Here, it is organic food that is invested with the hope of better quality and safety, a framing of organic food that has been found in a number of other studies (Connolly and Prothero, 2008: 135; Magnusson et al., 2003; Michaelidou and Hassan, 2008; Murdoch and Miele, 1999: 480–81). Still, to eat organic food is not the single defining activity of riskified performance as it was for environmentalised food performances and practices. There are also examples of studies where organic food is not necessarily understood as safer food, e.g. in Norway (Storstad and Bjørkhaug, 2003: 160–61).

A range of procedures in food activities or related to food activities work to help instil less risk in the family's food consumption. Such procedures include, for example, to read and react upon food content declarations, to establish rules in the family about candy eating, to cook meals from scratch, to treat raw eggs and chicken according to official advice about hygiene, and to watch and use recommendations from consumer programmes on television. The engagement in this risk-handling type performance is related to exerting agency and protecting the family. This kind of engagement resembles one of the so-called 'consumer rationalities' in de Krom's qualitative study of Dutch food consumers and how they react to food safety governance in the age of avian influenza (de Krom, 2009). The consumer rationalities are ideal typical ways in which these Dutch food consumers deal with poultry meat in their everyday food practices, and the theoretical framework of the Dutch study is practice theory. The Dutch consumption ideal type that is comparable with the worried way of dealing with food risk is the type called 'rationality of one for all', where consumer agency is actively used in order to improve the societal supply of food and to persuade members of the social network to do the same (ibid.: 13–14).

The worried way of dealing with food risks has at least one important parallel with the 'identifying' way of dealing with environmental challenges in Chapter 3. The two types have in common the positive understanding of consumer agency in society and the engagement in actively carrying out such agency; here on behalf of the family, especially the children. This is clearly expressed in the following quote from one of the rural focus groups:

> But I think it's terribly difficult, when you try to buy the right things and the sensible stuff … can you believe the things that are written on the different packages and … you know, right down to the cradle-stage of this product, really you don't know what they include and … so it's damn difficult. I so much want to offer my little child something proper, but I don't have many chances to get to the bottom of it. (Grete, female childcare assistant)

This practical procedural way of exerting consumer agency in order to protect oneself and loved ones can be recognised in a similar quote from Connolly and Prothero's qualitative study of Irish green consumers, where one of the women explains: *'You'd laugh if you saw me shopping – I read the ingredients of everything if it's something we've not had before – everything'* (Connolly and Prothero, 2008: 135).

Why not understand this type of risk-handling activities in relation to food as a consumption practice in itself? I would argue that in the data from the Danish case study, this type of dealing with risk challenges does not include sufficient practice elements to qualify as a kind of social practice in itself. Rather, worried risk handling should be seen as a particular type of performance within the food practices of the parents. There are very few statements in the focus groups where either social identification, recognition or distancing is explicitly related to a bundle of doings and sayings about risk handling. Neither are there systematic constructions of particular groups of consumers seen as good or bad risk handlers. This may, of course, be related to the method of data-production; namely, focus groups, which do not allow much space for long individual narratives with examples. On the other hand, constructions of socially recognisable categories of consumption and consumers were plentiful in the focus group data from the young food practitioners in the Chapter 3 analysis. It seems more likely that the lack of constructions of a clear ‘package’ of riskified food consumption could be related to the ‘missing’ single distinguishing activity in risk handling.

Furthermore, are identification and recognition more important than if the individual food practitioner performs the doings and sayings of the risk-handling activities in such ways that they amount to a practice project in the Schatzkian sense? Such a practice project could, for example, be to provide as many ‘safe’ meals as possible for your children, which could arguably be the case for the risk-handling food activities of e.g. Grete (who was quoted earlier) and Lone from one of the rural focus groups, and for Sara and Corinna from the two different big city focus groups. Here is how one of them expresses it:

> But I do feel at least that of course I want to give Ida [her daughter] the best of the best, and I also want to, how can you say this, try to buy … the best of raw materials, and what do I know, right, but I just also think that you can make it into … almost like a jungle to trace, because you spend oceans of time finding the correct of the correct, right? And that means that you have less time for your family when you actually come home and you’re completely confused … you know, I felt like that when Ida was little and I rushed around to buy her organic food, right, you know I think I simply spent oceans of time on it … and I have had to cut down on that and say, okay, if they have it where I shop, I buy organic, and otherwise it will just have to be as it is, because … it’s too far. (Corinna, female clerk)

However, as it is clear from Corinna’s statement, everyday conditions and the intersections of other practices weigh heavily among the parent food practitioners, limiting the amount of risk-handling activities (doings and sayings) that occur. Thus, it is questionable whether worried risk handling amounts to a practice project in itself.

Irritated

The second type of dealing with risk challenges of food can be called the irritated type. The main characteristic of this kind of risk-handling performance is the conflicts in the intersections with other practices. The medialised discourses about food risks are followed from the sideline, but only because food practitioners experience that they cannot escape it in the daily flow of their media practices. Hence, food risk knowledge has a tendency to work through ‘push’ – communication towards consumers as the target group in media campaigns, rather than ‘pull’ – communication where consumers actively seek out and pull knowledge to themselves, as in the worried type of risk handling (Cover, 2006: 148–50; Lull, 2007: 80–100).

Activities in dealing with the risk challenges of food vary considerably in this type of performance, both in terms of what is done and said as well as in the frequency of doings and sayings. Weeks can go by without the food practitioner performing any food risk handlings, and then the media or members of the social network may remind the food practitioner of a risk issue, and activities are changed for a while. This is expressed in the following quote from one of the big city focus groups that illustrates this shifting way of relating to food risk in everyday life:

> I thought about chicken, you know … it's so embarrassing or irritating. Because I have such a good short-term memory. So when I've seen one of these television shows I become deeply offended and think NEVER again. Then about ten days go by, and then I stand in Gobi[5] and buy five chickens for a hundred kroner.[6] Because then I'm too stingy. Then it doesn't work any longer. But you know, it works immediately, and it's very scary, but um … then I've got such a good filter up here [points to her head]. It's both economic, but also … a bit comfort, you know, because you could think differently. You know, one chicken could last for two rounds of something, right? ... But it doesn't last so damned long time … (Melissa, female childcare assistant)

Here, the risk-handling activity in other words consists in what not to do; namely, avoiding the use of cheap battery chickens, suspected of salmonella problems. This way of dealing with risk in food resembles another of de Krom's consumer rationalities; namely, the 'rationality of the centrality of the self' (de Krom, 2009: 12–13). Here, food consumption activities revolve around not over-reacting on information about food risks, and trust in members of the social network is more important for what is regarded as safe food than trust in abstract governmental regulatory systems.

Among the Danish parents, there are also irritated risk-handling activities where the construction of food as safer or less risky is shifting. In the following quote, Jes (electrician), one of the male food practitioners in one of the small-town focus groups, enacts his irritated understanding of organic food, stressing that the organic label can be fraud, referring to general knowledge from media stories. Katrine (nurse) is his wife, and Carl (male computer consultant) and Caroline (female bank employee) are their married friends:

> Jes: 'But then again, I have this a bit with ecology, right …'
> Carl: 'Yeah, what is organic there [Jes: 'Yeah.']. Yeah really …'
> Katrine: 'But, that …'
> Jes (interrupts): 'Is it organic butter from some organic cow that has been grazing on a sprayed field and …'
> Katrine (interrupts): 'But they're NOT allowed to.'

5 Gobi was at that time a discount supermarket chain.

6 Equivalent of 11–12 Euros. In Denmark, you would only be able to buy battery chickens at this price, and Denmark has witnessed several rounds of problems with salmonella infections in battery chickens.

> Jes: 'No. But you see it time and again, right … [Katrine: 'But then …'], then you find out it's no more than the letters that are organic.'
> Caroline: 'You know, sometimes you do think about it, when you see these investigations where they say, oh it wasn't quite organic anyway, then you have actually paid more for more or less the same product.'

On the other hand, when the group grapples with specific food products and their understandings of risky and secure in relation to them, Jes tells the others in the focus group that he and Katrine often drive to the local organic farm shop and buy vegetables. This may very well be related to composite relations of trust in food among food practitioners. Some types of organic food are not trusted because they are part of the abstract, institutionalised systems. Other more local forms of organic food are trusted, not so much because they are organic, but because they are local and hence are categorised as belonging to the 'knowable' in the same way as own produce and the social network's produce are (Halkier and Holm, 2004: 23; Lupton, 2005: 456; Misztal, 1996: 157).

The shifting of the risk-handling activities and procedures is related not only to the coming and going of risk issues in the medialised discourses, but also to the ways risk handling is viewed as conflicting with or threatening other everyday practices. This includes, for example, parental practices of letting children eat what they like best or what other children are allowed to eat. It also includes shopping practices of getting through the supermarket as quickly as possible without thinking too much about what lands in the trolley. And it includes food practices of eating what is enjoyable to eat and to share this pleasure in the family. In this way, the engagement in this type of dealing with the risk challenge of food is related to defending bodily and social pleasures in food practices. One of the food practitioners from one of the big city focus groups talked about this:

> I still think it's really annoying if these television programmes somehow … no information is good. But I still have this, I think that the quality of all kinds of food has somehow, to use that word, been made suspicious towards food and these kind of things, hng? I think that all food is infested with you having to be suspicious towards it, and you can … the sheer enjoyment and pleasure about it, and just being, just incorporating, you know without having to have those great reflections about whether it comes from one place or another. I think it's bloody annoying. And somehow I would really like to drop it. You know, completely stop thinking about it. Only say what I feel like and buy that and make it and end of story. (Jan, male childcare assistant)

The irritated way of dealing with food risk issues embraces as a type of performance even more diverse procedures than the worried type. However, what seems to unite the irritated risk-handling activities, apart from the conflicts with other practices, is that the food consumer displays a lack of recognition of societal consumer agency or a lack of confidence in the potential of such consumer agency. The ordinary food consumer is seen as a weak societal actor. Connolly and Prothero emphasise in their study of green consumers in Ireland that even among explicitly risk- and environmentally dedicated consumers, there are dilemmas, complexities of knowledge, and doubts about consequences of an individualisation of responsibility in relation to consumer agency (Connolly and Prothero, 2008: 137).

The understanding of the food consumer as a weak actor is expressed in the following quote from one of the rural focus groups in the Danish case study:

> But I am also tired of the media in the way that … they bring something up, right, and then I sit and work myself all up about it and saying that it's too bloody bad … but my possibilities for doing ANYTHING about it are not really there, are they? You know … the fish does not get better from them making such a television show, right? I've just got yet another problem thrown into my face, right? (Johannes, male social worker)

This is an understanding that irritated risk performance has in common with the distancing environmental performance described in Chapter 3; however, there are many other elements of mundane performance where the two types of challenge handling are different.

Pragmatic

This last way of handling the risk challenge to food can be called pragmatic. The main characteristic of this type of risk handling is the upholding of practical and social do-abilities; in this way pragmatic risk performance has a lot in common with the Chapter 3 type of appropriating environmental performance. This is reflected in the following brief quote from one of the small-town focus groups: *'We sort of listen to everything – and then we do what suits us anyway!'* (Jane, female fishmonger). The medialised discourses about food risks are known, and the practitioners' doings and sayings refer to their representations, for example pesticide residues in fruit, hormones in beef, salmonella in chickens and artificial additives in fruit syrup.

But the main understanding is neither that risk in food is an important problem that necessitates proactive engagement, nor that risk in food is media communication that interferes with pleasurable routines. The main understanding is that food risks are everyday problems to which there are practical solutions, just like there are practical solutions to getting the dinner made that fit family logistics, and there are practical and socially appropriate solutions for providing something sweet to go along with the coffee served for unexpected guests. A quote from one of the rural focus groups illustrates this understanding:

> I think about such things as fruit and the like, you can't assess when they say that it's not sprayed, but I don't believe very much in that, you know. I think it's

> sprayed in some degree all of it, you know. But really, you can't do anything else than, then you have to buy it and wash it and … eat it. (Helle, female nurse)

Here, the practical solution to pesticide residues in fruit – to wash the fruit before you eat it – has become routinised. This kind of risk-handling performance resembles the type called 'rationality of the mediators' from de Krom's study of Dutch food consumers and risk behaviour (de Krom, 2009: 14–15), where the routinisation of food practices and responses to food risks is important.

Thus, the activities involved in dealing pragmatically with food risk are as diverse as can possibly be imagined, since there is no primary, substantial understanding of what is perceived as less risky food and food procedures. For example, among the food practitioners who enact pragmatic risk handling, the status of organic food and Danish food varies greatly. Some practitioners understand these types of food as something to be routinely used as a practical solution to food risk, while other practitioners never include organic food in their consumption and in some food categories prefer foreign food, such as Italian ham and French cheese.

What ties together this type of risk performance is a combination of the main understanding of risk as mundane problems with concrete solutions; the attempts to establish and work mainly with routine procedures for the handling of food risk; and engagement in making food practices in everyday life work. This type of risk performance is comparable to ways in which Australian food consumers deal with the risks of food poisoning. According to Lupton's qualitative study of the risk-handling discourses and strategies among Australian food consumers, it is precisely the routinised procedures of, for example, keeping raw meat separate from other foods and washing fruit before eating it that form the core of the consumers' risk handling (Lupton, 2005: 458). What follows is an example of a media discourse-sceptical version of pragmatic dealings with food risks among the Danish parents, expressed by a couple from one of the big city focus groups, Marie (female university student) and Kristian (male civil engineer):

> Marie: 'Yeah, but you cannot live according to what's up and about currently, what's healthy at the moment, because … when we have reached our age, that has changed so many times what is healthy and what is unhealthy, so … if you should live according to this you would have to change your entire eating habits.'
> Kristian: 'Yeah, every six months!'
> Marie: 'And we can't be bothered to do so, you know. Then you have to say, okay, we choose this, what you believe, and what we by the way think is tasty. You will have to know that more or less though.'

In Lupton's Australian study, there is a similar quote from one of the male participants, illustrating the scepticism towards the medialised discourse that produces risk challenges in relation to ordinary food practices:

> I never believe anything I hear on the news about cancer scares and peanut butter or anything like that. I don't take any notice of any of that – over the years they've said everything's supposed to have cancer. Why bother listening to them. I don't take any notice of them. Now if you lay off all the foods they say are going to give you cancer, you wouldn't eat at all. Use a bit of common sense! (Lupton, 2005: 460)

The question of consumer agency in relation to this type of risk performance is neither a practical acceptance of societal consumer agency, nor is it a dilemma-ridden rejection of the same. Apparently, agency is both understood and performed as taken-for-granted procedures of solving problems, and food practices are negotiated and adjusted to such mundane problem-solving. It can be discussed to which degree such an agency is related to society, but for some of the practitioners who are enacting pragmatic risk performance it seems to do so. This is illustrated in the following discussion from one of the big city focus groups, beginning with comments about crisps that contain GMO (Buggles corn crisps) and dealing with the issue of societal consumer agency. Lea (female student) and Keld (male student) are married and have a baby, and they primarily enact the pragmatic risk performance type throughout the focus group. Lotte (female bank assistant) and Stig (computer consultant) are also married.

> Lotte: 'I haven't bought these [picks up the Buggles corn crisps] since I learned that they are genetically manipulated, I haven't bought one single package since.'
> Stig: 'You know, boycott the products, that's the way we can handle these problems ... and then we can shout at our politicians, right?'
> Lea: 'Think about it in the daily shopping, right?'
> Stig: 'Avoid the products.'
> Keld: 'I think I choose a handful of products that I trust in, and then I just buy them ... and if I find out something bad about them...about rye bread for example, then I will have to find another rye bread I can have confidence in ... you know.'

The question is, of course, whether consumers' handling of the safety of their food is seen as a societal question – or a private one.

Risk Performances and Food Practices

None of the three types of risk handling can in my view be understood as a practice in itself. There is no systematic social recognition among the parent food practitioners of risk handling as connected bundles of doings and sayings. Why is it important to discuss whether risk handling in food consumption can constitute a practice or not? One argument is that it enables us better to grasp what goes on in everyday life. In a practice theoretical perspective, practices and their carrying out are the most basic assumptions about how social life unfolds itself. This means that activities and performances that can be understood as practices probably have priority in people's daily lives, and other types of activities, performances, changes in conditions, etc., are manoeuvred in relation to the intersecting web of integrated practices.

Thus, dealing with risk in food consumption becomes integrated into food practices in various ways, because the organising of food practices generates needs, wants and occasions for choice. Lone, the housewife from one of the rural focus groups, carries out her food activities as a project for changing the world, by keeping a kitchen garden that allows her to be almost self-sufficient and by upholding vegetarian cooking and eating in the family. When the media discourses challenge ordinary food consumption with food risk issues, Lone and her family respond with an active search for information and discussions in the social network about what is risky or safe food and food procedures. They also begin to choose more organic goods and Danish goods, reconstruct their understanding of the goods into a risk discourse, and add a new understanding to their engagement in growing their own fruit and vegetables.

However, when comparing the patterns of the parents' participation in the different risk performance types with their enactments of different food practice types, there are no simple relationships between kind of food practice and risk performance type. The parents who primarily practice food as necessity participate in both worried and pragmatic risk performances. The parents who predominantly practise food as pleasure do not all perform irritated risk handling as might be expected. And among the parents who mainly practise food as project for changing the world or food as skill, there is also variation across all three types of risk performances. The next section of this chapter focuses on the details of the practical procedures of dealing with food risks. The aim is to emphasise the complexities of practical do-ability in dealing with riskified food consumption. This is done in order to discuss the relative importance of procedures versus engagements in relation to handling of risk-challenged consumption. The optimistic analytical position 'empowering consumers' from Chapter 1 has a tendency to lend primacy to elements in active consumption that relate to engagements. But practical procedures seem to be equally important in how everyday consumption agency is carried out.

Ambivalent Procedures

This part of the analysis focuses on the complexities of procedures (principles and rules of how to do) in doing risk handling in food consumption. Ambivalence is one kind of complexity in how to do consumption that often appears in the analytical discussions of food risk and ordinary consumption. Food risks fit into the modern complexities of the body and the management of control and desire, expressed in the many governmentalities of the modern bodily practices (e.g. Coveney, 2000; Dean, 1999; Gronow, 1997b; Hewitt, 1991; Lupton, 1999:

84–103; Macnaghten and Urry, 1998; Nielsen, 2008; Sassatelli, 2001). Also, food risk is a type of food consumption challenge that perhaps is experienced as closer to the food practitioners' own bodies and their children's bodies in real time than environmental challenges. This may enhance the prevalence of ambivalence in the everyday dealings with food risk. Ambivalence in the dealings with risk in everyday food practices is especially tied to the procedures in how performing is carried out. What procedures are used to deal with food risk, and in which ways do these procedures entail ambivalence for the practitioners?

Although ambivalence in practical procedures was present in the case study about environmentalisation of food, ambivalence seems to take up more social space in the carrying out of risk-handling performances among the Danish parents. At the time of the case study data production, a textual analysis was performed on different consumer positions in various texts in the public domain that were constructing the consumer's position in relation to food risks;[7] for example, the consumer as victim or the consumer as hero. A similar analysis on different consumer positions was performed on the data from the focus groups. This analysis showed that the dominant construction among the parents was the ambivalent consumer (Halkier, 2001a: 218). This was especially striking compared with the textual analysis of the same categories in the public texts, where the dominant construction was the consumer as victim.

Ambivalence as a part of food practices, however, works in a variety of socially do-able ways and not just as the conflict version that is typically associated with ambivalence (Bauman, 1991; Warde, 1997: 67–69; Ziehe, 1988), and which is also represented in the analyses in Chapter 3. Thus, the analysis in this section reveals a multitude of ways that ambivalence is carried out in practical procedures of risk handling.

Conflicting

This is the classical way of expressing ambivalence, where the bodily/mental procedures used in dealing with a challenge result in conflicting events and situations within food practices. Here, food practitioners will experience tension in the organisation of their daily food activities, if they include the explicit knowledge about food risk from the mediated discourses into their understandings and procedures of their food activities. The potential or realised awareness of these tensions interferes with the routinised procedures of how to acquire, cook and eat food.

The experience of tensions can, for example, occur when the food practitioner is being reminded of the explicit knowledge about food risks from food labels and commercials in the supermarket, while the practitioner just tries to get the routine

7 The public texts were the goods themselves (that were used in the focus groups), leaflets from public authorities about food risks on display in supermarkets, particular television shows on risk and food, and current television news on food risks.

food shopping over and done with. The conflicting ambivalence experience is related to being pushed into reflection in activities where practitioners usually go about with procedures without explicit reflexivity. Here, one of the parents from a rural focus group describes such a conflicting ambivalence situation, triggered by the label on a package of rye bread:

> I think about that one, actually it irritates me … baked without straw-shortening chemicals, right … you know, straw-shortened wheat … because it makes me think that it is put there because a while ago there was a debate about horses being less fertile or their sperm quality being much lower due to straw-shortening chemicals, right. And this is meant to make me think that straw-shortening chemicals is something terrible, which I think it probably IS … but I find it tiresome that they have to manipulate with such a bloody label there, it irritates me. And this is … if I go shopping, what I buy is directed by what irritates me. (Johannes, male social worker)

The conflicting carrying out of ambivalent procedures is one of the key elements in irritated risk handling.

Legitimising

Here, ambivalence still consists of contradictory procedures. But when food practitioners legitimise ambivalent procedures, the contradictions of dealing with food risk are 'placed' outside their own mundane agency procedures. Instead, ambivalence in how to do is placed as part of the conditions for consuming food in modern large-scale societies. This is an important difference from the first type, the conflicting ambivalent procedures, where the do-ability of dealing with risk in food consumption is incorporated in food practitioners' mundane agency. In this second type, consuming without carrying out ambivalences in the procedures is placed outside of the do-able; hence legitimising existing food procedures. Here is a typical example from one of the small-town focus groups, where the parents are discussing their understandings of different food risk types against each other:

> You just don't know … because then sometimes I start thinking about … the bacteria they might get you ill here and now, but you just don't KNOW about these additives, is it something in the longer run … and why are there, ARE there more cases of cancer, or is it just because now they discover them, right. Or IS it because there is something completely sick in our food, right? But you just can't … if you have to have food on the table every day, you just can't go around and think about it every day … (Katrine, female nurse currently on maternity leave)

The do-able is to get food on the table every day, and the routine procedures in this cannot be turned completely upside down by reflexivity about possible consequences of certain food activities. This situation is applied to food consumption in general by using the 'general you' instead of the 'personal me'. The same kind of legitimating ambivalence performing takes place at a group negotiation level. Here follows an example from one of the big city focus groups. Jan and Melissa are married, and they share a two-family house with Marie and her family:

> Jan: 'The chickens we had tonight, actually they are Easter food, right? But it's often difficult. In reality, it is limited to a couple of months where you can get chickens ... if you should follow the seasons, right?' [Marie: 'Yeah ...']
> Melissa: 'But that's also the ideal thought. You know, that's when you talk about it and think, oh, but what is it I would prefer to do. Now and then you remember that this is what you prefer to do – and then there are the days where you blody well just have to get the children from institution and shop and you are off at seven o'clock, right? Then it's roast pork and ... [Jan: 'Oh, you mean Monday to Friday?'] ... and French fries or such things.'
> Marie: 'You know, if the children can choose what we are having today, we are getting something roast with potatoes and gravy. And then you know there's peace and quiet! Everybody eats and is happy.'
> Melissa: 'This is what ... at least I think this is important to allow yourself to say, but that's the way it is then, right?' [Marie: 'Mmm.']

The ambivalence legitimised here is between the reflected ideal understandings of following the seasons with food in order to get better quality meals and on the other hand the do-able procedures of having to provide for meals in a busy family with young children every day of the week. The use of the 'general you' can also be noticed here as legitimising device. The legitimising performance of ambivalence resonates with Lupton's argumentation against the simplistic notion of reflexivity among laypeople in the writings on risk by Ulrich Beck (1992) and Anthony Giddens (1991). Lupton claims that empirical studies of risk dealings in daily life show that laypeople's use of reflections is broader and more complex, insofar that, for example everyday experiential understandings and relations with members of social networks are included (Lupton, 1999: 122).

The legitimising performance of ambivalence is not particularly connected with any of the risk-handling types.

Normalising

For some practitioners, however, ambivalence in the dealings with food risks in everyday life becomes incorporated into bodily/mental food procedures and thus also into mundane practitioner agency. Ambivalences between, for example, explicit discursive knowledge about risky food and implicit taken-for-granted ways of getting something to eat are adapted into the daily food practices by the help of bricolage (Gronow, 1997a: 170–71; Hall, 1992: 275–77). In a sociological sense, bricolage combines otherwise unrelated (or here potentially conflicting) elements (here food practice understandings, procedures and engagements) into a socially acceptable framework, such as in the narratives about food risk handling. This way, potential deviations and tensions can be adjusted into the normality of the food practice. This can be seen in the following quote from one of the rural focus groups, where one of the female parents explains how she combines the ambivalence between using organic food and fast food:

> I don't know … you know, I think I have a tendency to have ideological taste buds … someone once told me … [laughter] … I simply BELIEVE that organic tomatoes taste better than the traditional ones … so if they have something organic for sale … in the shop today … you know, if they for example have organic cauliflower, that can make me feel like eating cauliflower soup. I don't feel like it all winter, because … I don't know, I AM quite selective, because you know … I just pass by the vegetable shelves, because never mind about the traditional ones, it's about organic things, right … now they had cucumbers, right, so we are going to get tzatziki this week … so I go after the organic label a lot in this manner … then now and then we get a tin of non-organic sausages and bad consciousness. (Cecilie, female employed in clothes shop)

The normalising ambivalence experiences are particularly well represented among the enactments of the worried risk performance type, but they can be found in relation to pragmatic risk performances as well.

Escaping

Since ambivalence can create tension in the activities of food practitioners, ways of avoiding these tensions become worked into procedures for acquiring food, cooking meals and eating. In some ways, the two former types of ambivalence performances are accomplishing this: the conflict potential in food risk ambivalences is removed either by placing the conflict in society or by recognising the contingent character of one's own everyday life and adjusting the expectations for coherence. There is, however, a third way of getting rid of tension; namely, to make a choice about risk handling, turn this into a habit, and stop reflecting about risk discourses in this small area (see also de Krom, 2009: 14–15; Lupton, 2005: 458). This escaping ambivalence in procedures tends to be expressed under pragmatic risk handling. Here, engagement in risk performance is about making everyday life work, which is different from the engagement in worried risk performance to which the normalising ambivalence type is related. The food practitioner attempts to exclude risk reflexivity by routinising bodily/mental food procedures, which is different from normalising ambivalence, where reflexivity is incorporated into bodily/mental food routines.

Here is an example from one of the rural focus groups, where the parent enacts her tackling of ambivalence like this:

> I think about such things as fruit and the like. You can't assess it, when they say that it's not sprayed. But I don't believe very much in that, you know. I think it's sprayed to some extent, all of it you know. But really, you can't do anything else than – then you have to buy it and wash it and ... eat it. (Helle, female nurse)

Adapting to Ambivalence in Food Procedures

To handle risk challenges to food consumption in everyday life entails adjusting to ambivalences in practical procedural flows. The procedural adaptations made by the parents often resemble the procedural mixes between routines and reflexivity made by the young food practitioners in relation to environmental challenges. For example, complex bodily/mental procedures seem to be just as important as engagements in the ongoing accomplishment of dealing with the normative risk challenge in food practices. Even a high engagement in providing 'safer' meals for your children presupposes complicated and compound principles and ways of how to do this.

However, level of engagement seems to vary systematically between the different ambivalence procedures. Legitimising the daily use of meat products with many additives, because this is the kind of meat products that are supplied in the local supermarket, is connected to a lower level of engagement in food risks than normalising the 'part-time use' of tinned sausages. The analysis in the next section of this chapter focuses on the negotiations of the level and content of normative engagements in risk handling. This is done by showing how social interactions are part and parcel of shaping the normative content of categories such as 'safe food' and risk agency. The purpose is to question the individual-centred approach to engagement-like factors such as lifestyle, reflection, relevance, values and motivations – be that phenomenological life-world-centred or rationalistic cognitively centred. Engagement in handling food risks does not only get entangled in practical procedures, engagement also gets mixed up and reproduced and changed through social interactions in daily life.

Normative Negotiations of Risk-Challenged Consumption

In this analysis, three types of normative negotiations about risk handling are presented in order to discuss the place of social interaction in the processes of handling risk in food consumption. The three types of normative negotiations are: negotiations about the agency position of the ordinary food consumer in relation to responsibility for reducing food risks; negotiations about an important normative category (Danish food); and negotiations about exceptions to appropriate risk-reducing normative performances.

Negotiating the Agency Position of Ordinary Consumers

The normative content of this type of negotiation is constructing a particular normative do-ability. 'Cutting corners in risk handling is okay in a busy everyday life' is the normatively acceptable engagement. This tells us something about how much adjustment and change can be expected among ordinary food practitioners and thereby suggests that researchers adapt optimistic expectations to societal consumer risk agency. Supporting this interpretation is the finding that this normative construction is enacted and obtains consensus across the social differences (in, for example, educational background – A-level or no A-level – and habitat – rural, small town, big city) between the focus groups.

The following example comes from one of the rural focus groups near the end of the group discussion, where the participants are negotiating what the individual families can do about food risks. The sequence shows how the social interaction helps shape the normative content (there are everyday limits to what consumers can do). In the exchanges, the participants support each other in reproducing this normative content and forming an explicit consensus about the construction. They also legitimise the normative content by systematically referring to a generalised 'you' when talking about their own agency, meaning that these limits to risk-handling consumer agency belong to consumers in general and not just themselves.

The participants in the sequence are Helle (female nurse) married to Hans (unskilled worker), and Minna (female preschool teacher) married to Johannes (male social worker).

> Helle: 'Actually, it's belief, but also really to pay attention to the information you get now and then and then perhaps take it with a pinch of salt, you know.'
> Minna: 'Your common sense, right [Helle: 'Yeah.'], actually I think so too … but it's a lot about … you know, the information you get, right?'
> Helle: 'Yep.'
> Hans: 'Yeah.'
> Helle: 'And sometimes they are just more misleading than guiding. [Minna: 'Yep.'] … Because I think it's impossible for one family to dive into this, you ought to get into depth with the different things, and you can't, you know, you have to … eat something bad now and then, you know.'
> Hans: 'Yep.'
> Minna: 'Now and then it could be fun to become a little more knowledgeable, right, but that's how it is with those … solutions that you clearly could … but you know … it's again this, you don't want to be completely holier-than-thou in this world [Helle: 'Oh, no.'] … then it would be too …'
> Helle: 'No, the halo doesn't necessarily have to hang ABOVE your head, hng?'
> Minna: 'No … it's also about what's realistic, right.'
> Hans: 'Yep, that's realistic.'
> Helle: 'And to feel good, to be able to defend what you eat, you know.'
> Minna: 'Yeah.'

The social shaping of the explicit consensus about the normative content suggests that engagements in practising food and risk handling are not just expressions of emotional and normative orientations of the individual food practitioner, based on his or her trajectory through food practising and the multiplicity of intersections with other everyday practices. Rather, engagements are also co-constructed as practitioners go along in mundane social interaction.

The sequence also shows that there is an implicit construction of some 'other' food consumers, who are categorised as being very dedicated to handling risk in food (holier-than-thou), and from whom these parents wish to distinguish themselves socially (Bourdieu, 1984). However, as it has been pointed out earlier in this chapter, there are no concrete examples of known members of the network or specific stories of doings and sayings that would make it clear what 'holier-than-thou' risk handling might consist in.

Negotiating the Category Less Risky Food

Earlier in this chapter, I referred to quantitative studies with Danish consumers which show that a majority of Danes associate less risky food with food they have some kind of personal relationship with, either because they have produced it themselves or because someone they know personally has produced it (Halkier and Holm, 2004: 22–23). A variation of this normative construction of less risky food at a societal level is to construct food that is produced in one's own country as safer food or less risky food, compared to imported food. The construction of the category 'less risky food' as 'food nationalism' is shared across the social differences of the six focus groups. This normative content of the category less risky food in everyday food risk handling is also reflected in representative samples, not only of Danes but of a variety of Europeans (Berg, 2000; Kjærnes et al., 2007: 132). Interestingly, this norm of 'food nationalism' was not found in Lupton's study about handling of food risk among Australian consumers (Lupton, 2005: 463), which could be related to the institutional context that Australia is an exporter of fresh food, with little import of food.

The following example is a negotiation where consensus is formed about this 'buy Danish' normative content of the category 'less risky food'. The example shows how the content of 'less risky food is Danish food' becomes normatively 'filled out' as a result of the social interaction in the group. The participants keep reminding each other of their memories and sensate experiences, and more criteria become crammed into the category – seasonality, variety, no spraying, no additives and no perfection.

The sequence comes from one of the small-town focus groups, where Katrine (female nurse) is married to Jes (male electrician), and Caroline (female bank employee) is married to Carl (male computer consultant).

> Katrine: 'And then one thing that has made me think a bit about vegetables and such. I remember some time on the morning television, I heard something

> about … where they talked to the chefs there who cooked, and they said that in principle … yeah, not always, because they couldn't count on it, but they actually used the season's vegetables [Caroline: 'Yeah.'], because then you can have Danish vegetables, then you don't have to have them imported. And actually, that's proper, then you also get some variety, so that you don't always …'
> Caroline: 'Do you know what, I can actually remember when I was little, when I had rye bread with liver pate with green cucumber on top of it,[8] I did not get that all the year round, [Katrine: 'No, that was only during summer time, right?']. Yes, exactly.'
> Katrine: 'And I MUST admit, with cucumbers and such things, there I look for you know … or with most vegetables I have begun to see whether they're Danish. I don't know if they are less sprayed [Caroline: 'No, no.'] or what they are, but …'
> Caroline: 'But at least they are not artificially grown such as the apples we now hear about that lie around for a whole year before we get them, right. Typically, that's not how it is if it's season's fruit, right, that is from our home country, then it's grown here and now.'
> Jes: 'Then you also have to pay a bit more, right? You know, I will rather … if for example you have to buy a bag of apples or something … I buy these apples that are slightly more expensive, you get a little less, if I can see that … it's proper apples, not so polished or how to put it.'

In the negotiation, the participants make explicit self-positionings (using 'I') in relation to risk performance. They refer explicitly to their own doings or own food memories (Caroline's first input) and own uses of their bodily senses, such as Jes's account of 'not so polished apples'. This way, their social interaction helps shape the normative content of the construction 'Danish food as less risky food'. A number of different understandings of safe food are tied together to produce the practical guideline for doings, such as the uses of varied food, less sprayed food, less artificial food, and less perfect-looking food. Hence, practitioners can have a normative engagement in consuming less risky food, but to perform less risky food consumption is part of an ongoing social negotiation and adaptation about what this might consist in.

Negotiating Inappropriate Risk Handling

The discussion of normative negotiations in this subsection does not produce consensus. On the contrary, the negotiation in question contains normative conflict over what appropriate risk handling should consist in. The example shows how reactions in social interaction can influence the content in legitimising exceptions from proper risk-handling.

8 Rye bread slices with liver paté and a cucumber slice on top used to be perhaps the most classic lunch packet content for Danish schoolchildren in the 1970s and 1980s.

The sequence of negotiations comes from one of the big city groups, and the participants are three couples, consisting of Marie (female university student) and Kristian (male civil engineer); Melissa (female childcare assistant) and Jan (male childcare assistant); and Sara (female unemployed academic) and Steffen (male schoolteacher). They are discussing how they deal with the hygiene around raw eggs and risk from salmonella bacteria. The two couples who live in a two-family house together (Marie and Kristian, Melissa and Jan) construct a humoristic alliance in order to handle normative accusations from Sara and Steffen about behaving inappropriately in relation to risk from raw eggs:

> Marie: 'But it's not different than … we made lemon mousse[9] for … how many people [Sara: 'Uh!'] on New Year's Eve, what was it, sixty people?'
> Melissa: 'Yes, it was.'
> Kristian: 'It was all right.'
> Sara: 'With organic or non-organic eggs?'
> Kristian: 'With eggs.' [laughter]
> Sara: 'With eggs???'
> Marie: 'Come on, didn't they boil for a second?'
> Kristian: 'We usually boil the shells.'
> Jan: 'No-o-o, we didn't get around to that.'
> Sara: 'Well, you just talked about it???'
> Melissa: 'We don't know if they're alive! [laughter]. But we haven't heard any rumours.'
> Jan: 'But they can't if …'[laughter]
> Marie: 'At least they had enough.'
> Jan: 'Yes, YES!'
> Melissa: 'There was damn well enough!'
> [laughter]

Marie, Kristian, Jan and Melissa sustain their narrative about risk performance at the New Year's Eve party cooking as acceptable because they position themselves as a 'group in the group' through humoristic exchanges. Sara, however, questions the normative appropriateness of their handling of raw eggs. But her expressions of worried normative engagement in proper risk handling do not seem to influence the content of the normative conclusion much: namely, that exception from normatively expected risk-handling conduct can be made acceptable.

The use of humour in the interaction can be seen as an indicator that the participants are aware of the potential inappropriateness of the food performances discussed. This kind of risk performance could also be seen as an example of how the participants gain pleasure from doing risky activities (eating potentially

9 Lemon mousse is a classic Danish dessert that mainly contains sugar, lemon juice and lemon peel, and raw egg whites that are whipped stiff.

salmonella-infested raw eggs), because it represents a transgression of an otherwise sustained self-regulation (Lupton, 1999: 171).

Food Risk and Normativity

The normative content of engagements in risk handling is not just the result of food practitioner involvement; rather, it is related to the ongoing processes of social regulation of suitable conduct performed in everyday interaction. Hence, practitioners can carry out doings and sayings with a normative engagement in consuming less risky food, but to perform less risky food consumption is part of an ongoing social negotiation and adaptation about what this might consist in.

Doing Disciplined Consumption?

What are the consequences in everyday life when food risk issues challenge ordinary food practices? Food risk is a field in society where regulations have been reorganised during the last decade in European countries (Kjærnes et al., 2007). In Denmark, ordinary food consumers have been made a direct part of societal governance through, for example, the Smiley system (see pp. 75–6) in shops and restaurants (Nielsen, 2006). This way of involving the change in habits of individual actors in the governing of social and political problems is exactly what the governmentality approach calls 'the conduct of conduct' (Dean, 1999: 10), and governmentality is governing by making people discipline and normalise their bodily practices (Hewitt, 1991: 228–30), including food practices (Coveney, 2000: 139–40).

The question is whether society can expect a rise in the disciplining of food practices in relation to food risks on the basis of current knowledge about how food practitioners deal with the risk challenge to ordinary food consumption. This is, of course, a question that cannot be answered decisively, but merely discussed. The analysis of risk handling among Danish parent food practitioners through a practice theoretical perspective provides some insight into this debate.

The patterns in food practices and risk performances are not unidirectional. On the contrary, even in this small, qualitative sample there is a lot of variation in how food practitioners deal with food risks. Such a pattern of diversity in consumer dealings with risk in food is supported by the other qualitative studies in the international literature (e.g. Connolly and Prothero, 2008; Knight, 2009; de Krom, 2009; Lupton, 2005). Investigating and analysing the diversity in practical, everyday life reactions to the risk challenge of food consumption are important, because the risk-handling diversity and the diversity in social conditions for sustaining and changing food habits are often underestimated in the international research.

This underestimating of the complexities of everyday life practices and conditions is typical for much of the current research that operates from cognitivist assumptions about consumption behaviour and therefore tends to recommend better information in order to influence consumer attitudes for risk communication (e.g. Frewer et al., 2002; Hagemann and Scholderer, 2007; Hughner et al., 2009).

The underestimation of everyday life complexities is also found in research where it is recognised that consumers may act according to broader and different types of risk-understandings than experts, food producers and regulators. This research tends to recommend that more participatory and dialogical modes of risk communication are employed (e.g. Lofstedt, 2006; Renn, 2006). However, the influences on consumption agency from practicalities and social negotiations in everyday life are not included in these suggestions, which seem to involve only mental reflexivity. Hence, the participatory approaches keep the attention focused on individual mental attributes in riskified food consumption, instead of *'redirecting attention from risk perception and communication to focus on consumption practices and food institutions'* as Kjærnes puts it when arguing for her relational perspective on risk and trust in food (Kjærnes, 2006: 919).

In the Danish case study, the diversities can be seen at the level of types of risk performances. Worried risk handling seems to be related to an understanding of the disciplining of everyday conduct, since it involves constant monitoring of and reflecting on one's own food practices. But both irritated and pragmatic risk handling contain understandings, procedures and engagements that manoeuvre around disciplining without getting involved in it. Furthermore, the analysis showed that not even the worried risk-handling type could analytically be categorised as a practice in itself. This suggests that such activities will probably not gain priority in everyday life activities compared to integrative practices. This also counts against a hypothesis of increased disciplining.

Furthermore, a similar, divided pattern is observed when the analysis zooms in on the practical procedures in risk-handling food performances. It is perhaps only the normalising ambivalence experiences that can sustain an argument about increase of disciplining. Finally, when looking at the normative negotiations, the examples demonstrate how social interaction can contribute to the rationalising and disciplining of consumption conduct (e.g. use national produce). But the examples also show adaptations of consumer agency to practical do-ability and reactions towards inappropriate food conduct that embody anti-rationalising understandings and engagements in the pleasures of food.

However, disciplining should not be crudely equalled with oppressing; disciplining has enabling aspects as well (Clegg, 1989: 153–59; Dean, 1999: 12–13). The disciplining involved in worried risk handling and in keeping food risk anxiety in check can at the same time be seen as ways in which food practitioners gain control of their lives, exert protective agency in relation to their children, find pleasure in minimising choice, and contribute to the changing of procedures for food risk handling by practising them.

Chapter 5
Dealing with Challenges of Cooking from Scratch

Celebrating Everyday Life?

'Bake your own healthy, homemade buns for your toddler's lunch packet.' 'Pick elderberry flowers in nature to make the best cordial for the Saturday picnic.' 'Sample lavender flowers from your grandmother's overgrown garden to add flavour to your jars of sugar for the autumn cakes.' These are all very likely headings in the new types of media text in Denmark. In this chapter, I will analyse and discuss a challenge to ordinary food consumption that comes from medialised discourses and representations that normatively identify good cooking with cooking from scratch and home-made food. Research from other national contexts has shown a rise in the status of cooking from scratch (Bugge and Almås, 2006: 207), where homemade cooking has become a kind of medialised food discourse in itself. In the American context, this cooking-from-scratch discourse and the related social expectations on cooking practices become directly linked with lifestyle media products such as women's magazines and especially the Martha Stewart phenomenon (Julier, 2004: 18; Moisio et al., 2004: 379).

In relation to several other food issues such as nutrition, food safety and deskilling of food work, the questions of whether and how everyday food practitioners cook food and meals from scratch often play a role in both potential problems and solutions (Caraher et al., 2004; Jabs and Devine, 2006; Lyon et al., 2003; Short, 2006: 4–10). The deskilling issue deals with concerns about whether people's abilities to prepare food and cook meals have decreased and food work in everyday life has become less skilled, but this is debatable. Some scholars claim that although traditional routine skills are probably reduced due to the increase in availability of already processed foods, a re-skilling of new abilities is also taking place due to the rise in the variety of available food items, the broad exposure to multiple cultural cuisines, and the technological development in kitchen tools (Lyon et al., 2003).

The Danish Context

Regarding the use of cooking from scratch in relation to other food issues, the arguments typically run along the lines of 'if only consumers could cook themselves, they would not eat unhealthy fast food and ready-made food with hidden large amounts of fat and sugar'. This type of argumentation can be found at the current website of the Danish Food Agency (www.foedevarestyrelsen.dk). There is a subpage called 'Food at home', and under the subheading of 'In the kitchen', the agency argues in favour of involving children in cooking meals because 'children with kitchen experience become adults who are interested in healthy food'. The arguments can also run along the lines of 'if only consumers were experienced in proper practical hygiene procedures in cooking, there would be fewer incidents of salmonella poisoning'. This type of argument can be found at another page on the Danish Food Agency website (www.foedevarestyrelsen.dk). This page, called 'family and consumer', is intended to communicate directly with ordinary food consumers. Under the heading 'food safety' there is a piece of consumer information, called 'Do you use dirty tricks in the kitchen?', which gives three pieces of advice on hygiene procedures when cooking.

However, public policy makers in Denmark have found support from the private sector in their efforts to promote cooking from scratch. In recent years, Denmark has witnessed a growth in the amount of magazines, lifestyle sections in news media, television shows, coffee table books, and web pages that all seem to celebrate ordinary, everyday life activities traditionally associated with domestic femininity (Hollows, 2007), such as, for example, cooking home-made meals from scratch, baking, preserving, cleaning, producing and maintaining clothes, decorating the home and gardening.

Similarly, though for a slightly longer period of time, other ways of re-launching everyday life through Danish media have been produced, underscoring the medialised representations of the normatively 'good' about daily life practices. The mixed genre of docu-soaps, where everyday human psychological and social relations are being dramatised, has gained popularity (Hjarvard, 2002; Jerslev, 2005), and analyses of the development of Danish television news suggest a rise in the use of populist repertoires (Hjarvard, 1999), whereby ordinary, everyday actors gain more room for speaking and discursive references to interests of everyday actors gain stronger legitimacy. This development is also analysed in the medialised political communication in other countries (e.g. McNair, 2000: 105–21).

Women's magazines of different types have been with us for around a century (Griffen-Foley, 2004), and they have traditionally dealt with practical advice on all sorts of everyday issues relating to what was historically constructed as belonging to female interests (Hermes, 1995). With the 1960s growth in female employment and the 1970s rise of the women's movement in Denmark, magazines focusing on ordinary, everyday reproductive skills and practices gradually became mainly targeted to women above 50. In the late 1990s, a new type of magazine about such practices appeared, which are expensive, glossy and explicitly targeted to so-called younger women, age 25–50.

The group of food practitioners who are being targeted or who subscribe to the discourses of the everyday life celebratory media texts are women with allegedly busy lives. Danish women in this age group are likely to have younger children and be in full-time employment or education. Danish women in this age group also still on average spend five hours more per week on domestic chores than Danish men do (Deding et al., 2006), and a recent Danish survey reports that 48 per cent of the women cook dinner every day, whereas only 13 per cent of the men do this (Poulsen, 2006). This gendered division of labour in food work is found in most of the international literature (Beagan et al., 2008; Blake et al., 2009). At the same time, the consumption of fast food and ready-made meals that is typically framed as the opposite of meals cooked from scratch has increased in Denmark. Among children and young food practitioners the use of fast food has increased by one-third compared with 10 years earlier (Fagt et al., 2008). This increased use of fast food and other types of convenience foods is also observed in other Western and European national contexts (Ahlgren et al., 2005; Jabs and Devine, 2006; Lyon et al., 2003; Moisio et al., 2004; Prim et al., 2007).

Current Studies

The current literature on cooking seems to be fairly limited. For the purposes of this chapter, the literature can be divided into roughly three types. First, there are studies that analyse specific food elements of cooking, rather than the cooking processes themselves, such as understandings of traditional food products in cooking (Guerro et al., 2009), recipe use differences in different social groups (Hertzler and Bruce, 2002), relations between food choices, meal occasions and locations (Marshall and Bell, 2003) and the position of ready meals and fast food in cooking (Ahlgren et al., 2005; Brembeck, 2005; Prim et al., 2007).

Secondly, there are studies that focus on the cooking processes and the cooking practitioners themselves, but with the specific approach of seeing cooking as part of the overall food work and food work skills (Beagan et al., 2008; Blake et al., 2009; Bove and Sobal, 2006; Carahan et al., 2004; Lyon et al., 2003). A Canadian qualitative study of family division of food work among food practitioners of three different ethnic groups (Beagan et al., 2008) is typical for this kind of study. One of the main results described here is an ideal typology of female food practitioners' rationalisations of the gendered division of food work in their families, which is resonated in the quote in the title of the article, 'It's just easier for me to do it.'

Thirdly, there are studies that focus on the variety of processes of cooking, and which also tend to comment upon the normative discourses of cooking from scratch. Moisio et al., (2004) did a qualitative study of how American consumers from three generations construct their family identity and the social reproduction and transformation of cooking practices through home-made food. Bugge and Almås (2006) reports a qualitative study of Norwegian women's cooking practices with a special focus on what is constructed as a proper domestic dinner. Frances Short (2006) has undertaken a qualitative study of English cooking practices among adult everyday cooking practitioners, focusing in particular on cooking skills, where she expands the concept into covering less technical skills such as planning, timing and organising. These cooking studies as well as the food work studies are closely related in knowledge interest and theoretical perspective to the classic sociological and anthropological empirical studies of cooking and the proper meal (Douglas and Nicod, 1974; De Vault, 1994; Murcott, 1983).

The Danish empirical case study upon which this chapter is based is analytically related to the studies that focus on the variety of cooking processes, as well as to the studies that see cooking as part of the overall food work.

The Danish Case Study: Cooking in Medialised Society

This chapter is based on an empirical project entitled 'Cooking in medialised society' (Halkier, 2009).[1] The research is a qualitative in-depth study of how women cook and how they relate to cooking from scratch. Part of the sample consisted of eight female readers of the Danish women's magazine *Isabellas. Enthusiastic about Everyday.*[2] The sample of eight women displayed a variation according to age (20s, 30s and 40s), according to educational level (with or without high school degree), according to family status (with or without children), and according to habitat (city, suburb, village in Zealand, Jutland and Funen). For one part of the data production the eight female readers of *Isabellas* were individually interviewed and re-interviewed about their life stories of cooking, their cooking routines in everyday life, the similarities and differences between their own cooking and the cooking of their social network members, and their uses of the women's magazine *Isabellas*. The individual interviews drew upon techniques from ethnographic (Spradley, 1979), biographic (Atkinson, 1998) and active interviewing (Holstein and Gubrium, 2003).

Another part of the data production consisted of auto-photography (Heisley and Levy, 1991; Hurdley, 2007), where the participating women took photos of their own cooking during one or two weekday evenings (ingredients, food, tools, places, activities and the cooked food or meal). These photos were used as part of the second individual interview as a help to embody and materialise stories about cooking activities, and the pictures were also used as data in themselves.

The third part of the data production consisted of focus groups (Barbour, 2007; Puchta and Potter, 2005). Three of the individually interviewed women each selected three women from their own social network to participate in a focus group. The individually interviewed women were also asked to make sure that at least one of these three network members did not like the magazine *Isabellas*. This resulted in three focus groups: one with women in their 20s, one with women in their 30s,

---

1 The study was financed by Department of Communication, Business and Information Technologies, Roskilde University, 2006–2007.

2 *Isabellas. Enthusiastic about Everyday* is a glossy lifestyle magazine, targeted at women between 25 and 50, dealing mainly with cooking, gardening, and home decorating. As a magazine it is connected to a web-shop that sells a large variety of cooking tools, kitchen decor, other types of home decor, cleaning devices, and gardening equipment. The title *Isabellas* is named after the founder and first editor of the magazine and owner of the web-shop, Isabella Smith.

and one with women in their 40s. The focus group discussions were about what preoccupied the participants about cooking, about what was understood as 'good cooking' and 'bad cooking', and about how the participants related to the specific representations of cooking in the magazine *Isabellas*.

The presentation and discussion of the Danish case study on cooking from scratch follows the form for all four empirical chapters, outlined in more detail in the general methodology section (see the last section of Chapter 2). The following briefly summarises the outline.

First, the analysis describes and categorises the specific varieties of cooking practices that are carried out among the Danish female magazine readers. This is done in order to understand the basic configuration of which food consumption is already a part; namely, the food practices. This lays the groundwork for inferences later in the analysis about the ways in which people react to having their food consumption questioned.

Second, the analysis describes and categorises the different ways of handling cooking from scratch in an ideal typology. The purpose of this second part of the analysis is twofold: first, to demonstrate the variety in reactions to the challenges of cooking from scratch, second, to discuss when everyday life performing constitutes a practice in itself and when it does not, in order to contribute to the discussions about consumer agency.

Third, the analysis zooms in on the details of how cooking-from-scratch activities are performed by focusing on the practical procedures. The purpose of this third part of the analysis is to highlight the significance and complexities of the practical do-ability involved in everyday reactions to challenged food consumption.

Fourth, the analysis gives examples of negotiations of the normative engagement in cooking from scratch and how the negotiations reproduce, adapt, change, improvise and experiment with the normative content of three issues: agency of ordinary consumers, the category of 'good cooking', and exceptions to appropriate cooking conduct. The purpose of this analysis is to question the balance in current cooking research between an individual life-world focus and a focus on social processes.

Practising Cooking

This section describes the diversity in cooking practices among the Danish female magazine readers. This is done – as in the other chapters – in order to get a detailed picture of the food context that is potentially challenged, in this case by the discourses and representations of cooking from scratch, thereby getting to know the practices that are generating consumption activities.

Instead of using the broader category of practising food, in this analysis I am focusing on a relevant sub-activity of food practices; namely, the practising of cooking.[3] There are clearly similarities between some of the kinds of practising food described in Chapters 3 and 4, and some of the kinds of practising cooking in this chapter. This might be due to similarities in the social background and age of the participants in the three projects. But it could also be due to a more general relevance of the characteristics of the practising of food and cooking in the Danish case studies. These characteristics tend to resonate with types and results that are described in the qualitative food studies in the current international literature (e.g. Bove and Sobal, 206; Holm and Kildevang, 1996; Lupton, 1996; Moisio et al., 2004; Murcott, 1983; Short, 2006; Warde, 1997).

Cooking as Improvisation over Pleasure

This way of practising cooking is coordinated by understandings, procedures and engagements that revolve around pleasure. Here is an example of pleasure enacted in the lunch-making activity:

> I made such a sandwich with salmon and such delicious all sorts of organic stuff, so people went a bit, 'all right, relax', they thought it looked a bit wild, just because you make a salmon sandwich for your lunch, it's just a bit [laughs], hello you know! I really like that it's … I don't know, I have just never been the type who would just put myself off with a slice of rye bread that has gone soft on the edges and such, I just really can't get it down, you know. (Martha, student, 20s)

Cooking is mostly done on the basis of what the practitioner feels like eating on that particular day and what kind of food is found in cupboards, fridge and freezer, including leftovers. This is described by one of the women in her 40s:

> But a lot of what we do for dinner is something where we improvise, you know just what we've got, like I said before then … if we make chicken in the oven for example, but then the vegetables are the ones that we have, you know. (Pia, self-employed, 40s)

Shopping is done without a plan for specific meals but in order to have storage of food with which to improvise. Some of the women, for example, subscribe to a weekly organic vegetable box delivery service, where the providers decide what is in the box. As for use of cookbooks and recipes – if the ingredients are not there, the practitioner improvises and replaces with something from the cupboard or fridge, or she phones her mother or a friend to discuss what would be

3 I am grateful to the journal *Food, Culture and Society*, published by Berg for permission to draw explicitly on analysis for this section earlier published with them in B. Halkier (2009): Suitable cooking? Performances and positionings in cooking practices among Danish women, *Food, Culture and Society*, 12, 3, 357–77.

a proper replacement. This parallels one of the findings in a quantitative American study, where a sample of nutrition educators was found to exhibit a high level of experimenting with recipes (Hertzler and Bruce, 2002: 341–42).

Food and cooking is discussed intensely around the dinner table, and cooking is understood to be a relaxing activity that makes family and friends happy and thereby gives pleasure to the cook. This is enacted in the following quote:

> You know, if I have baked bread or something, that's a lovely, tangible activity compared to what I do in my job … and then some meal comes out of it, and often the children go yum-yum, and you can see they shove it in, and that is some kind of satisfaction. (Ellen, academic employed in private firm, 30s)

In a qualitative American study of cooking and homemade food in three generations, there is a very similar quote which is interpreted as an example of how cooking home-made food becomes a satisfaction for the cook through the social recognition about the labour of love she gets from those who enjoy the meal:

> When you sit down and they say, oh this is good mom, or if I've tried a new salad or something you know, they're like oh, yeah this is good, can I have the recipe for that? Yes, it does make you feel good and it kind of … it boosts your ego even though it's a lot of work and it would be easy to just order pizza like some people do. (Moisio et al., 2004: 374)

One of the first memories of cooking that Ellen from the Danish study recalls in the biographic part of the interviews also focuses on the pleasure of food work. She remembers how her father filled their large bathtub with water and curly kale to wash it, and she used to imagine how wonderful it would be to jump in and immerse herself like a mermaid in all the wet kale.

Cooking as Craft

The different activities, understandings, procedures and engagements of this way of practising cooking tend to revolve around a notion of the craft of cooking. This parallels the notion of mastery of cooking, analysed in other studies of cooking (Bove and Sobal, 2006: 76–79; Moisio et al., 2004: 374–75). What follows is an example of how this is enacted by one of the women in her 40s, who gives a very detailed description of how she made the vegetables for one of the evening meals that she auto-photographed:

> But the most important thing about this meal was … it was the root vegetables, it was actually to get the root vegetables in … in nice pieces, and how to say it, equal pieces, so they would finish at the same time in the oven. And then it was the composition, you know, the beetroots and the onions, they get such a sweet taste, those red onions, when they are heated, right, and then you have parsley

> root and parsnip and when you see them you never know what kind of taste you get into your mouth, because they look so much like each other, right? (Dorte, bank assistant, 40s)

To have well-working kitchen tools is also very important for the processes of turning raw materials into meals. According to Dorte, for example, a knife must be sharp enough to '*pass the tomato-test*' – can the knife cut easily through the skin of a ripe tomato?

These practitioners do not reflect much upon how cooking is done; rather, they have a naturalised notion of knowing what and how to do in order to cook a meal. The do-abilities of the craft and the related cooking procedures have been incorporated by lifelong experience with practising cooking, beginning from early childhood. When Dorte is interviewed biographically, the very first memory of cooking she mentions is a memory of participating in the slaughter of a pig and the making of sausages etc. at her great-grandmother's farm. This demonstrates the importance of cooking practitioner trajectories over time for the use of tacit procedural knowledges.

The significance of practitioner trajectories is also found in the current literature. In Bove and Sobal's qualitative study of food work among newly married couples, the previous cooking experiences of each of the two partners in a marriage determined their division of cooking, their negotiations of food work, and their enjoyment of cooking (Bove and Sobal, 2006: 74–78). In Moisio et al.'s qualitative American study of cooking across three generations, cooking from scratch is closely tied with biographic memories of shared cooking events and family members participating in these, whereby understandings and procedures of homemade food have been embodied. One of the female cooks in the project expresses such ties by explaining what homemade food is to her: *'Oh gosh, cinnamon rolls, um, probably the time I spent with grandma helping her make these and playing with the dough. Helping to sprinkle the cinnamon over the dough'* (Moisio et al., 2004: 366).

In the Danish study, cookbooks and recipes from friends, magazines and the Internet are mostly used for new inspiration. To cook meals from scratch is taken for granted, and shopping is planned and organised in order to provide a storage of food with which cooking can be carried out that results in proper, tasteful and healthy meals. Organising, planning and timing seem to be particularly significant to the cooking procedures in this type of cooking practice, similar to the findings in Frances Short's British qualitative study of cooking practices (Short, 2006: 117–18). Birte, a woman in her 30s whos is expecting her first child, always cooks on the basis of running bi-weekly plans for evening meals, and she is hoping to acquire a second freezer in order to store not just the meat and the home-made, prepared dishes but also the vegetables and berries from their newly established kitchen garden.

> It's something about keeping that freezer … going, I suppose and empty it out or eat from it … and a bit from this we make our meal plans, and then of course from what we feel like … or what we are doing … and then of course now that I'm pregnant, we have had a lot of focus on this with a vegetarian day and a fish day and … trying to eat a bit more healthy than we probably otherwise would do. (Birte, sales assistant, 30s)

The importance of organising, planning and timing is also analysed and emphasised in qualitative studies of cooking and food work in Canada (Beagan et al., 2008), Sweden (Prim et al., 2007: 243), and the USA (Blake et al., 2009).

Cooking is understood as a taken-for-granted ability that is capable of producing a multiplicity of happenings in the family life – from pleasurable experiences, over fuel for other activities, to regulating the food intake, and to socialising children into the skills of cooking food and meals. Tilde, a nursing aide in her 30s, explains her procedures in this last type of engagement when she involves her daughter in the cooking:

> Yes, it does take longer time when she is with me, because sometimes it's just like having a little pupil where you have to explain and … sometimes it's just faster to do it myself … I know exactly what to do and when … but it's also healthy to bring someone into it. You get to … get questions all the time, and you get to say some things out aloud, that 'now we have to do like this and this because …'. (Tilde, nursing aide, 30s)

The engagement in involving her daughter in the cooking in order for the girl to incorporate the routine procedures and tacit knowledge is negotiated in relation to the timing of cooking in the multiplicity of other everyday practices. This way, part of Tilde's quote almost echoes the title of a recent article about how women rationalise the division of labour in relation to food in the family: 'It's just easier for me to do it' (Beagan et al., 2008).

Manageable Cooking

This kind of cooking practices is mainly coordinated by understandings, procedures and engagements related to manageability. Cooking is performed on the basis of what the practitioner feels she can handle fairly easily, such as a bowl of rice porridge or a home-made pizza. One of the young cooking practitioners explains this:

> It's nice it's so easy … it is as if you can just walk around the supermarket and put those things in the basket you want on top of your pizza, and there isn't really so much to do about those things before they come on top of the pizza crust, so it's very easy to see, and I like that. I like it when cooking becomes manageable … (laughing) … you know, twenty pots boiling and remember to

> cut things in particular ways and … have you also remembered to put this in the oven and, you know … that really stresses me out completely. So chop, chop, chop, on top of the pizza, into the oven, twenty minutes later there is food … I like that very much. (Martha, student, 20s)

Part of the biographic interviewing with Martha consists of her narrative about how her mother never involved her in cooking, and how difficult it was to move away from home, not knowing what to do and trying to *'look over the shoulders of friends'*. This resembles the cooking practitioner trajectory of one of the male cooks in Bove and Sobal's study of food work among newly married couples, who was not allowed to cook by his mother but learned to cook by doing cooking with his wife supervising (Bove and Sobal, 2006: 78).

Shopping is done almost every day according to what the practitioner and the partner/husband or children feel like eating, in order to supply the small storage in the fridge and cupboards. It is often the same type of meals that are cooked in a kind of a rotation of a standard repertoire of cooked meals. To use a standard repertoire of specific meals seems to be the case for cooking practitioners in other national contexts as well. Bugge and Almås report how variations over minced meat are part of standard cooking for Norwegian young mothers (Bugge and Almås, 2006: 217–18). In their qualitative study of food coping strategies in American families, Blake et al. show how the division of food work between husband and wife can result in the use of standard repertoire meals, here exemplified in a quote from a male cooking practitioner:

> I'm sure she [wife] would like to have someone cook for her more but … I will [cook] once in a while, cause once in a while like if she's only gonna be home for a certain amount of time, I'll [cook]. One of our compromises is we have spaghetti, cause it's easy. (Blake et al., 2009: 5)

This standard repertoire can also be adapted to how to cook when moving in with a partner, similar to Bove and Sobal's notion of food negotiations (Bove and Sobal, 2006: 84). Susy, who is studying to become a school teacher, recently moved in with her partner; here, she explains how her standard repertoire of vegetable-based cooking was adapted:

> And then … but now we have weaved our dishes together so that if I, for example, want to make moussaka, well but fine, then it's actually okay to put meat in, you know … the dishes have just become … broader, and that's really fine. (Susy, student, 20s)

This standard-repertoire cooking often requires a lot of chopping, but ends with most of the ingredients in one bowl or dish, such as salads, oven dishes and wok stir-fries. Recipes are torn from magazines and put in a folder if they have been tested and are found easy to follow.

Cooking is ambivalently understood as a complicated activity that has to be do-able, but which at the same time must produce tasteful and pleasant meals. One of the more experienced cooking practitioners expresses the difficulties of do-ability in manageable cooking in the following:

> I would like to feel confident in a kitchen. If for example my husband came home and said, um, I would like to have … some dish, but fine, I'll make that. Not that you have to know the recipe by heart, but just so that you can … see yourself do it … you know, that you dare tackle it. Because sometimes I still phone my mum and dad or ring my mother-in-law, ho-o-ow is it just now you do with this. (Tilde, nursing aide, 30s)

Such ambivalences in the manageable-ness of cooking homemade food relate to the discussion about cooking skills in the current literature and whether practices of ordinary cooking have become increasingly deskilled or if we are instead witnessing a re-skilling. Lyon et al. (2003) question whether historically everyday cooking practitioners from two generations ago were necessarily more skilled than present-day cooking practitioners, but they also conclude that routine skills have probably diminished for a majority of people in the UK (ibid.: 73). Short argues on the basis of her English qualitative study that the level of skills among ordinary cooking practitioners probably is underestimated because of a narrow conception of skills, meaning mainly technical skills for cooking from scratch, thus underestimating the skills employed in, for example, organising meals (Short, 2006: 117–18).

Cooking as Healthiness

This way of practising cooking is related to 'doing healthy' in a broad sense of the term. Cooking is being done preferably in such ways that either the practitioner feels she is doing something good for herself, her husband, and her children's wellbeing, or by using procedures and products that are constructed as more healthy – such as organic food and low-fat products. The last type of healthiness is typically balanced with the first type, which includes tastiness. This is how Susy enacts this balancing:

> There has to be everything in it, you know, vitamins and such things, enough of it. Right now, um, I'm trying to become pregnant … [Interviewer: 'Okay, good luck with that.'] … Yes, thank you. So it's a lot with … for example, I'm trying not to eat too much fat, fish or such. I'm trying to find out what's in it and what I feel that I need in my body. So I sense myself very much, um … and get a bit of everything all day. (Susy, student, 20s)

The 'doing healthy' way of cooking corresponds with a common finding in the current literature about how female cooks often become the family manager of healthiness in food (Beagan et al., 2008: 661–62; Bove and Sobal, 2006: 85). In this quote from the Canadian qualitative study, one of the female cooking practitioners positions herself as the healthy food manager:

> If my partner decides to cook I know that he would cook with probably oils that I wouldn't want to cook with, or prepare it in a way that I probably wouldn't prepare it. I know my way would be a healthier way. (Beagan et al., 2008: 661)

Shopping is done every other day, to supplement storage from which to compose meals, and recipes are not necessarily used, except for inspiration for new, different and healthier cooking. Dorte explains how she sometimes uses the Internet for this:

> Oh, but among other things, there is one called www.fedtfattig.dk,[4] there you can go in and write, 'I've got yogurt and I've got yellow peas and I've got beetroots in my fridge, what can I make from that?' And yes, you can use that for something, and then you can say is it for a starter or a main course or is it for baking, so you get a bit of ideas this way, all right, that sounds fun. (Dorte, bank assistant, 40s)

Cooking is understood as a relaxing activity that brings about well-being both for the practitioner herself and for those she cooks for. This is enacted in the following quote by one of the women in her 30s:

> I think I have found out that when I make things myself … it gives me a greater pleasure to eat it, and I gain a better, I don't know if you can call it a better conscience, but it makes me feel better, I think I am doing something good for myself by not jumping over the lowest part of the fence … (Thea, clerk, 30s)

This particular linking of healthiness with pleasure invites a comparison with Hollows' argument about post-feminist cooking being about pleasing oneself (Hollows, 2003).

Cooking as Necessity

This way of practising cooking is primarily coordinated by necessities. It is necessary for the family to get something to eat, and thus it is necessary that somebody provides these meals. The husband, partner or boyfriend is usually positioned as not possessing cooking agency, so the female cooking practitioners feel they have to cook every day. This way of going about cooking activities resonates with results about division of food labour in other qualitative studies, where it is shown that men often choose voluntarily to cook, whereas it is usually

4 'Fedtfattig' means low-fat.

only women who are ascribed with cooking or take cooking upon themselves (Beagan et al., 2008: 666–67; Bove and Sobal, 2006: 86; Bugge and Almås, 2006: 210; Prim et al., 2007: 246). This process seems to be related to the normative expectations experienced by female food practitioners in their interactions with their social network. In Erickson's quantitative study of division of household labour and emotional work among American families, she argues that 'women recognised that they are held accountable for the performance of this work in ways that men are not' (Erickson, 2005: 348). This is parallel to a practice theoretical perspective on such processes, which would emphasise the importance of the social expectations and recognitions of appropriate behaviour. One of the women in the Danish study says that she cooks every day, although she repeatedly positions herself as neither particularly skilled nor interested in cooking. In this quote, her cooking agency is compared to the cooking performances of her sisters:

> For them it has been natural to cook their own meals, even when they moved away from home, where my food was hotchpotch … I remember once I didn't have any money I ate patty shells with salami. This was what I had and for me it was just about getting full … but my sisters would never ever do something like that … they have had a kind of minimum limit as to what you … put in your mouth. (Tilde, nursing aide, 30s)

Cooking practices are dominantly organised according to do-abilities. Cooking meals has to be feasible, and the activities are manoeuvred in relation to the intersections of all the other practices of a busy everyday life. Only major shopping is planned, and often cooking is done on the basis of experimenting with what is already in fridge, freezer and cupboards. Here follows how Tilde expresses the conditioning of cooking:

> I have worked many night shifts. Then it's not the great culinary expeditions I embark upon, it just isn't …. And the food gets marked by that immediately, it does. Then it's pasta and minced meat and … what I have the energy to do. (Tilde, nursing aide, 30s)

Important engagements are that the food must be sufficiently varied, but at the same time prepared so that everyone in the family feels like eating the food. Cooking is primarily understood as a necessary, important everyday chore along with other everyday routine chores. In the following, Pia expresses this understanding:

> Yeah … you know, I must admit, I think it's hard to stand there and, oh, what am I going to come up with tonight … what is it we haven't eaten for a while … and I also think about, are we covered, so we get what we need of vitamins and proteins and … such things … Some times I think it's like that … also, some times you would just like to do something else than just cooking, I think … I think a lot of time is spent on cooking every day. (Pia, self-employed, 40s)

This way of cooking seems to revolve around providing for others, similar to the analysis in Anne Murcott's classic article on cooking among women in south Wales (Murcott, 1983) and her follow-up analysis, based on a nationwide British study (Murcott, 2000).

Cooking Practices, Food Practitioners, and Cooking from Scratch

The female magazine readers as food practitioners rarely stick to one way of practising cooking. For example, Pia, one of the women in her 40s, does both pleasurable improvised cooking and knows her cooking craft inside and out, yet feels stuck with having to cook every day. In this respect, the performing of cooking among the female magazine readers seems to be neither less nor more composite than the food practising among the young Danes and the food practising among the Danish parents. Hence, this diversity must be considered when analysing how cooking from scratch is handled among the magazine readers.

However, there is a particular characteristic about the cooking-from-scratch challenge to food consumption that is different from both the environmental challenge and the risk challenge. These specific cooking-from-scratch discourses are as historically recent as the environmental challenge and the present risk challenge of food consumption. But cooking from scratch as a particular performance within cooking practices obviously has a much longer history of already being or becoming integrated in food practices for generations of cooks (Floyd and Forster, 2003; Lyon et al., 2003; Moisio et al., 2004), in times when ready-made meals and semi-manufactured products were an exception, used only by a small minority of the population.[5] This makes it more difficult in this case study (compared to the studies on environment and risk challenges) to distinguish between food practising (cooking) and the handlings of challenged consumption (dealings with cooking from scratch). At the same time, the participants in the research project on cooking were sampled after the criteria that they subscribed to a magazine that represents the cooking-from-scratch discourses. It seems reasonable to assume that there is some identification with the cooking from scratch going on in the doings and sayings of these female readers. Thus, the analysis now turns to the differences in ways of cooking from scratch.

Ways of Cooking from Scratch

In this section, the different ways of handling cooking from scratch among the Danish female magazine readers are described and categorised with the help of an ideal typology. The aim of establishing this typology is to highlight the variety in reactions to the challenges of cooking from scratch, but also to discuss if and

5 This, of course, depends on how 'ready-made meals' and 'manufactured products' are defined historically.

when such consumption performing can constitute a practice in itself. Such a discussion can inform the wider debate about the potential societal agency of ordinary consumers.

However, this ideal typology differs from the other Danish case study-based ideal typologies in one important respect: This typology does not contain a category for negative performing or non-performing, unlike the ideal typologies of handling environmentalisation (distancing from environmentalised food) and food risks (irritated risk handling). Such varieties are not expressed in the data from the case study on cooking from scratch, not even in the data from the focus groups, where women who did not read or did not like everyday life celebratory women's magazines were participating. This may be related to the point that was made in the section above: Cooking from scratch has had a much more practice-integrated historical trajectory in relation to food consumption than using organic food or tackling salmonella bacteria. It may also be related to understandings of perceiving a 'proper dinner' as a home-cooked meal as a long-standing normative ideal (Bugge and Almås, 2006; Kjærnes, 2001; Murcott, 1983). One might surmise that nobody wants to talk too much about their take-away pizzas and ready-made sauces.

The lack of non-performing to a degree that it can amount to a separate type may also be related to the cooking trajectories of the individually interviewed participants. Across all the social differences of the women in the sample, the participants grew up with parents who cooked food from scratch and kept kitchen gardens. But there are still variations in levels and types of dealing with cooking from scratch among the participant women, and it is these variations that form the categories in the typology.

The variations in ways of cooking from scratch point to another issue. There is no strict definition of what cooking from scratch consists of among the cooking practitioners, but that is also the case for social science analytical accounts of food and cooking (Moisio et al., 2004: 372; Short, 2006: 7, 88–89). How far back in the food production chain you have to go in order to'cook from scratch' is socially and historically relative. Do you, for example, buy a whole chunk of beef and mince it yourself for the spaghetti Bolognese sauce? Or is it enough to buy freshly minced beef in a store in order to cook a home-made meal? In this study, the participants associate a number of specific activities with cooking from scratch; namely, to cook so-called old-fashioned meals,[6] to *not* use semi-manufactured articles and processed foods, to bake, to preserve and to maintain a kitchen garden. Across the social differences in the sample, the participating women all bake their own

6 'Old-fashioned' meals in a Danish context usually mean the kinds of meals that people's grandmothers produced. Thus, the content of this category depends on the age group and the social background. To the women in their 40s, old-fashioned meals are, for example, various stews with cabbage, peas and pork, and various types of porridge. To the women in their 20s, old-fashioned meals are, for example, pork with potatoes and brown gravy.

bread, buns and cakes; Ellen, Dorte, Birte, Pia and Susy make their own preserves, including jam, pickles, cordials, syrup, herb salt, flower sugar and schnapps; Ellen, Dorte, Birte, Pia and Tilde maintain small or large kitchen gardens.

Cooking from Scratch is Taken for Granted

To cook meals from scratch can represent something that is completely taken for granted, not in any way questioned. Cooking from scratch is simply how one cooks most of the time. The following quote about an ordinary cooking activity from one of the women illustrates the matter-of-fact practicality of such cooking:

> About three weeks ago, we made soup, when we got that cow, or rather bought it, we had a lot of bones and … leftovers from this cow that I boiled, and we made … 8–10 litres of beef soup … and then I have just frozen it as portions in plastic bags so it can be taken out and used. (Birte, sales assistant, 30s)

Thus, to cook home-made food from scratch as a taken-for-granted performance is organised through routinised practical procedures and understandings of 'knowing' the food and cooking. In this sense, taking cooking from scratch for granted comes close to 'cooking as craft' practising. The element of 'knowing the food' comes forward in the following expression from one of the experienced cooking practitioners:

> But you know, we both like to make these home-made things, I make stewed strawberry[7] or … jam, we make jam once in a while, but you know, of course we also buy jam, but you know … I like that thing about making things from scratch, you can see what kind of things you've got your hands in, right, and proper raw materials and such things. (Dorte, bank assistant, 40s)

So, the practical understanding here is that you get to know your food by becoming bodily acquainted with the different elements of it, and cooking from scratch enables you to do just that.

This way of performing cooking from scratch is related to a trajectory of having had parents who cooked from scratch and actively involved their children in these activities. Hereby, the women have learned to cook from scratch as the unquestionable way of cooking. When interviewed biographically about her cooking, Pia explains how she learned to cook:

> We had regular chores. Both in the kitchen garden and, you know, we helped … We also rushed around and played and then came in for dinnertime. But you know, I've always baked, made cakes and … you know such things, I've always

7 Stewed strawberry is a traditional Danish dessert where strawberries are cooked together with sugar to a kind of porridge and served hot with milk or cream.

> baked buns. You know, it's always been like this, if we wanted a cake, we could bake cookies or whatever it was. [Interviewer: 'Did you not go to the bakers?'] No, that's not something we've done … and we don't do that ourselves today, you know. (Pia, self-employed, 40s)

Taking cooking from scratch for granted as a result of cooking trajectories is observed both among the oldest and the youngest generations of cooking practitioners in other studies. In the American study of cooking in three generations, the oldest generation understands homemade meals as cooking from scratch with fresh raw ingredients and taken-for-granted procedures (Moisio et al., 2004: 380–81). In a British qualitative study of children's understandings of cooking, the children's drawings and explanations about the meal they could serve for the fantasy figure 'Grubb' included elements of cooking from scratch (Caraher et al., 2004: 268).

Cooking from scratch as taken for granted seems to be such an encompassing performance, that the food consumption involved in this – using as many raw ingredients and as few processed foods as possible – could be categorised as a specific consumption practice, because it amounts to a whole project in the Schatzkian sense. To recap, this means that concrete groups of activities (doings and sayings) and their coordinating elements (understandings, procedures and engagements) are combined in tasks, and these tasks are combined to form a socially recognisable project – such as cooking as many of the meals from scratch as possible. To attempt to cook as many of the meals from scratch as possible also entails that the practitioner consumes (shops for, provides and uses) as basic types of food as possible.

On the other hand, the element of engagement in the organisation of this food consumption practice is fairly tacit, if we compare the cooking from scratch as taken for granted type with the kind of engagement in, for example, the identification type from Chapter 3 on environmentalisation. So the question is how much explicit engagement do we require before a highly encompassing food consumption performance can be understood as a practice in itself? An answer to this question is related to the question of whether such food consumption performances are socially recognised by other food practitioners. This brings us to the next way of dealing with cooking from scratch.

Cooking from Scratch is Expected

Cooking food and meals from scratch can represent something that is socially expected, both from others and from the practitioners themselves. It is expected by the other parents and the teachers that the cake you bring for your daughter's school party is home-made (Clarke, 2007). Or it is expected that non-home-made dinners on ordinary weekdays are an exception (Bugge and Almås, 2006: 219–21; Prim et al., 2007: 244). Hence, not performing in the appropriate way can produce expressions of offence, bad conscience and legitimations. The breaching of expectations usually produces clear examples of what is considered appropriate cooking from scratch.

In this example Thea expresses clearly what is considered appropriate cooking by telling a story about how she discovered inappropriate cooking at Christmas in her parents' home:

> We were over there for xmas, and she [the mother] had, yes she had bought ready-made rice porridge in one of those plastic bags, right, to make the ris a la mande ,[8] and it was really like this, when I opened the fridge, they were just lying there, and I was just like, okay we are going to have a good xmas, I am not going to make a scene, and then I just went out to Emil and said, do you know what's in the fridge (laughs) … she obviously doesn't bother to make the porridge … it didn't taste too good either, that was really a bit of a miss, not stirred with love! (Thea, clerk, 30s)

The element of suitable cooking that Thea's mother does not perform properly here is how cooking labour turns food into home-made gifts of love (Bove and Sobal, 2006: 80–81; Moisio et al., 2004: 370–71). Cooking from scratch is here clearly socially recognised.

The social recognition of cooking from scratch as something socially expected is also expressed among the female cooking practitioners in relation to the medialised representations of the cooking-from-scratch discourse in the everyday celebratory women's magazines such as *Isabellas*. One of the younger women expresses such a social recognition in the following quote:

> It signals that you take your time to do the cooking. Which I actually don't do so often, right … you know, I take the time to make food quickly, hmmm, but then it usually turns out lucky and tastes nice anyway, even though I haven't spent 1½ hour on it but only 1 hour, right … (Susy, student, 20s)

Social recognition of cooking from scratch as something expected often leads to such legitimising enactments. In the Norwegian qualitative study of cooking and domestic dinners among young mothers, similar legitimising arguments and positionings are enacted. When the Norwegian women speak about their mothers' cooking, the mothers are positioned as people who cook everything from scratch, and the women position themselves as people who do not cook like that because, as one of them says, 'but then again I'm not a housewife either' (Bugge and Almås, 2006: 214).

However, there are also a number of ambivalent expressions in relation to cooking from scratch as socially expected. This resonates with arguments in the current

8 'Ris a la mande' is the most traditional Christmas dessert in Denmark, made from cold rice porridge mixed with blanched chopped almonds, whipped cream and vanilla and served with warm cherry sauce.

literature about how cooking practices have become more visible performances on display for others, which relates to worries about social expectations (Julier, 2004: 18). In the following, one of the experienced practitioners tells a story that places her cooking practices as on the one hand living up to expectations by practising cooking from scratch, and at the same time distancing herself from the normative control in drawing upon predictable expectations:

> Right, yes, I thought it was really funny when coming down to Anders' school, and you knew that you had got this vegetable box from Årstiderne,[9] very nice with recipes, and you had got those turnips, and then when we put all the food on a common table at the school, you could see that there where at least three of us who had made the same salad with vinaigrette and the turnips from the Årstidernes box, and it's just ... oh no (laughs) ... it just becomes so politically correct and predictable. (Ellen, academic employed in private firm, 30s)

'Cooking from scratch as socially expected' is a much more discursively explicit type of performance than the previously discussed type, 'cooking from scratch as taken for granted'. Cooking from scratch as expected contains the element of social recognition, central to the concept of practice. However, cooking from scratch as expected does not necessarily entail large amounts of doings and sayings with the practitioner itself; thus, it should be kept at the level of a performance within cooking practices. The same goes for the next two ways of cooking from scratch.

Cooking from Scratch brings Control

In this type of cooking from scratch, knowing the raw materials and knowing how to organise and perform the cooking procedures enable the practitioner to exert control over the food and eating in the household. Moisio et al. (2004: 368) describe the same kind of defence against the dangers of processed food in their study of three generations of American cooking practitioners. In another American qualitative study, the female cooking practitioners are even labelled 'default family food managers' (Blake et al., 2009: 6). The control can be performed on the basis of different types of engagements in food and cooking, but one engagement that comes out clearly among the female magazine readers is an engagement in avoiding certain kinds of bodily risks.

> I like to make things from scratch, so you can see what kind of things you are using, right, decent raw materials and such...all those chemicals and stuff, things they put into ... which is crap to say cause you don't know, but ... all those useless colours and ... such things ... I'd rather avoid it cause you don't know about long-term effects yet. (Dorte, bank assistant, 40s).

9 Organic vegetable box delivery program in Denmark. 'Aarstiderne' translates as 'The seasons'.

In this example, Dorte connects her cooking-from-scratch practices with an engagement in controlling what kind of materials are taken into the body via the food eaten. This is an engagement in food practices that has been found in empirical research many times, and it forms a basic element in the theorising over food consumption (Falk, 1994; Fischler, 1988).

Constructions of risk in relation to food are never just bodily, but always also social, as shown in Chapter 4. This duality is particularly obvious in relation to control of the food served for children. The next quote shows an example of how cooking meals from scratch can form a part of the engagement of teaching your children to eat what is considered proper meals. *'I thought they* [her daughters] *had to learn how to cook food, because I did not want us to have children who could only get by with fast food'* (Pia, self-employed, 40s). Pia explains how she has included her children in cooking since they were young, and how both daughters now can cook from scratch. Pia's example shows engagement in control over food, but with the purpose of passing on cooking skills to her children, in the hopes that they can practise the production of what is seen as decent meals.

Cooking from Scratch brings Pleasure

To make home-made food and meals can also be organised according to an engagement in what is understood as pleasurable about food, eating and cooking. Cooking from scratch can result in pleasant sensate, emotional and social experiences for the practitioner herself, just like in the following narrative from Birte:

> I could just sit in the sofa [refers to her condition as highly pregnant], but I don't really think … that's perhaps not exactly what I want … but then again, I DO like to stand in a kitchen, right, so … you know, I've got this friend, she really thinks it's over-energetic that I bother to make all these things, but I actually enjoy it, you know, uh, so I don't think about people cutting corners … people don't have to cook from scratch, if they don't think it's fun, you know. (Birte, sales assistant, 30s)

Cooking from scratch can bring pleasure in other ways; for example, by pleasing others, which brings us back to the notion of the labour of cooking as a gift of love or even 'the delivery of a devotional performance' (Moisio et al., 2004: 371). Martha, one of the younger food practitioners, expresses this result of cooking from scratch in her account about making cakes for her friends:

> It's often I make a layer cake for my friends as a birthday gift … and I just think that, that it is the princess in me feeling so good about all the pink, the white and the flowered, you know, coloured sugar decorations and such … I love it and strawberries and such, and again because it's manageable and simple, right, well you could say not many people would find it manageable to bake their own

> layers for a layer cake, but it's incredibly easy … and making it from scratch instead of going out and buying one of those packages that just tastes like old cardboard. (Martha, student, 20s)

In this quote, Martha also touches upon a third element in 'performing cooking from scratch brings pleasure'; namely, the taste of the meal and the food. Interestingly, the taste of food is not directly discursively connected with cooking from scratch as pleasure. But pleasure of taste as an important part of cooking seems to be implicitly present in the narratives of the case study participants when they are talking about their favourite meals, about what constitutes good cooking, and how they have photographed their own cooking and meals. Maybe the assumption and experience of better taste in home-made food is so self-evident that it does not have to be put into so many words?

Cooking from Scratch – Already a Practice?

There seems to be less diversity in the ways of dealing with the food consumption challenge of this chapter, compared to the challenges in the other empirical chapters of this book. Cooking from scratch has had a much more food practice-integrated history compared to using organic food or buying salmonella-free chicken. Hence, it is a difficult question whether it makes analytical sense to try to categorise any of the different ways of cooking from scratch (such as the taken-for-granted type) as a practice, if cooking from scratch in itself can be seen as an integrative practice. There are also some unresolved questions about how much weight should be put on the extent of concrete and taken-for-granted performances of cooking from scratch and how much weight should be put on the degree of explicit social recognition of cooking from scratch, if the aim is to conceptualise certain consumption activities as potential practices.

Thus, the analytical relationship between food practising and ways of handling the specific food consumption challenge is not straightforward in this case study. In order to pursue the issue of the taken-for-granted-ness of cooking from scratch, the next part of the analysis focuses on the procedures in 'doing cooking from scratch'. The aim is to highlight the embodied and composite character of such performances.

Bodily/Mental Procedures in Cooking from Scratch

Earlier, I argued that the cooking-from-scratch challenge to food consumption is different from the environmental challenge and the risk challenge, because cooking from scratch has a historical trajectory of being done as an integrated procedural element of cooking practices. To use as many raw materials and own cooking labour as possible is already present in both food practice and food practitioner trajectories to some degree, which neither using organic food nor avoiding salmonella-infested pork is, at least not yet. A consequence of this difference could be that the cooking-from-scratch challenge is much easier to appropriate and adapt than the environmental and risk challenges. One way of seeing this is in the degree to which cooking from scratch is organised by routinely embodied procedures. This section shows a number of examples that illustrate the importance of the embodiment of the bodily/mental procedures of cooking from scratch.

Relations with Food

Across the many differences in social conditionings, the participating women express their relationship with raw materials for cooking as a combination of important tastes, smells, looks and feels with explicit understandings of what constitutes proper raw materials, such as 'natural', 'fresh', 'following the seasons', 'organic' and 'healthy'. The procedural relations explained by the women consist of routinised and embodied knowing-how-to-dos with food.

One example of this is where Pia explains why the auto-photography was never carried out in her case, because the family ended up eating sandwiches and left-overs: [10]

> All right, Jane [daughter] was in full swing and making the salad and everything she was preparing for those shrimps … she had grated the orange peel and the lemon peel and everything. Then the shrimps were put onto the frying pan, and all of a sudden she thinks it smells weird, and so do Arne and I, we definitely also think so, so the shrimps are dumped in the bin. (Pia, self-employed, 40s.

Pia uses her bodily experience with how raw seafood, such as shrimps, must smell to be edible, and it appears that her daughter has incorporated this know-how, too. Pia has involved both of her daughters in cooking activities since their pre-school years.

Another example of a similar experience with tacitly embodied know-how in relation to food comes from one of Ellen's narratives as part of the biographic interviewing. This example shows the bodily/mental practical learning from the daughter's perspective:

> I sat on the kitchen table or heard her [her mother] talk about how her mother used to make particular things and … I think, I have sort of seen how to do some things without actually doing them myself, but I can see that I know. And the reason why I know this is that I remember when I moved into a shared house after high school and began to study and so, I could see that there were some of these guys in the shared house, when we had to cook ourselves and knead dough and bake rye bread and make liver paté and such … to see such a guy, Jan who

10 Apparently, sandwiches and leftovers are not considered good enough as a meal to become photographed.

> studied music, right? To see him stand with the dough and not knowing how to collect a dough for a bread for example. And I think, not because I have baked much bread as a child, but I have seen the movements, how to do it, and if it feels too greasy then you pour more flour into it and such. (Ellen, communication planner, 30s)

This description of knowing how to do through a combination of watching, hearing and trying comes close to what Loic Wacquant labels embodied simulation (Wacquant, 2004). Embodied simulation is one of the dynamics of practical learning that Omar Lizardo (2009) suggests should be integrated into practice theory. Lizardo criticises practice theory for having lost the concept of socialisation and needing a more dynamic concept for how practices are learned. Regardless of the potential merits of this particular conceptual suggestion, the empirical example also illustrates the practice theoretical point of always seeing acting (and interacting) as embodied as well as discursive.

Relations with Tools

Just like the female magazine readers' relationship with food, their relationship with tools in cooking from scratch are highly embodied. The procedural element of using various tools is an integrated part of body-related functionality and thus also practical do-ability. Tools have to 'feel good in the hand' when being used. Here, one of the women explains and rationalises her bodily sensation of a tool:

> This is just a Rådvad[11] knife. Not anything particularly fancy or expensive but … it has a bit of weight in the hand, but it's not a particularly expensive design, oh no … I work better with this, I think, it's a bit better stuff than those light ones, right. (Thea, clerk, 30s)

The knowing of the tool can become as important as the knowing of the food in order to perform practically do-able cooking from scratch. The next quote from one of the experienced cooking practitioners shows how difficult it is to turn this embodied do-ability into discursively explicit and precise guidelines. Dorte explains what happened when a favourite tool was worn out:

> My mother thinks I am being a bit silly … my old parsley mincer broke down after 15 years or so, and I went completely hysterical, and then I got a brand-new one for xmas, and it was a completely different model, and it could not at all mince parsley, and it had to be like I used to do it, so my mother succeeded in finding it at a jumble sale, it had to be that, silly maybe, but when you have

11 Rådvad is the oldest knife-producing firm in Denmark, located in and named after a locality close to Copenhagen where production of various tools began in the late medieval era because of the location of watermills along a small river.

> been used to using that piece of tool and it works for you, right … (Dorte, bank assistant, 40s)

Apparently, it was difficult for Dorte to explain to her mother exactly what the parsley mincer had to be able to do. The easiest way back to well-known procedures in mincing was to find a recycled version of the exact same model with which Dorte tacitly knows how to do in order to produce the food when she needs to mince something. Interestingly, the 'newer' food work technologies such as freezers and microwave ovens seem to be taken for granted and are not talked about as tools, which can be related to the argument made in Lyon et al. (2003: 170–71) that these technologies are easier to use or require skills different from traditional tools.

Relations with Recipes

Recipes for cooking are more explicitly rule-regulated types of knowing-how-to-do than the knowing-how-to-do with raw materials and with tools, although recipes are used in a multitude of flexible ways (Floyd and Forster, 2003). Interestingly, though, recipes are seldom used as rule-regulated procedures in practical cooking from scratch in the Danish study, except in two situations. The two kinds of situations where recipes are used as rules for procedures are when the women cook for guests or when the women try out new meals. Otherwise, the narratives about recipe uses among the female magazine readers are characterised by much more hybrid procedures, which is consistent with other studies of recipe uses (Forster, 2003; Heck, 2003).

Such hybrid procedures include using bits and pieces from a recipe (which can simply be the picture and nothing else); substituting various raw materials in a recipe with what is found in fridge, freezer and cupboards; imitating a taste composition with different means; asking friends and family how they would cook a particular meal; and letting a website make a do-it-yourself suggestion for procedures on the basis of information on raw materials in the household. In two cases of the auto-photographs and the narratives explaining them, recipes are mentioned, but only for one part of the meal. Martha cooks rice porridge for dinner in her auto-photograhy, and she looks at the instructions at the package of rice to see how long to boil it. Tilde cooks a home-made pizza for her auto-photography, and she looks in a recipe book in order to make the dough for the pizza. Meanwhile, Ellen cooks fatty smoked sausage with stewed curly kale, Dorte cooks hamburger steaks with oven-baked root crops, Birte cooks spaghetti with smoked salmon and vegetables, Thea makes shrimp salad and bakes buns, Pia makes sandwiches and serves them with leftovers, and Susy cooks meat lasagne – all without referring explicitly to recipes. So, even the most discursively explicit type of bodily/mental procedure in cooking from scratch is embodied and composite.

However, cooking from scratch is at the same time discursively constructed, socially recognised, and normatively expected and negotiated. The following section in this chapter brings the analysis back to the social expectations and normative content of cooking from scratch among the female cooking practitioners.

Normative Negotiations about Cooking Home-made Food

The aim of the analysis in this section is to highlight the influences of social interaction processes on the content of the normative categories and engagements in cooking from scratch. Thus, this section gives examples of negotiations of the normative engagement in cooking from scratch and what the negotiations do to the normative content of agency of ordinary consumers, the category of 'good cooking', and exceptions to appropriate cooking conduct.

Negotiating the Agency Position of Ordinary Consumers

The normative content negotiated in this example has to do with what food consumers can realistically expect from each other in the field of providing meals. The negotiation contains a conflict between a position of normatively prescribing cooking from scratch and a position of trying to adapt such a normative prescription to the workings of everyday life.

The empirical example comes from the focus group with women in their 20s. The example shows how normative engagement in interaction processes can lead to social control and legitimising adaptations of cooking performances.

The sequence comes from halfway through the focus group. The participants are Susy (student), who was interviewed individually, Anna (sales associate) and Paula (zookeeper). The women are working on a group exercise where they have been asked to collectively sort a pile of food into two piles: one pile with food they would serve for guests, and one pile with food they would absolutely not serve for guests.

> Susy: 'There were green grapes, they are really good, and then there are these cantuccini, these biscuits with almonds, and such things that are …'
> Paula: 'They taste really nice, yeah.'
> Susy: 'Yes.'
> Anna: 'And you could also serve these, okay?'
> Paula: 'Yeah, OKAY mum.'
> Anna: 'Then there is pesto, right …'
> Paula: 'Mmm.'
> Anna: 'Yes.'
> Paula: 'No, because I would NEVER serve such a pesto, because if I were to serve pesto, I would make it myself.'
> Susy: 'Okay. But that's fine. But I ACTUALLY don't have the time to make it myself, so I buy it.'
> Paula: 'Time to make it, it doesn't take any time to make a pesto.'

> Susy: 'That doesn't matter, because I …'
> Paula [interrupts]: 'You just need a blender and some basil and some pine kernels and a little bit of other good things.'
> Susy: 'Yeah, yeah.'
> Paula: 'And then you have made a pesto.'
> Susy: 'But I DON'T [Paula makes farting noises with her mouth] always have the time for it … um, and it's not always that I have it in the cupboards … because then Morten has eaten it.'

Paula engages normatively in favour of making pesto from scratch for guests, and she does not change her position on accounts of Susy's attempts to refer to practical problems of time use in daily life. Rather, Paula backs up her normative argumentation by also referring to practical procedures (it doesn't take any time to make pesto), thereby undermining Susy's position. As a result, it seems that Susy experiences the interaction as social control of her cooking routines, because her reaction in the end is to legitimise her lack of cooking a pesto from scratch by positioning her boyfriend as someone who hinders her in doing appropriate cooking (claiming he eats everything in the kitchen cupboards).

Thus, the legitimising element here is referring to practical do-ability in social conditions. Similar legitimising explanations are used in the Norwegian qualitative study on proper domestic dinners. When, for example, ready-made pizza is served for the family, it is explained with statements such as 'My daughter was going to a handball match' or 'I had such a terrible cold that I couldn't bring myself to cook' and other practical do-abilities (Bugge and Almås, 2006: 221).

Negotiating the Category of 'Good Cooking'

One of the consistent findings of the qualitative studies of cooking is that everyday food practitioners associate take-away, ready-made food and processed foods with bad or inappropriate cooking (Ahlgren et al., 2005; Blake et al., 2009; Bugge and Almås, 2006; Moisio et al., 2004; Prim et al., 2007). The construction of the category 'good cooking' as synonymous with cooking food and meals from scratch therefore is a particularly relevant category for analysing reproductions, adaptations, experiments and changes to the normative content of engagements in cooking.

The first example of normative negotiations of the category 'good cooking' comes from the focus group with women in their 40s. The example shows how the social interaction of the negotiation makes one of the participants change the content of her understanding of good cooking.

The sequence is from the first half of the focus group discussion, and the participants are Dorte (bank assistant), who was interviewed individually, Sonja (personal assistant), Birgit (self-employed) and Karen (clerk). As an exercise, the participants have just sorted pictures and recipes from the broadest possible range of women's magazines, and they are now in the middle of discussing what they understand as good and bad cooking.

> Sonja: 'When I was a child, when we had fish it was these frozen fish fingers …'
> Karen [interrupts]: 'Yes, THAT is disgusting [Sonja: He, he …] … that is bad cooking.'
> Dorte: 'Yes, it is.'
> Sonja: 'That is simply YUKKY.'
> Birgit: 'Yes, my kids love them …'
> Dorte [interrupts]: 'No, nobody likes fish fingers.'
> Birgit: 'Yes, I like them.'
> Karen: 'It's the same with that breaded fish you can buy, it's only breading.'
> Birgit: 'No, that depends on which ones you buy … some of it is okay to buy …'
> Karen [interrupts]: 'I will rather buy it without breading, and then … [pause]'
> Birgit: [interrupts]: '… where there is a lot of fish … [pause]' [Karen: 'do it myself'] but that is [Sonja: 'You don't know what's in there'] obvious …'
> Karen: 'No.'
> Sonja: 'It looks like such stuff.'
> Karen: 'Yep.'
> Sonja: 'Oh yes, that's bad cooking too. To me bad cooking is doing it with deep-frying.'
> Birgit: 'Yes, all right I can only admit that [Karen: 'Yes'] to you … we don't use that either.'
> Karen: 'I also think …'
> Sonja [interrupts]: 'But then again, it's that fat.'
> Karen: 'I actually used it, I used it to deep-fry those camembert cheeses for dessert,[12] but I have begun to make that in the oven … that's actually the only deep-fry …'
> Dorte: 'It's a long time since you have made that dessert for us.'
> Karen: 'Yes, he he.'
> Birgit: 'It's actually quite a while since I've had it, you know with a little bit of homemade blackberry preserve …'
> Dorte: 'Yes.'

There is a lot of mutual positioning going on in the negotiation, and the positionings result in the women discovering that they disagree about the appropriateness of the use of certain prefabricated food products, but they also succeed in re-establishing a consensus on the normative content of 'good cooking', which is then defined as not using processed food and fatty food products. Sonja, Karen and Dorte position

12 Deep-fried Camembert with blackberry preserve was a typical 1980s dessert in Denmark.

themselves as agreeing about the normative engagement against the use of prefabricated frozen fish fingers – in contrast to Birgit, who argues that processed food can be fine. But in the end, Birgit is included into the group formation again after she has changed the normative content of her expressions (preserve should be home-made) and agreed to the construction of good cooking formed by the rest of the group.

The second example is a negotiation that produces an opposite consensus compared to the first example. In this second example, the women form a normative consensus in favour of a ready-made product. Thus, the whole group changes the normative content of suitable cooking through their social interaction processes, unlike the adaptation of one of the participants to the group construction seen in the first example. This example shows how social interaction can work as making normative expectations more flexible, whereas the first example showed that social interaction can work to reproduce normative regulation.

The excerpt is from the focus group with women in their 30s. The participants are Ellen (communication planner), who was interviewed individually, Anja (communication planner), Britta (researcher) and Connie (public head of division). We enter the sequence in the beginning of the focus group, where the women are discussing what occupies them currently in relation to cooking in their everyday lives. They are discussing 'koldskål',[13] a popular Danish buttermilk dish:

> Anja: 'It doesn't happen so often, but it happens sometimes, it's really handy. Or sandwiches, or now it's season for … buttermilk pudding …'
> Britta: 'And I'd like to do that, but not really with all those small rusks in it, my son would eat most of a bag of small rusks [Anja: 'Why, mine just don't get so many, he, he'], oh can't I have some more mummy, please …'
> Ellen: 'That thing about small rusks, it's cool to know that the eggs have become unhealthy, because before I would never buy buttermilk pudding in a carton … because I just think it was, I don't know really, um … I did not grow up with it and my mum cooks everything from scratch, so I think, no you just can't, but now I think okay, it's cumbersome anyway and you are not allowed to eat those raw eggs, so now that's how it is.'
> Connie: 'Got a good excuse.'
> Ellen: 'Yes, now I've got such a good excuse for trying out all those different … and some of them are a bit more eco-ish …'
> Britta: 'And with little dots in …'
> Ellen: 'Oh yeah … with real vanilla …'
> Connie: 'I saw that on television, I haven't seen it myself [he, he].'

13 Koldskål is a cold buttermilk dish made with buttermilk, sugar, raw eggs, lemon juice and vanilla, served with small rusks in it. Traditionally, it was a sweet 'starter' along with other milk, fruit and porridge dishes, aimed at filling people's stomachs, so they did not eat too much of the expensive meat. But since the 1970s, it has become a dessert dish.

> Britta: 'I actually got it this morning, mummy, when are we going to have buttermilk pudding? So now you just sit here and pick up on that, I think I'm going to HAVE to no matter what, it has to be fun also now and then …'
> Ellen: 'For dinner, can you do it for dinner? WASN'T that what you said?'
> Britta: 'Yes.

Especially Ellen, Britta and Anja position themselves in relation to what can be seen as proper dinner cooking in this sequence. Through their exchanges, a particular cooking performance is being legitimised; namely, to serve ready-made buttermilk pudding for dinner. This way, the construction of appropriate dinner cooking is expanded from at first not entailing the use of neither ready-made products nor dessert/lunch formats, and then to constructing ready-made buttermilk pudding as an appropriate evening meal.

Negotiating Exceptions to Cooking from Scratch

The practical and social appropriation and adaptation of the normative requirement for women to do cooking from scratch is done in a multitude of little ways in everyday living that juggles conditions of stability with processes of changes. Across the different ways of dealing with and doing cooking from scratch, the female magazine readers express many negotiations of exactly *how* home-made or made from scratch a food item or a meal has to be in order to be recognised as such. The data material is full of expressions of ambivalences, exceptions, legitimations and negotiations around what constitutes sufficiently homemade food, also relating to the everyday life conditions of the cooking practices of the women. Thea explains this in the following manner: *'So a home-made soup is completely made from scratch, but preferably in an easy way, not like having to boil a chicken for three hours (laughs)'* (Thea, clerk, 30s).

For example, there is a whole vocabulary of categories expressing more or less legitimate exceptions from what is considered 'real' home-made food and meals. The most used categories for such exceptions are 'jumping over the lowest part of the fence', 'cutting corners' and 'cheating'. Cheating as explicit category for not producing meals made from scratch is also found in the study of cooking among three generations of American food practitioners (Moisio et al., 2004: 376). The examples of negotiations of whether food is recognised as sufficiently homemade to count as proper cooking from scratch are parallel to some of the negotiations among participants on how to improve the appropriateness of ready meals in order to serve them for dinner in a Swedish study (Prim et al., 2007: 245). The examples are also comparable to negotiations among participants in the Norwegian study about what constitutes a proper dinner (Bugge and Almås, 2006: 219–21).

The following example of negotiating exceptions to cooking from scratch shows how the normative content of even a strong engagement in constructing proper food as food cooked from scratch can be changed through the forms of the social interactions in the group.

This example comes from the focus group with women in their 20s and the excerpt is from the part of the focus group discussions where the women are sorting different food items into two piles, one they will serve for guests and one they will not serve for guests.

> Paula: 'Honey cake slices, I also don't fancy that.'
> Susy: 'Honey cake slices, they're absolutely fine.'
> Paula: 'No, no, no, no, no, no!'
> Susy: 'Yes.'
> Paula: 'No, no, no girls … cake, you make that yourself.'
> Susy: 'Yeah, but I could … [Paula: [interrupts] 'Even if it's Amo[14] …'] … put them on a dish and serve them for guests, honestly really Paula, you could do that too.'
> Paula: 'No, no.'
> Anna: 'There are different guests.'
> Susy: 'Yep.'
> Paula: 'I could never … [pause][laughter, everybody talks at the same time] … serve honey cake slices …'
> Susy: 'No, honey cake slices, they are good.'
> Anna [he, he]: 'They are good.'
> Paula: 'IF I should serve something ready-made, then it had to be, you know, cookies, REAL cookies, not clammy Karen Wolff[15] cookies, but … [Anna [interrupts]: 'I have never tasted those …'] … such cookies that have been treated and … such luxury stuff.'

Paula begins with a clear self-positioning as somebody who will not serve ready-made cakes for guests. Susy positions herself as someone for whom it's fine to do so, and Anna forms an alliance with Susy about defining the honey cake slices as normatively acceptable guest servings. Paula then expresses a different self-positioning in which she can now serve cake that's not home-made, but only certain kinds of ready-made cakes, which are different from the one on the table. Thus, the normative content of Paula's construction of what counts as suitable guest servings is changed through the flow of social interaction.

Other qualitative studies in the current literature on cooking also contain examples on how the definition of a proper meal is negotiated and adapted in practical food work. Blake et al. describe different coping strategies among especially the female participants in their American study on gender and food-choice satisfaction, such as trading off nutrition for saving time (Blake et al., 2009: 5). Prim et al. show how the participants in their Swedish study turn ready-made

14 'Amo' refers to a brand of flour and other baking products, including ready-made cake powders and bread mixtures.

15 Karen Wolff is the most common Danish brand of cheap ready-made biscuits and cookies, which you can get in every store.

meals into 'real cooking', for example, by cooking the trimmings themselves and adding spices to the ready-made stew (Prim et al., 2007: 245).

Normative Engagement in Cooking from Scratch – Conventions or Social Visibility?

Earlier in this chapter, I discussed whether cooking from scratch can be analytically understood as a particular food consumption practice. The type cooking from scratch as taken for granted comprises a large amount of bundles of activities, of connected doings and sayings, in relation to using as few ready-made and semi-processed food products as possible. These bundles of activities are taken for granted by some of the women in the case study. The activities are also discursively voiced as normative engagements at a project level of practices by some of the women. Furthermore, the normative negotiations about appropriate and inappropriate cooking make it clear that cooking from scratch is socially recognised as a package of activities with fairly clear social markers such as using raw materials, not using ready-made meals and processed foods, and possessing traditional cooking skills such as baking.

The question is whether cooking from scratch can be seen as a consumption practice, because cooking from scratch has been such an integrated part of the historical trajectory of food and cooking practices? Or whether cooking from scratch can be seen as a consumption practice, because the recent medialised discourses have constructed a normative sounding board for the engagements of some food practitioners whereby cooking from scratch becomes socially visible?

Doing Suitable Consumption?

What are the consequences in everyday life when ordinary cooking practices are challenged by representations and discourses which communicate that proper cooking is to bake, preserve and cook everything from scratch with raw materials? The range and variety of food supplies in stores in European countries have increased considerably (Lang and Heasman, 2004), and the possibilities for food consumers to use all types of specialised goods such as semi-manufactured and ready-made food products are greater than ever before (Dixon, 2008). Thus, there are multiple opportunities for doing unsuitable food consumption in present-day society. But there is no strict definition of what cooking from scratch entails among the cooking practitioners, among public policy makers in the food area, or among social scientific analyses of food and cooking (Moisio, 2004: 372; Short, 2006: 88–89). This creates space for manoeuvrings, negotiations and adaptations when people seek to accomplish acceptable cooking conduct.

Another characteristic about the cooking-from-scratch challenge that supports a space for manoeuvrings, negotiations and adaptations is the trajectory of cooking from scratch as practical performance. Cooking from scratch has formed an integral part of the organisation of food practices for generations of food practitioners, and it seems to play a part in all the ways of practising cooking. There is no connected and organised pattern of 'non-performing' home-made food among the Danish female food practitioners in this study. This may mean that the distinction between suitable and unsuitable consumption is fairly negotiable.

The negotiability of cooking from scratch and the food consumption activities linked to such practices is also described in other current studies of the detailed processes of cooking in everyday life (Blake et al., 2009; Bove and Sobal, 2006; Bugge and Almås, 2006; Prim et al., 2007; Short, 2006). One Swedish qualitative study takes the negotiability of appropriate family dinners so far as to comprise family visits to fast food restaurants such as McDonalds (Brembeck, 2005), but that argumentation rests upon a focus on the social forms of the eating rather than the provision of the meals.

The question is how this negotiability of cooking from scratch in everyday life interacts with the attempts in, for example, public campaigns to use cooking from scratch as part of the solution to other food issues (such as food safety, nutrition and lack of food work skills). It probably does not make it easier to frame consumer responsibilities for e.g. dietary health problems in a context of cooking from scratch more often, if cooking from scratch is such a potentially volatile pursuit.

The Danish female food practitioners may not be celebrating everyday life in the manner of the lifestyle magazines. But they certainly show skilled practical and social agency in their manoeuvrings in everyday life.

Chapter 6
Dealing with Nutritional Challenges

Integrating Nutrition?

The last challenge to ordinary food consumption discussed in this book deals with the multitude of nutritional advice, guidelines, initiatives and interventions. Internationally, nutritional discourses have a relatively long history (Beardsworth and Keil, 1997: 125–49; Coveney, 2000; Falbe and Nestlé, 2008; Gronow, 1993; Lupton, 1996; Turner, 1984) regarding attempts to influence and change food practices of ordinary citizens, compared to environmental discourses and modern food-risk discourses. However, nutritional discourses change across historical societal trajectories, and in Europe and other Western societies, a current focus seems to be the so-called obesity epidemic (Coveney, 2000: 143–47; Lang and Heasman, 2004: 63–70) where over- and mal-consumption of food put people at risk of a variety of chronic diseases such as type-2 diabetes, coronary heart disease and high blood pressure. In a governmentality-inspired analysis of the social technologies and practices of nutrition, John Coveney argues that the obesity epidemic enables a pluralisation of societal actors and forms of regulation around nutrition, resulting in 'new opportunities to problematise everyday life' (Coveney, 2000: 155). This is an argument parallel to the main viewpoint in this book: that ordinary food consumption activities become challenged through the medialised normative discourses within different issues and the social actions related to such discourses.

The Danish Context

Denmark, like the rest of Scandinavia, has a strong tradition for public health promotion via information campaigns about smoking, exercise, alcohol and diet (Vallgårda, 2001). In relation to diet, The Agency of Consumer Affairs has informed the general Danish population about what has been considered proper nutrition since 1936. A content analysis of information materials from The Agency of Consumer Affairs to households from 1936 to 1985 showed that proper nutrition increasingly and exclusively became discursively framed as prevention of specific modern lifestyle food-related diseases, such as obesity. As a part of this development, proper food practices were also constructed as being based upon scientific nutritional knowledge and rational planning instead of other everyday considerations such as satiety, economic resources, taste preferences or cooking skills. Communication about food practices also became targeted to individuals as the ones to be nutritionally regulated, rather than families and other communities

(Christensen, 1998). This is a development that is also found in other national contexts (e.g. Coveney, 2000: 96–106; Lupton, 1996: 68–73; Warde, 1997: 80–81).

This construction of nutritional food practices as building upon scientific knowledge, aimed at preventing lifestyle diseases, and placing the responsibility on the individual, can also be recognised today in public Danish initiatives on healthy food practices. In April 2009, The Danish Commission for Prevention launched a report with recommendations for national initiatives to improve public health. The report recommends a large number of prevention initiatives in relation to especially diet, alcohol, smoking and exercise. These recommendations are grouped into two main types: socially targeted prevention offers such as school lunches, and individually targeted regulations such as taxes and prohibitions. In the area of food and diet, there are twice as many individually targeted regulation recommendations as prevention offers (Forebyggelseskommissionen, 2009). This tendency to individualise the responsibility for a nutritionally healthy diet in Denmark was also reflected in the empirical results of a recent comparative European study. An analysis of the construction of the food consumer among a broad variety of representatives of societal actors – producers, manufacturers, retailers, public authorities, scientists, media, and consumer organisations – showed that in relation to solving problems related to nutrition and health, all types of actors in Denmark ascribed the main responsibility to individual consumers themselves (Halkier et al., 2007: 389). This was different from the constructions made about food consumers in relation to environmental issues, where consumers were framed as co-responsible, as well as in relation to risk issues in food, where the state was constructed as responsible (see Chapters 3 and 4). This resonates with an earlier Danish study of how consumers were blamed for the decline in food quality in Denmark (Holm, 2003a).

A comparison of the content of individually targeted, public nutritional communications in the four Nordic countries concludes that the main dietary advice in all of these countries is more or less the same, both regarding the content (more vegetables and fruit, more fish, more whole grain products, less sugar and animal fat), and regarding the way suggestions for changes in routines are simplified in the medialised discourses (Andersson and Bryngelsson, 2007: 36–38). But just as the development in environmental, risk and cooking-from-scratch issues has shown (see introductions in Chapters 3–5), food producers and retailers are also part and parcel of the challenging of ordinary food from the nutrition angle. Another characteristic of the dietary advice (as reported in several national studies) is the importance of interactions between public sector actors and private business sector actors in constructing, adapting and communicating about healthy food habits (Asp and Bryngelsson, 2007; Falbe and Nestlé, 2008; Holm, 2003a; Kjærnes, 1997). An example from Denmark is the recent launch of a labelling system for nutritionally better foods, called ‘the keyhole’.

Current Studies

The potential consequences of these challenges to ordinary food consumption for food practitioners have been discussed in the international literature for the last 30 years. An important contribution to the debate is Crawford's thesis of the medicalisation of everyday life (Crawford, 1980). In his analysis of the social effects of modern individualised and nutritionalised health prevention strategies, he highlights the 'victim blaming' of so-called unhealthy eaters, which among other things carries the consequence of neglecting structural conditions of malnutrition and diet-related illness. Based on Crawford's thesis and other studies (e.g. Coveney, 2000; Lupton, 1996), it has indeed been argued that it is almost impossible for the individual food practitioner nowadays *not* to reflect upon health in relation to cooking and eating as something that is normatively required (Nielsen, 2008: 18). In a comparative qualitative study of food and eating in families in four different European cities (Copenhagen, Frankfurt, London and Stockholm), the women who were interviewed began unprompted to reflect and judge themselves normatively, just talking about what they were eating in daily life to an interviewer (Holm et al., 2003). The self-reflections of the interviewed women in this study point towards ambivalences in everyday life in relation to the nutritionalisation of food consumption as shown in other qualitative studies of food and eating (Ekström, 1991; Holm and Kildevang, 1996; Lupton, 1996). Interestingly, even an English qualitative study from the 1970s showed that when women where interviewed about their food practices and understandings of 'good food', they talked about the gastronomic part of good food in personalised everyday life terms, whereas they talked about the nutritional part of good food in scientific and abstract terms, unrelated to the everyday life food experiences (Murcott, 1993).

In the current literature about food consumers' handling of nutrition and health issues of food, there is recognition of the social conditionings and complexities of modern food practices. This is, for example, the case in the empirical studies carried out from a Foucauldian perspective and in the empirical studies that view food provision, cooking and eating as part of everyday life routines. John Coveney's governmentality analysis of Australian families and their food practices is an example of the Foucauldian strand; it shows how nutritional discourses become the government of food choice through the self-regulation of individuals based on nutritional knowledges (Coveney, 2000). Other empirical studies highlight different social conditions influencing how people in everyday life tackle nutrition and health claims on food. These studies show, for example, how social resources and procedures in food routines enable and constrain food choices (Delormier et al., 2009); how time scarcity influences people's food practices in less healthy directions (Jabs and Devine, 2006); how nutritional self-disciplining can clash with other disciplinary regimes (Balfe, 2007); how embodiment of food routines in social identification can create conflicts with nutritional advice and health care in the family (McKie et al., 2004; Warin et al., 2008); and how family negotiations shape nutritionalised food practices (Bassett et al., 2008). Typically, these studies contain social criticisms of how communications and interventions about more healthy food are conducted, as this example shows: *'Nutritional advice typically focuses on what to eat, but seldom on how to fit those recommendations into busy daily lives'* (Jabs and Devine, 2006: 202).

However, there are also in the nutritional area of food challenging a number of studies that are based on more cognitivist analytical assumptions, towards which the Foucauldian studies remain critical, seeing them as exaggerating rational choices in eating and underestimating how eating is embedded in the social practices of everyday life (Delormier et al., 2009: 216–17). Many of these cognitivist studies build on the theory of planned behaviour (see Chapter 1) and focus on so-called individual variables such as information, intention, attitude and behaviour among selected target groups (e.g. Aikman et al., 2006; Blanchard et al., 2009; Carrus et al., 2009). There is also a parallel theoretical position in communication theory, focusing on the cognitive factors in constructing effective health communication (Fishbein and Cappella, 2006).

In the field between the broader sociological analyses of how people deal with constructions of healthy food and the rational-choice studies of how individualised nutritional communications can improve their efficiency, there is a group of studies focusing on the social dimension of public health in relation to food and nutrition. In these studies, there is recognition of how food consumption is socially embedded and at the same time a clear goal of attempting to improve nutritional public health initiatives on the basis of such more social knowledges. Examples of such contributions are analyses of social marketing (see Chapter 1) (Bellows et al., 2006; Piggford et al., 2008), media literacy (Livingstone and Helsper, 2006) and health activism (Bandesha and Litva, 2005; Zoller, 2005).

The Danish case study upon which this chapter is based belongs to the group of studies with broader sociological analyses of how people handle constructions of allegedly healthy and unhealthy food, cooking and eating.

The Danish Case Study: Nutritional Challenges to Food Consumption

The empirical research project that is the focus of this chapter is called 'Network communication and changes in food practices'.[1] The research is a qualitative in-depth study of the food habits among ethnic Pakistani Danes and how 'doing healthy food' is handled among them. The overall sampling strategy was one of maximum variation regarding the following criteria among the participating Pakistani Danes: age, education, gender, whether participants were born in Denmark or Pakistan, whether a person in the family had been diagnosed with type-2 diabetes, and whether participants worked in the health sector. A total of 19 Pakistani Danes participated in individual interviews, family interviews or group interviews.

---

1 Associate professor Iben Jensen, CBIT, Roskilde University, was senior partner in the research, and the study was financed by the National Danish Social Scientific Research Council (FSE), 2008–2010.

The qualitative data in the study were produced by several methods. One part of the data was produced by individual in-depth interviewing with the main cooking practitioner in the family. Participants were interviewed about food provisioning, cooking and eating in everyday life, about cooking and eating in relation to other people in their network, and about cooking and eating in relation to constructions of healthy food. These interviews were conducted using ethnographic interviewing (Spradley, 1979) and active interviewing (Holstein and Gubrium, 2003). Some group interviewing (Frey and Fontana, 1993) also took place in cases where it was impossible to do individual interviewing; the same interviewing techniques were used.

Another part of the data was produced by auto-photography (Heisley and Levy, 1991; Hurdley, 2007), where the participating main cooking practitioners and other members of their family households took photos of everything they ate and drank in the course of an ordinary weekday and of some food from the weekend. These photos were used as data in themselves. But the photos were also used in the family interviews that followed the interviews with the individual main cooking practitioner, in order to help embody and materialise the stories about food activities and food understandings in relation to constructions of, for example, healthy food. The family interviews included those family members who wished to participate. Family interviews obviously also take on the character of group interviewing, and in all of these interviews, which were held in the home of the family, ordinary participant observation field notes were taken, especially since snacks and meals were always served. Participant observation (Hammersley and Atkinson, 1995) was also used at an opportunity to attend a wedding.

The presentation and discussion of the Danish case study on nutritionalised consumption follows the form for all four empirical chapters, outlined in more detail in the general methodology section (see the last section of Chapter 2). The following briefly summarises the outline.

First, the analysis describes and categorises the specific similarities and diversities of food practising that are carried out among the Pakistani Danes. This is done in order to understand the basic configuration of which food consumption is already a part; namely, the food practices. This lays the groundwork for inferences later in the analysis about the ways in which people react to having their food consumption questioned.

Second, the analysis describes and categorises the different ways of handling nutritionalised food consumption in an ideal typology. The purpose of this second part of the analysis is twofold: first to demonstrate the variety in reactions to nutritionalisation of consumption, second to discuss when everyday life performing constitutes a practice in itself and when it does not, in order to contribute to the discussions about consumer agency.

Third, the analysis zooms in on the details of how nutritionalised consumption activities are performed by focusing on the practical procedures. The purpose of this third part of the analysis is to highlight the significance and complexities of the practical do-ability involved in everyday reactions to challenged food consumption.

Fourth, the analysis gives examples of positionings and negotiations of the normative engagement in nutritionalised food consumption and how the positionings and negotiations reproduce, adapt, change, improvise and experiment with the normative content of the three following issues: agency of ordinary consumers, the category of 'healthier food', and exceptions to appropriate 'healthy' conduct. The purpose of this analysis is to question the balance in current everyday life analytical research on nutrition and consumption between an individual life-world focus and a focus on social processes.

Hybridised Food Practices

In the first three empirical chapters, the analysis of the variety in dealing with the food challenges began by looking at the food practice configurations into which the consumption contestations enter. This was done because it is important for a practice theoretical perspective to establish what the basic integrated practices in everyday life consist of. For each of the other three Danish case studies (the young people, the parents and the female magazine readers), a diversity of food practices was described. It was found that within all three groups of food practitioners, distinctly different groups of food activities (doings and sayings – what is prepared and eaten, and what is said about this) are carried out. Each of these groups of food activities are organised by a coordinated set of distinct understandings of food, procedures in provisioning, cooking and eating, and engagements in food. Each of these groups of activities is also socially recognisable as a distinct way of practising food.

The data from the case study with the Pakistani Danes, however, show much less diversity in food practice types. An analysis of the data indicates one shared type of food practice, which is more or less culturally hybridised between Pakistani and Danish food formats and adapted to different patterns of time use. This analytical categorisation is made because the reported, specific food activities – the patterns of what is prepared and eaten, and what is said about it – are fairly similar across differences in age, gender, educational level and whether participants have grown up in Denmark or Pakistan.

To a large degree, the food activities consist of the same meal patterns and dishes. On weekdays, food practitioners begin the day with porridge, cereals or toast, sometimes supplemented with fried eggs, and they have lunches of rye bread or toast bread with vegetables, cheese and eggs, or leftovers from dinner the day before. Evening meals usually include rice or chapattis[2] with chicken, lamb or

2 Dry-roasted pancakes.

beef in masala[3] or with dhal,[4] sometimes supplemented with a salad. Studies of Pakistani immigrant food habits from other national contexts such as England, Norway and Canada show that a 'proper' Pakistani meal is understood as chapattis with curries (Jamal, 1998; Mellin-Olsen and Wandel, 2005; Ristovski-Slijepcevic et al., 2008). Evening meals also include generalised Westernised dishes such as pizza, pasta and lasagne, and generalised Middle Eastern dishes such as kebab. The acquisition of food is done as bulk purchasing so families always have a sufficient stock of everything necessary to cook meals:

> So I think we think it's easy. You know, it's fairly easy to make food. Because it's simple. You don't have to think about shopping, because you already have all the stuff, you always have the stuff at home. You can make that at any time. (Rushy, female academic)

Food and drink supplies for unexpected guests are also kept in storage at any time, covering soft drinks, ingredients for Asian chai,[5] biscuits, nuts and a variety of fried snacks such as samosas[6] and kebabs, kept in the freezer. On weekends and when invited guests come over, several dishes are served at the same meal, meat is always included, extra trimmings such as chutney are provided, as well as puddings. Cooking food takes more time on the weekends.

The understandings of food are also shared among the participants, but without a clear pattern of being linked to particular other elements in the organisation of the food practices, whether it be activities, procedures or engagements. The main distinction in food understandings here relate to constructions of Pakistani food and Danish food. Pakistani food refers to the majority of the evening meal formats that are prepared and consumed, while Danish food refers to boiled food with food items separated, to lasagne and pasta dishes,[7] to the breakfast cereals, and to the rye bread for lunch. Food is an important signifier of identification, especially for ethnic minority groups (Holtzman, 2006: 365), and dishes that are considered Danish become incorporated into the food-based identification by adding Pakistani spices to turn the food into 'our food'. Here is an example from a family interview with a food practitioner, Sada (female nurse), and her sister-in-law, Maria (female childcare assistant):

3 Masala is the common denominator for the basic sauces in Pakistani cooking, often made with oil, tomatoes, onions and spices.

4 Dhal is the common denominator for dishes made with lentils, peas and beans.

5 Tea made with milk and spices, with sugar added.

6 Packages of puff paste filled with vegetables and deep-fried.

7 A Swedish study of the multicultural lunch table at work shows that pasta and lasagne are constructed as Swedish food by Swedes with ethnic minority background (Lindén and Nyberg, 2009). However, pasta dishes are frequently served dishes in majority Danish evening meals (www.food.dtu.dk).

> Maria: 'Lasagne is also something, that's full of seasoning, it tastes all right.'
> Sada: 'But we use our own spices.'

This cultural appropriation through the spices reflects the findings of other empirical studies of the food habits of people with Pakistani or Punjabi background in Sweden (Lindén and Nyberg, 2009), Norway (Mellin-Olsen and Wandel, 2005) and Scotland (Bush et al., 1998).

Among the Pakistani-Danish participants, other understandings of food are expressed that resonate with food understandings in the other three Danish case studies, such as necessity of food, pleasures of food, and food as an element of care for others. But these understandings of food are not systematically linked with any of the other organising elements of a food practice (specific activities, procedures and engagements). The same is the case for the participants' engagements in food. Food performances among the Pakistani Danes only become distinctly different from each other when the element of nutritionalised food is included in the analysis, and this is the topic of the next main section of this chapter.

There is, however, one element of food practices in general that varies considerably in the practising of food among the Pakistani Danes. This has to do with procedures of cooking. How meals are produced and the amounts of time or the timing of the work allocated to meal production vary among the participants. For some of the food practitioners, it seems inappropriate not to cook most of the food from scratch. Almost all food procedures explained by these participants are detailed descriptions of how masalas are made with fresh raw ingredients, how chappatis and naan bread are baked, how stocks of home-made samosas are made for the freezer, and how complicated desserts and chutneys are fabricated. Here, weekday cooking cannot be done in less than one hour, and guest dinners can take seven hours to prepare during weekends.

Other food practitioners also stress the importance of cooking meals from scratch, but at the same time describe ways of cutting down on the time spent on food preparation in order to make room for the logistics of two full-time jobs and two to four children. Examples of this include serving ready-made fish fingers and French fries or ready-made poultry meat balls and pitta breads and add masala and potatoes; using frozen vegetable mixes; using tinned mackerel in tomato sauce for a fish masala; and, of course, buying take-away pizza or shawarma. One of the women explains:

> It's when it has to be quick. Where it just gets used, um, the few times where we just you know have to have some fish fingers and French fries to go with them, right [laughing]. When the children just want something, um burger, home-made burger, right, where I also get to make some fish quickly. (Sada, female nurse)

Another way of handling the time juggling of the multiplicity of everyday practices is to make the time use more flexible by cooking at other times of the day and the week than just before the food is served. This includes, for example, cooking dinners the evening before or early in the morning in order to heat it later, or to cook during the weekend and store it in the freezer.

This variation in procedures of food practices is related to another part of the cultural hybridisation of the food practices among the participants; namely, the globalisation of Western food industry, frequently referred to as McDonaldisation (Ritzer, 1993/2008), and an internationalisation of food tastes (Holm, 1996; Warde et al., 1999). Here, larger amounts of processed food, ready-made meals, soft drinks and culinary variations are incorporated into food practices. This tendency is also described for food practitioners with a Pakistani background in other national contexts, for example in England (Jamal, 1998), Norway (Mellin-Olsen and Wandel, 2005) and in Scotland (Bush et al., 1998).

The last element to notice in the hybridised food practices of the Pakistani-Danish food practitioners is the importance of guests and food for guests. The food practitioners give accounts of a comparatively high level of guest activity, and this includes the unexpected as well as the planned or invited guest occasions. Depending on where guests are placed in the social network of the food practitioner and their family, whether they are in the in-group or in the larger part of the network, different types of food are expected and deemed appropriate. Members of the in-group (especially family) can more easily drop by unexpectedly and take part in the ordinary evening meal or only get chai and biscuits served. Guests from the larger social network and invited guests, on the other hand, are expected to be treated to soft drinks, deep-fried snacks from the freezer, or an elaborate guest meal with several courses, with different types of meat, oily masalas and heavy, sweet desserts. Again, this is a pattern in this type of hybridised food practices that is reported in other studies as well (Bradby, 2002; Bush et al., 1998; Mellin-Olsen and Wandel, 2005). In Mellin-Olsen and Wandel's study, the Norwegian-Pakistani participants explain how they may try to cut down on the fat intake in everyday cooking, but that guest curries must look 'glossy' with oil (ibid.: 325). Here, one of the women in the Danish study explains the difference between ordinary masala and masala served for guests by referring to a similar metaphor for the richness in oil in guest meals:

> Have you ever seen any of these curries, oh yeah, you have seen them at my party, right, there is a lot of oil, but the same curry doesn't shine so much when you put less oil in it. It's probably just a question of habit. (Rushy, female academic)

This woman also explains that Pakistani food is never boiled; it is always roasted. Boiled food or food with less oil or butter or without meat is considered inappropriate to serve for guests. One of the other food practitioners puts it this way when being asked whether it would be possible to serve less fatty food for guests: *'[laughter] Then they would never come again!'* (Zabel, female employed in kindergarten).

This first section of the analysis described and categorised the similarities – and the few differences – of food practising among the Pakistani Danes. The purpose was to establish the basic configuration of which food consumption is already a part; namely, the food practices, in order to lay the groundwork for the following analysis of the reactions towards the nutritional challenge of this food consumption.

Ways of Handling Nutritionalised Food

The previous section showed how the hybridised food practices of the Pakistani-Danish participants were intersected by activities, understandings, procedures and engagements in relation to Pakistani food, Danish food, appropriate food and inappropriate food. This section describes and categorises different ways of handling nutritionalised food consumption in an ideal typology. The purpose of this second part of the analysis is to demonstrate the varietiy and complexity in reactions to nutritionalisation of consumption. As in the first three empirical chapters, the goal is also to pursue the discussion of whether and when such patterns of reactions could be understood as practices. This discussion is one of the ways in which a practice theoretical perspective can contribute to the more general analytical debate about societal consumer agency.

Engaging Proactively in Healthier Food

Here, expressions of the participating food practitioners suggest that everyday life contains a relatively large amount of doings and sayings in the food practices that are directed towards handling nutritionalised food, and that healthiness of food is a taken-for-granted normative assumption. Just like in the comparative study of food habits in families in four European cities (Holm et al., 2003), food practitioners talk without being prompted about what constitutes healthy and unhealthy food and explain the food procedures they use to make healthier food. There are references to all the main elements of public Danish dietary advice: more vegetables and fruit, more fish, more whole grain products, less sugar and less animal fat (Andersson and Bryngelsson, 2007: 36–38).

Examples of procedures constructed as healthier are to make chicken, fish and kebab in the oven instead of in a pot or pan in order to use less oil; to steam vegetables instead of roasting them for a long time in a curry in order to maintain more vitamins; and to make 'biriani' instead of 'pilao'[8] in order to use less oil. All these examples correspond to current public Danish nutritional advice. Here,

8 In biriani, the roasted ingredients (vegetables, spices etc.) are mixed into the steamed rice just before being served, whereas in pilao the rice is roasted together with the other ingredients, requiring more oil in order for the rice not to stick to the pot.

one of the food practitioners describes how she makes her 'Saturday chicken',[9] marinated in yogurt and spices:

> One of the days where it's being called, my elder brother always makes fun of us, 'oh, are you having your Saturday chicken', right. [laughs]. But it's usually that chicken in the oven. … Because the only thing is just to peal off the skin of the chicken. Some people make it with the skin, but as I've told you, I prefer not to because of all that fat. So, you know, off with the skin, and it also becomes better marinated. It gives more taste of the spices instead of the skin just getting it. (Sada, female nurse)

So, the procedures of cooking activities have been changed in order to make what is constructed as healthier food. A large part of the understandings sustaining the procedures seem to correspond to what is called 'the mainstream healthy eating discourse', referring to modern nutritional terms in order to control the effects of eating. This discourse is analysed in a Canadian qualitative study, comparing discourses of healthy eating across three different ethnic groups (Ristovski-Slijepcevic et al., 2008: 172–73).

Eating activities and procedures have been changed, too. Food practitioners claim, for example, that they have cut down on how often they eat the traditional Pakistani breakfast meal, parathas. It is a flat, unleavened bread or thick pancake where the dough is made with wheat flour and ghee,[10] roasted in butter on a pan and buttered once again before eating it. Typically, food practitioners eat it only on weekends, instead of every morning, and to avoid it is constructed as reflecting and taking care of your body:

> The whole family eats it, um, I think parathas are a bit heavy, I like the dry ones better, gradually a lot of people … you know, those who are conscious about their bodies, they probably don't eat them so often. They love them, but they don't eat them so often. (Rushy, female academic)

As mentioned in the section on hybridised food, Pakistani-Danish guest food is understood as tasty but also unhealthy due to the high contents of fat and sugar. Thus, the food practitioners performing proactive engagement in healthy food find ways of handling these situations. Here is an exchange about such procedures from one of the family interviews, where the two women (Sada, female nurse and her sister-in-law Maria, female childcare assistant) have just discussed scraping off oil from dishes:

9 To use the expression 'Saturday chicken' is to make an ironic reference to the first type of ready-made meals you could buy in Denmark back in the 1980s, which consisted of pre-roasted chicken pieces dripping with frying oil and packed in aluminium foil trays.

10 Ghee is butter that is melted into a concentrate.

> Interviewer: 'Is it allowed to take it off when you are at parties and so?'
> Sada: 'We try.'
> Maria: 'With quick movements!' [showing with her hands]
> Sada: 'But you cannot avoid it. I can feel that it's probably one of the cheap kinds of fat that is usually being used in that sort of food.'

The Canadian study about different discourses on healthy eating across three different ethnic groups covers participants with Punjabi background, and one of the Punjabi quotes illustrating the mainstream healthy eating discourse clearly resonates with enactments of proactive engagement in healthy food in our study:

> Our culture uses a lot of butter and margarine, you know, when they're making their curries. It's almost part of the base. I try to cut down on a lot of the stuff that I'm using, like cut the quantity down so, you know, instead of using a tablespoon I'll try to use a teaspoon of it. (Punjabi BC woman, 45) (Ristovski-Slijepcevic et al., 2008: 173).

In this type of handling nutritionalised food, new knowledge about what is healthy and what is not healthy is questioned, discussed and actively sought in magazines, books, from television shows and the Internet, and from other people in the social network. Communication about food in a health context is being initiated with members of the 'in-group', typically family members such as mothers, daughters, sisters and sisters-in-law. Sada and Maria, for example, call each other on the mobile phone if they learn something new. However, one of the activities that clearly distinguish this type of handling nutritionalised food from the other three is that communication about healthy food is also initiated with members of the larger social network. Some participants discuss healthy food with colleagues, the nurse Sada strikes up conversations with every Pakistani Dane with type-2 diabetes whom she encounters, and some participants initiate discussions with their medical practitioners about healthy food by telling him or her about their own experiences with herbal medicine and traditional Pakistani healing properties of food:[11] *'Yes, we told our doctors, they are very happy and they said, you must tell us, afterwards if it works, then we can tell other people'* (Meghana, female employed at nursing home). This understanding of healthier food mirrors another discourse on healthy eating from the Canadian study; namely, a cultural/traditional healthy eating discourse, where the positive aspects of e.g. Pakistani food conventions are promoted (Ristovski-Slijepcevic et al., 2008: 170–72). In our Danish study, one of the participants has even made a living out of networking about health and food. Ali has taken a new short education course called 'Healthy in your own language', making him a 'health ambassador' in the social networks of ethnic minority Danes, and members of his larger social network come to him for advice

11 For example, the system of dividing all food into 'hot' and 'cold'.

on food and nutrition: *'And when you are health ambassador, you cannot help telling about and talking about health'* (Ali, male health ambassador).

The engagement in healthy food in this type of dealing with nutritionalised food includes making healthier meals for others, not just members of the in-group, but also members of the larger social network. Here is an example where the food practitioner explains what might happen in such situations:

> But as I told you, I have experienced that I have made some special food … somebody with diabetes comes and I make it with that sugar additive, sweetener, so I make two bowls, but then she doesn't even want to eat it, she'll rather have the one with sugar in it, right, and then I think, why do I slave … (Rushy, female academic).

Sada has also baked cakes for larger gatherings without sugar and gotten similar reactions. She draws a parallel between 'doing healthy food' in her larger network and 'doing religiously appropriate food'[12], explaining how she has to make sure that her children do not eat inappropriately in their larger network:

> And then I have a cousin, when we where travelling together, she also brought some wine gums, and I said to her, you shouldn't give this to your children, because it contains gelatin. She said, 'yeah, yeah, fine with you', that's what she said and she began to dish it out to her children, right, and my children knew of course that they shouldn't eat that. (Sada, female nurse)

The religiously-based commitment resembles the third discourse on healthy eating found in the Canadian study, called complementary/ethical healthy eating discourses, where healthy eating is embedded in other social concerns (Ristovski-Slijepcevic et al., 2008: 173–74). Apart from this discursive parallel, a more bodily-procedural parallel can be seen. Making sure that the children learn to discipline themselves as part of carrying out appropriate food practices – such as not eating wine gums – is a process some authors in the field would characterise as part of the nutritional disciplining expected in modern societies (Coveney, 2000: 125). Disciplining – also for Coveney – should not be exclusively understood as oppressive and limiting. Rather, disciplining of food practices also entail enabling aspects for the food practitioners, such as creating space for action.

Fitting in Healthier Food

This way of dealing with nutritionalised food revolves around the practicalities of tacitly adjusting some of the procedures in daily food practices to become healthier. As in the first type, constructions of healthier food correspond to both

---

12 In this case with muslim participants, to eat 'halal', e.g. not to eat pork, including gelatin, and meat from animals not slaughtered in the correct way.

mainstream 'nutritionalised' discourses as well as cultural/traditional discourses on healthy eating (Ristovski-Slijepcevic et al., 2008). There are references to getting knowledge about nutrition and healthy food from books, television, the Internet, cooking programmes and the children's schools, and understandings of nutrition and healthy food are taken for granted as something that is already a part of the activities of food practitioners. One of the husbands from a family interview puts it like this: *'Actually, we know already really well what is healthy and what is not healthy ... And we also try to make that, so actually we don't have to seek any advice ... But we do what we can'* (Ahmed, male taxi driver). Taking for granted that one's own cooking and eating is sufficiently informed by appropriate knowledge about healthy food is a common self-positioning expressed by food practitioners whose expressions inform this type of performing healthier food. One of the women clarifies this by including the interviewers: *'No, we don't talk about it. Why don't we? Not about that. ... Because, um, we have the way of ... I, too, know what is unhealthy and what is healthy. So do you, right!'* (Solejma, female office clerk). Such expressions resemble statements from a New Zealand interview study on food provisioning in families and how the participants acquired food knowledge (Bava et al., 2008: 492).

Some of the cooking and eating procedures in the food practices of the practitioner and her family are adapted to the understandings of healthy and unhealthy food. Examples of these include making balanced meals, using less oil in masalas, baking chappatis with wholewheat flour, tricking children into eating vegetables without knowing by blending the vegetables, boiling vegetables instead of roasting them, and making juice from fruit leftovers instead of using soft drinks. The tacit adaptation of certain elements of nutritionalised food can be seen from the trajectories of these food procedures. Shabana (female school teacher), married to Ahmed, began to make her own fresh juice, because her husband at that time worked as a driver for an organic vegetable box delivery service and brought home lots of leftover fruit. Sunanah (female unskilled worker) sometimes serves boiled vegetables, because they form part of a quick meal with oven-roasted chicken legs, hybridised with Danish meal components. Solejma (female office clerk) allows her children to 'wash off' the oily masala from the meat because this is how she can make them eat such traditional Pakistani dishes.

As a part of this 'fitting in' healthier food handling type, the food practitioners communicate mainly with members of their social in-group about healthy and unhealthy food. Amisha (female housewife) explains that members of her family seek her advice on good and healthier cooking, and her teenage daughter proudly clarifies this in the family interview: *'I don't think we doubt about that sort of things in relation to Pakistani food, it's probably more Danish food you can wonder about'* (Ishita, high school student). There is not necessarily as much discussion and communication going on as in the first ideal-type way of handling nutritionalised food, but it seems on the other hand to be socially legitimate to talk about it with people in the intimate circles of the social network. One of the food practitioners explains after having been asked if she serves her less oily masalas for guests: *'Then we just tell them that this is what we have made and that here in our home we don't use very much oil. And that's how it is'* (Shabana, female school teacher).

The next example also shows that healthy food is not just discussed with members of the food practitioner's in-group, but that healthier food is also practically done with such members. When people with diabetes come for dinner, Sunanah cooks masalas with a specific vegetable, 'karela', which is understood to be good for those with diabetes in traditional Pakistani medicine. Solejma explains that she is frustrated about her sister-in-law making dishes with lots of fat and sugar for her brother, who is diagnosed with type-2 diabetes:

> You know, I tried, um, to explain to her from these leaflets my brother has from the organisation about, um, how he has to relate to food and what he must eat and what he should not, um, and tried to explain it to her. This is just where it goes wrong, that she doesn't understand what is written in these leaflets and catalogues that my brother has got. (Solejma, female office clerk)

Solejma makes different dishes for her brother when he visits her home.

But 'eating healthier' can also just sort of happen practically in everyday life, here for the children:

> You know, my husband bought pizza, so he took some home. He ate a little, and then he took it home, and then I asked the children, do you want, do you want, no, no. This is the third day, it's still in the fridge, they haven't eaten a single piece. (Sunanah, female unskilled worker)

Doing Healthier Food Ambivalently

Tensions characterise this way of dealing with nutritionalised cooking and eating. Understandings of healthier food correspond to public Danish dietary advice (less fat, less sugar, more vegetables and fruit, more wholegrain staples), just like in the two first ideal types, and there is also engagement expressed in cooking and eating more healthy dishes and meals. But other engagements than health in food practices are expressed as being more important. What is constructed as healthier food activities and procedures are incorporated when these do not conflict too much with the other types of engagement in food practices. One such type of engagement is in the pleasures of cooking and eating, which is clearly described here by one of the women:

> Everything that tastes good is bad … you could say … but I just think you have to learn to limit it so that it doesn't become a daily routine. Because if you eat it once in a while, nothing actually happens. But that thing about making it into a daily routine to eat bread with butter and cakes and chocolate and such for snacks. Like in the office, it's really nice to sit and eat candy, you know, you're

> so concentrated and then you just sit and eat. That's what makes it so unhealthy. (Aysha, female medical secretary)

Across all the social differences among the participants in the research project, the pleasure of the taste of good food is never questioned. Food practitioners who express engagement in healthier food and specific procedures for how to cook, also express how unpleasant and inappropriate healthier food can be. Here is an example where one of the food practitioners, Maria (Sada's sister-in-law) provides an account of her own sister's cooking:

> Maria: 'My sister, do you know what she does? She only uses two teaspoons [of oil], and then when the onions have coloured, she takes the oil out and throws it away. And then she finishes the dish, that's why her food tastes to bad.'
> Sada: 'That's not good. That definitely doesn't taste nice.'
> Maria: 'No, it doesn't taste good, but then she feels she has done a good deed, right … NOW we're eating healthy!'

Another source of ambivalence is lack of engagement in cooking and eating. Aysha, the medical secretary, puts forward a self-understanding as someone who is not good at cooking and not really interested in it. Her husband does a lot of the cooking, and the overriding everyday engagement for Aysha is to juggle the time commitments of two full-time jobs, four children, and both regular and religious school: *'I don't care as long as we make something.'* This resembles the findings in a Norwegian study on Pakistani Norwegians with type-2 diabetes, their food habits and their experiences with communication with health workers. Coping with extra commitments in everyday life related to their minority conditionings was expressed by participants themselves as a constraint on their management of healthier eating (Fagerli et al., 2005: 300).

Thus, adapting healthier food activities and performances into the food practices has to be done in ways that do not create too much conflict. The food practitioners use some of the same procedures as in the first two ideal types to incorporate healthier food, such as using less oil in masalas, making Pakistani staples with whole grain products, etc. But at the same time, procedures of balancing pleasure with health are used. For example, when talking about situations in which food constructed as unhealthy is eaten, the food situation is constructed as an exception. Such exceptions can be understood as being beyond the control of the individual food practitioner. It is the social framing of the situation as e.g. festive with particular conventions that mainly influences the cooking and eating:

> Now I'm having guests on April 10. Then we have to read, you know the Koran and sit and sing verses and such, right. And then you make, then I would typically make, my sister-in-law and me, we are organising it together, right, just at my place, but in this case, um, we would use a lot of oil. Because then the

> consistency becomes better. It doesn't look so delicious when we don't put so much oil in. (Rushy, female academic)

Exceptions can, however, also be constructed as part of a strategy to handle the ambivalences of doing healthier food, such as countering unhealthy eating with exercising, or allowing oneself to eat unhealthy dishes on weekends if cooking and eating on weekdays are understood as sufficiently healthy. Negotiating the ambivalent relations between the pleasures and anxieties about eating is analysed in other qualitative studies of food habits, for example in John Coveney's study of Australian families (Coveney, 2000: 134–37), where such negotiations are analytically understood as part of the bodily/mental self-technologies of nutritional disciplining.

Communication about healthier food is initiated in the social in-group of close friends and family, including the older generation. Aysha, for instance, has six sisters with whom she discusses such matters: *'We stick our noses in everything!'* (Aysha, female medical secretary). These discussions are usually based on the practical efforts to strike a balance between healthy and pleasurable cooking that the food practitioners try out for procedures in their own daily lives. If it is inappropriate to serve healthy food for even in-group guests here is one solution: *'You know, I try to make low-fat food, um, I don't make heavy sweet desserts, I bake a cake instead'* (Rushy, female academic).

Ignoring Healthier Food as Social Practicality

In this last type of handling nutritionalised food among Pakistani Danes, the performances do not show any engagement in healthier food. Rather, the engagements in food practices revolve around the pleasures of food, around understandings of appropriate Pakistani food, and around prioritising the practising of food as care and maintenance of family relations. Food practitioners know and reproduce elements of public Danish dietary advice such as the food pyramid[13] to consume less fat and less sugar, to eat more vegetables and whole grain staples, and to incorporate variation in the meals across the week. But these understandings are not necessarily put into practical procedures in their everyday lives, since the other engagements in food practices fit better into the social do-abilities of cooking and eating. This goes, for example, for the engagement in taste and pleasure of eating. This way of handling nutritionalised food resembles the type of food consumers who are categorised as rejecting nutritionally correct eating in another Danish qualitative study (Holm and Kildevang, 1996: 9).

In a discussion about how much oil is used in respectively everyday cooking and cooking for guests, one of the women concludes: *'It tastes very good if you*

---

13 The food pyramid has staples in the bottom, vegetables and fruit in the middle, and meat, eggs and dairy products in the top. The advice is to eat most from the bottom and least from the top.

use a lot more' (Zabel, female kitchen worker). Cooking as family care also fits the social do-abilities of food better than 'doing healthy food'. To be able to cater to every family member's individual needs is a way of showing family love and reproducing the bonds within the family (Holm, 2004; Moisio et al., 2004). Here, Zabel's teenage daughter offers her interpretation of her mother's care-giving understanding of cooking:

> You know, all of us are a bit spoiled, right. You know, a lot of times when my brother comes home from work, or maybe just suddenly at 11 o'clock in the evening, then he just feels like eating French fries or something like that, right. So sometimes he makes it himself, but he also says, mum, I need to have something now at eleven o'clock, and then she has to make it.

It is more important to make the food that the son loves (when he wants it!), than to make a healthier dish.

Hence, food activities and procedures are not changed according to constructions of what constitutes healthy food. One of the women in the interviews expresses that using too much oil is unhealthy and that she doesn't use very much, and after this comes the following exchange:

> Interviewer: 'How little is "little oil"?'
> Imran: 'Two decilitres perhaps, for a potful … when there's meat in it, it needs more, with vegetables less.' (Imran, female housewife)

Compared to expressions of how much 'little oil' is among the other food practitioners (usually two spoonfuls), this amount of oil in cooking does not seem to have much to do with practical advice on reducing fat.

The health aspect of cooking and eating is hardly discussed in the social network, although food definitely constitutes a popular topic for conversation in general. If food becomes framed in the context of healthier cooking and eating, it seems to be initiated by some of the members of the younger generation. Here is an example with Zabel's teenage daughter: *'Actually, I usually say to them that it is a little bit unhealthy to eat that paratha for breakfast, and that you ought to begin with something small, fruit and such. But they like to eat that unhealthy thing.'*

The Do-abilities of Handling Nutritionalised Food

The four different ways of handling nutritionalised food in the Pakistani-Danish hybridised food practices among the participants bear some resemblance to the young consumers' ways of handling environmentalised food and the parents of young children's ways of dealing with food risk. 'Engaging proactively' in nutritionalised food has much in common with worried risk handling and identifying with environmentalised food. 'Doing healthy food ambivalently' resembles in some ways irritated risk handling. And 'fitting in' nutritionalised food resembles both pragmatic risk handling and appropriating environmentalised food.

The engaging proactively way of handling nutritionalised food consumption could be discussed as a candidate for a practice in itself, since a sufficient amount of nutritionalised activities (doings and sayings) are carried out and the activities are organised by their matching understandings, procedures and engagements. It is, however, difficult to find expressions of social recognition of such bundles of 'health-proactive consumption' in the data, and it is also hard to find examples where such a category is associated with specific people from the social networks of the Pakistani-Danish participants. There are mentions of Pakistani Danes who are conscious about their bodies and do not eat parathas. There is also the story about Maria's sister who is seen as someone who prioritises health to the point that it gives her a reputation for bad cooking. But overall, it is not possible to sustain an analytical argument for seeing the proactive handling of nutritionalised food as other than a type of performance.

Just like the patterns of food performance in the other case studies, the food performances of the Pakistani Danes also exhibit contradictions, exceptions, and processes that glide between categories. To make the chicken in the oven, avoid parathas, seek information on the Internet and serve fat- and sugar-free cakes at parties do *not* mean that fish fingers and French fries are not served on an ordinary Wednesday or that a mother-in-law does not get her chai with sugar and full-fat milk. There seems to be many specific procedural processes in the flow of practical cooking and eating among the participants that are implied in whether and how nutritionalised food becomes practically integrated. Thus, the next section of this chapter takes a closer look at three such procedural processes.

Procedures in Organising Nutritionalised Food Consumption

In this section, the analysis zooms in on the details of handling nutritionalised food by focusing on the practical procedures. The purpose of this third part of the analysis is to highlight the significance and contingency of everyday reactions to the nutrition challenge.

In the section about hybridised food practices, it was shown that the only patterned variation in the food practices of the participants comes from the procedure element in the organising configuration of their food practices. This makes it particularly relevant to analyse potential patterns at the procedural level, in which condition when and when not, how and how not, healthier food is incorporated. Such an analysis aims at specifying some of the contextual practical and social do-abilities in the specific hybridised Pakistani-Danish food practices. Three procedural processes seem to be particularly important in organising the inclusion and exclusion of nutritionalised food consumption among the participants; namely, caring, timing and socialising. All three procedural processes can organise both what is constructed as unhealthy food activities and as healthy activities.

Caring

Understanding the provision of food and meals as a part of caring for others is one of the central assumptions in the everyday life approaches to qualitative empirical studies of food practices (Delormier et al., 2009; Holm and Kildevang, 1996; Moisio et al., 2004; Murcott, 1983, Warin et al., 2008). There is also consensus about how caring for healthiness in the families via domestic work such as provision of food and meals is gendered (Gregory, 2005; McKie et al., 2004), and that female food practitioners tend to take such informal responsibilities upon them. Hence, social expectations will point towards female cooking agency for caring. However, as the qualitative empirical food literature shows, caring is not only about fulfilling health needs but also about fulfilling all sorts of everyday needs. One example can be taken from a Swedish study of women in families with young children. The women here express a well-known ambivalence between caring for the family in terms of serving proper and healthy food, and on the other side caring for the family in terms of serving food that expresses her love for the family members. There is a telling quote from one of the Swedish informants: *'I give them what they love, not what would be good for them'* (Ekström, 1990: 160). Similar ambivalences can be seen in the workings of the caring procedures in the food practices of the Pakistani-Danish women.

The recurring example of caring for healthiness through changing the food provided is enacted when a family member becomes chronically ill. Sunanah, Rushy, Solejma, Aysha and Sada have close family members who have been diagnosed either with type-2 diabetes or with coronary heart disease, and they cook differently, with less fat and sugar, for the sick family member. They also try to discuss concrete procedural changes with them in order to help them regulate their health. Sada discusses diabetes diet with her sister whose husband is diagnosed, and they have started to 'invest' in sugar free and light food products. Sunanah's husband has had a stroke, and she has begun to use less oil in the masalas or to scrape the oil off when the dish is ready to eat. Solejma negotiates with her sister-in-law about the cooking of meals for her brother who is diagnosed with type-2 diabetes, and Aysha tries to change the eating habits of her mother who has a heart condition. Here Aysha describes such a situation:

> My mother has a very bad heart and problems with her lungs and such, and um, every time she is about to take something, some cake, but you know, she really does take care of herself, right, but she can set her mind on taking just a small piece of cake, and then I say … you know very well it's not healthy. (Aysha, female medical secretary)

The same type of procedures is used in relation to caring for children. This happens, for example, when Solejma hides the vegetables in the dishes by blending them before adding them to the food, or when Maria (Sada's sister-in-law) only leaves a couple of ice lollies in the small freezer in the fridge where her son can find them and the rest of the ice lollies are kept in the larger freezer in the cellar. These examples illustrate when and how food procedures organised as caring tend to pull food activities in directions that are constructed as healthier.

Food procedures organised as caring can, however, also pull food activities in directions that are constructed as less healthy. Here, examples are particularly salient in relation to caring for children. When children don't want to eat healthy food or when children want snacks, food procedures organised as caring for the children's happiness and love can go into provisioning of less healthy food. Zabel keeps a supply of ready-made kebabs in the freezer for her teenage children to eat on the days where she and her husband eat vegetable dishes. Solejma gives her young children deep-fried chicken nuggets for snacks; however, she points out that they cannot have it every day. Shabana serves take-away pizza and shawarma for children guests, and some of the teenage children take for granted that their mother will cook deep-fried snacks for them at any time. This was evident in the example where Zabel's teenage daughter explains such food procedures in their family:

> You know, all of us are a bit spoiled, right. You know, a lot of times when my brother comes home from work, or maybe just suddenly at 11 o'clock in the evening, then he just feels like eating French fries or something like that, right. So sometimes he makes it himself, but he also says, mum, I need to have something now at eleven o'clock, and then she has to make it.

Timing

How the temporal organisation of food practices in everyday life takes place is another procedural element that can pull specific food activities in both less and more healthful directions. Food practices are just one set of practices in a multitude of intersecting practices that are done every day, and the procedures of food practices have to be coordinated, timed, fixed and flexed in relation to other practices that also have to be carried out in sufficiently appropriate ways (Southerton, 2006). There have been few empirical studies of how temporal organisation influences people's cooking and eating, but a recent overview article argues that time-scarcity typically draws food choices towards more convenience and ready-made food, assuming that meals cooked from scratch in general are more healthy (Jabs and Devine, 2006).

This tendency can be seen among the Pakistani-Danish food practitioners. Aysha, the medical secretary, and her husband describe in the family interview how busy their family life is with two full-time jobs and four children, but that they try to make homemade food as often as possible:

> Hussein: 'We keep an eye on what it is we, you know, we don't eat so much from outside the home.'

> Aysha: 'We don't eat so much take-away.'
> Hussein: 'Because we hate that junk food.'
> Aysha: 'We make it, even though we hardly have time to cook when we come home. He's just arrived too.'

The previous week, we visited Aysha and her family briefly in order to deliver a camera. They were eating take-away pizza for dinner and they explained that this kind of dinner happened very rarely. This type of ambivalence in specific food procedures is prevalent in the enactments across the social differences of the participants. Even Sada, the nurse who attempts to regulate food activities of people in the larger social network and who disciplines herself into peeling the skin off her 'Saturday chicken', serves unhealthy convenience food when pressed for time:

> It's when it has to be quick. Where it just gets used, um, the few times where we just, you know, have to have some fish fingers and French fries to go with them, right [laughing]. When the children just want something, um burger, homemade burger, right, where I also get to make some fish quickly.

However, timing can also enable food procedures to become healthier. This can be observed when time is not just seen as a scarce resource but rather as a multidimensional, organisational set of processes (Southerton, 2006). Timing does not have to be about providing food quickly, it can also be about providing food in ways that allow flexing of the temporal organisation. For example, Sunanah (the unskilled worker) uses the oven to make chicken legs with steamed vegetables on the side instead of chicken masala. The amount of time it takes before dinner is ready is roughly the same, but using the oven enables her to do other things simultaneously, hence flexing an otherwise fixed time-use. Using the oven to cook chicken, fish and kebab instead of making it in a pot with masala is repeatedly constructed as a more healthy food procedure by the participating women, because it enables use of less oil and butter in the cooking. This quote comes from a discussion in a family interview about the use of oil:

> Kebab for example, you make that too, right, when I make kebab, I make it in the oven as a way of avoiding it, it's also because I have some children who are very healthy, you know, they are a bit big, so you have to constantly think about how to save, right. (Rushy, female academic)

This kind of flexibility in timing, where you save time while simultaneously producing healthier meals, takes place when the women cook the evening meal at other times than just before serving it, e.g. the evening or morning before. Finally, what is considered proper time-consuming home-made meals in the hybridised food practices of the Pakistani Danes does not necessarily constitute better nutritional meals as otherwise suggested by Jabs and Devine (2006), who contrast such meals with fast food. Sada (the nurse) sometimes steams defrosted vegetables for dinner instead of roasting fresh vegetables in a pot with oil and tomatoes for a long time. This constitutes quick food for her, which saves some time, but it also enables her to preserve vitamins in the vegetables by using a food procedure different from the traditional Pakistani method. Solejma refers to the same procedure in her cooking, and she comments upon the lengthy roasting of vegetables in Pakistani food practices in the following manner: *'There are a lot of healthy things, where when we are using them, we make them unhealthy'* (Solejma, female office clerk). When Sada and Maria looked at photos of homemade Pakistani dinner dishes in the family interview and explained the details in the cooking procedures, Maria suddenly burst out: *'I guess you can see that the basic ingredient here is oil!'*

Socialising

Perhaps it seems obvious that socialising as a kind of procedural conditioning can enable both what is constructed as healthier and unhealthier food practices. The interaction in socialising is the social space where the bodily/mental recognisability and appropriateness of food practices is enacted. The specific content and direction of social regulation through interaction depend upon what is practically and socially do-able in specific situations, and also what constitutes the situational relationship between routinisation and reflexivity in food procedures. Across all the social differences among the participants in the study of Pakistani-Danish food habits, everybody talks about sharing recipes, giving and taking advice on food, and sharing food and health worries and possible solutions to food and health worries with others in their social network. Some of the women describe systematic exchanges of information and opinions on how to cook and eat healthier, including Sada, the nurse, and her sister-in-law Maria, whereas others pick up specific knowledge where they find it in their social network, as Zabel here explains: *'My friend has told me that it's good for your health if you use olive oil instead of other types of oil and not at all butter ... I have to use green oil, corn oil ... it's Zahica, she's my neighbour'* (Zabel, female kitchen worker). The examples of how the participating food practitioners themselves initiate discussions about healthy food and practical advice on how to do in the different parts of their social network in the typology of handling nutritionalised food are also examples of how socialising can enable the organising of potentially healthier food procedures.

However, socialising can also enable the reproduction of what is constructed as unhealthy food procedures, because social expectations to food and eating when being together in the social network typically revolve around other kinds of engagements and commitments than nutritional composition of the food. This is typically the case when guests are coming (both invited and unexpected), when outings are arranged with others, and when parties are held. When we interviewed

Solejma, she served soft drinks and snacks such as kebab, samosa and pakora[14] and commented upon it in the following manner:

> No, it's all right. You know if, um … you know when we have guests, then the first thing you serve is something to drink and then we can make deep fry, you know deep fry something for them. That, although it is unhealthy, this is how we do it. That's a kind of tradition among us Pakistanis. (Solejma, female office clerk)

Enactments about the large amounts of oil and sugar in party dishes are present across the social differences among the participants, referring both to the pleasure of such party food as well as explaining about the difficulties with the disciplining of one's own and other people's intake of unhealthy food at these social events. The descriptions of the party and guest meals compare with studies of Pakistani and Punjabi party and guest food in other national contexts, such as Norway (Mellin-Olsen and Wandel, 2005) and Scotland (Bradby, 2002; Bush et al., 1998).

A more mundane kind of socialising that tends to enable doing unhealthy eating is when members of the elder generation of the close family come for dinner or when the whole nuclear family is gathered for a longer breakfast during weekends. The elder generation is positioned as expecting appropriate Pakistani food, made, for example, with masala in the pot and with large amounts of oil or preferably ghee. The family breakfasts on weekends revolve around parathas, the flat breads with butter in the dough, fried in butter and buttered afterwards. Across social differences among the participants, parathas are reported eaten and enjoyed thoroughly as part of the weekend family socialising. One of the members of the younger generation, Ishita, teenage daughter of Amisha, claims that eating parathas for people with Pakistani background, *'It is like eating rye bread in Denmark'*.[15] Part of the socialising also seems to consist in the role of parathas in shaping the social eating trajectory of food practitioners. Here is an example where one of the women recalls weekend breakfasts of her childhood:

> My mother for example, when I think about childhood I often think Sunday, ah, I really feel like this chickpea bread she makes, and it's chickpea flour with all sorts of green and chilli and everything she puts in. And then lots of Lurpak[16] butter on top of it and then you eat it together with a drink made of natural yogurt. It's just … then I go straight back into childhood. That's not something I do myself. (Rushy, female academic)

14 Pakora is usually vegetables that are battered and deep-fried.

15 An overwhelming majority of majority Danes eat rye bread every day for lunch, and rye bread is one of the food items Danes report that they miss when travelling abroad.

16 Lurpak is the traditional brand of Danish butter, also an export article.

The Contingency of Procedural Processes

This analysis underscores both the importance and the contingency of the procedural processes in handling nutritionalised food. Both caring, timing and socialising can as procedural processes pull food consumption into unhealthier as well as healthier directions. This questions the primacy of normative engagement in healthier eating (or the lack of same) as driving nutritionalised food performances.

However, although caring, timing and socialising all constitute bodily/mental procedural processes, the normative engagements and expectations to proper food and healthier food keep cropping up as part of these procedures. The following section gives examples of how the normative engagement in nutritionalised food consumption is shaped in social interaction.

Normative Positionings in Relation to Nutritionalised Food

The analysis in this section gives examples of positionings and negotiations of the normative engagement in nutritionalised food consumption in order to show how social relations and interactions reproduce, adapt, change, improvise and experiment with the normative content of engagements in healthier food. The analysis focuses on the influence of social processes as equally important as individual, life-world sense-making in engagements in food performances. As in the other empirical chapters, the examples presented are about the normative engagement in agency, about normative engagement in a field-specific category (healthier food), and about exceptions to performing appropriately.

Normative engagements around nutritionalised food among the Pakistani-Danish participants are composite and seem to be revolving around a dichotomous mutuality of the Pakistani and Danish way of performing the relationship between the body and food. Danish food practices are constructed as being characterized by knowledge of nutrition and health issues relating to reducing fat and increasing physical activity. Denmark is equalled with modern social organising, car driving, cell phones, fitness centres, shopping options and less hard work. Pakistan is represented as hard work, walking, spending lots of time on cooking and eating loved and well-known meals and no knowledge of or interest in healthiness, except from the knowledge related to food as medicine.

Pakistan and Pakistani food practices are constructed in typical 'homeland terms', which means that Pakistan holds the contradiction between being described as the paradise on earth and a place it is important to leave in order to get a better life in a materialistic sense (Cohen, 1997). The homeland also represents the original Pakistani culture and a common national identity, which, for example, includes expressions such as 'our food' and a common national or ethnic expression of what is normal 'for us to do', referring to a Pakistani national community with primarily relations to Pakistan. As in other ethnic groups living in diasporas (Appadurai, 1996; Cohen, 1997), Pakistan is 'alive' as a lived experience.

Pakistan is represented through the satellite dish, through Pakistani magazines, through travelling to Pakistan, through visits from Pakistan and not least through marriages. In our sample, all marriages, except a young couple, consist of one spouse who grew up in Denmark and one spouse who grew up in Pakistan, a pattern that is the same in, for example, Norway (Mellin-Olsen and Wandel 2005: 313). Furthermore, if couples live in extended families, it is the parents of the husband with whom they live. This means that especially the daughter-in-law is assigned with the task of being responsible for the kitchen in the house of her mother-in-law, and this also places her close to the negotiations of the Danish versus Pakistani food.

The examples on normative positionings in relation to nutritionalised food relate to this mix of Pakistani food practices as both homeland identification and unhealthier traditional food ways and Danish food practices as both inappropriate, tasteless food and modern knowledge of food that enables healthiness.

Positioning on Agency of Ordinary Consumers

The normative content of the following example relates to the socially acceptable ways in which the food practitioner can act out her normative engagement in changes of food habits, also of other people in the larger network. The example shows how the narrative form with the shifting self-positionings shapes the content of the acting out of the normative engagement. The example is from the individual interview with Sada, the female nurse, and the sequence comes after she has described what she will and can serve for her female friends who are coming to dinner the next Saturday:

> Sada: 'And then I know there is one of them who has got diabetes, who can't … who has to be careful. She always has problems, but I sure understand why, she eats cakes and all these things.'
> Interviewer: 'Yeah.'
> Sada: 'Because last time, when I was at a party last Saturday, then I made this little cake where I sort of said that it's for those who have got diabetes, and I put something else in it.'
> Interviewer: 'Mmm, right.'
> Sada: 'I put sweetening agent in … But actually, it was eaten, but not by those who were supposed to have eaten it [laughter]. It's difficult to comply with in that way … And then there are some who can really do it.'
> Interviewer: 'Mmm. Do you know any of these?'
> Sada: 'Yes, but I think it's difficult, um, but I'm saying that it's not my problem, it's their problem. They do know that themselves.'
> Interviewer: 'Mmm. What do you think makes it difficult for them?'
> Sada: 'I don't know. The sight of food and then … I do understand a bit, I feel sorry for them that all sorts of things are served and they are not allowed to eat them, right? But you know, you really can try not to take those things.'

Sada begins by taking a superior position in relation to one of her friends who as a cake-eating diabetic gets positioned as someone who 'ought to know better'. The narrative afterwards about the alternative cake for the party sustains this positioning of others as people who ought to comply when she is trying to help them to do the nutritionally right thing. Sada then goes on to negotiate the normative assumption that knowing what is right to do nutritionally obliges one to cook and eat according to such knowledge. Here, she takes a more equal position with the others and expresses an emotional and social recognition of their difficult situation at parties with temptations of tasty food and the related difficulties of disciplining oneself. But she finishes where she began in identifying with and prescribing nutritional self-regulation. This way, the forms of social positioning help shape the expressions of normative engagement: from expressing the right to help others change their food routines by offering them practical solutions, towards recognising the difficulties in changing food routines. Thus, the space for acting in everyday life is negotiated in relation to others in the social network.

Positionings in Relation to the Category of 'Healthier Food'

The normative engagement in the first example is about constructing 'healthier food' as related to nutritionally knowledgeable cooking and eating. The empirical example comes from the individual interview with Solejma, the female office clerk. The example shows how the social positioning processes construct Pakistani-born people as less capable of practising 'healthier food'.

The sequence begins after the researchers have asked whether she talks with friends her own age about health and food.

> Solejma: 'No, no, we don't. Why don't we do that? Not with that.'
> Interviewer: 'But you can't answer these questions if you don't do it?'
> Solejma: 'Because, um, we have a way of … I also know what is unhealthy and what is healthy. Like you do … right.'
> Interviewer: 'Where does your knowledge come from?'
> Solejma: 'Um, because we were taught in school, we have learned it here – when we look at programmes and …'
> Interviewer: 'Yes.'
> Solejma: '… and if we search on the Internet, you know, we get to know from many different places, also from the media, yes, … um, in contrast to us, our sisters-in-law and the others who are not so much into this, they have to learn – they have to be taught a bit …'

In the interaction sequence with the interviewer, both majority and minority Danes are positioned as knowledgeable on healthy diets and Pakistanis (represented by the sisters-in-law) are positioned as those who are in need of nutritional education. This way, the normative engagement in using modern nutritional understandings and procedures to guide the practising of healthier food is reproduced in the social interaction between a minority Dane and a majority Dane. Solejma positions herself as taking part in the Danish nutritionalised way of handling health issues in food by stressing that she knows what is healthy in just the same way as the researchers.

The identifications with public nutritional discourses are related to a kind of normative positioning described under the section of 'fitting in healthier food' in this chapter. This is where the Pakistani-Danish food practitioners firmly position themselves as 'already knowledgeable' as an important element of their engagement in healthier food. Healthier food here refers to nutritional categories in order to control the consequences of eating, and it corresponds to 'the mainstream healthy eating discourse' described in the Canadian study that compared discourses of healthy eating across three different ethnic groups, including one with Punjabi background (Ristovski-Slijepcevic et al., 2008: 172–73).

The second example in this section refers to a normative engagement in acting 'already knowledgeable' in relation to healthier food practising. The example shows how social interaction in an intercultural setting is part of shaping the content of the normative engagement in healthier food for the food practitioner – here in the direction of acting already knowledgeable. The sequence comes from the individual interview with Shabana, the female school teacher, who has recently moved to Denmark from Pakistan:

> Interviewer: 'How do you find out what you think is healthy food?'
> Shabana: 'Those that contain proteins, carbohydrates and vitamins.'
> Interviewer: 'Yes, but how do you find out about it?'
> Shabana: 'I know for example that eggs contain proteins.'

Shabana positions herself as equal in relation to the interviewer already in her first utterance by stating a rather precise definition on healthy food, drawing on mainstream nutritional terms. The interviewer then poses what she thinks is an 'innocent' procedural question in relation to this use of nutritional terms. This seems to be interpreted as a silly or inappropriate question by Shabana, who then goes on to position herself as 'already knowledgeable' regarding what to do about the health aspect of food. This type of self-positioning suggests that Shabana and others of the Pakistani-Danish food practitioners have had a trajectory of being offered inferior food practice positions in interactions with majority Danes. This is likely, since in Denmark there is still a tendency for dietary information and public nutritional campaigns to minority Danes to build upon the aforementioned 'deficit model', where consumers are seen as lacking in knowledge and resources.

Negotiating Exceptions to Appropriate Eating

This last example of normative positioning is a negotiation about dealing with exceptions to proper eating. This example shows how exceptions to proper healthy eating are entangled in handling exceptions to proper (and pleasurable) Pakistani eating, thereby suggesting that interaction processes can make the practical carrying out of a normative engagement in healthier food rather socially complicated.

The sequence is an exchange from the individual interview with Solejma, where her acquaintance Rushy took part, and they are discussing traditional masalas and how such masalas are too fatty and whether it's okay to scrape oil away from your portion:

> Solejma: 'It tastes really good when there's oil in it. Real Pakistani food, then it tastes really nice. That's the original way. That's always the most delicious. But um ...'
> Rushy: 'Or butter, umh!'
> Solejma: 'Umh!' [laughter]
> Rushy: 'That's the kind of thing you only get once a year. [laughter] Twice a year.'
> Interviewer: 'But is it acceptable to scrape oil off with a spoon afterwards?'
> Solejma: 'You can do that, you can do that ...
> Interviewer: 'Someone did that at the last wedding with the carrot cake. They took the napkins and removed the layers of oil.'
> Solejma: 'They do what they want.' [laughter]
> Interviewer: 'And you knew just who it was?'
> Solejma: 'What it was.'
> Interviewer: 'All right, what, not who.'
> Rushy: 'Can I please get the names of who it was?' [laughter]

The sequence begins with Solejma and Rushy relishing bodily memories of tasty Pakistani masalas with lots of oil or butter in them, when the interviewer reminds them of what they just discussed: can you scrape off oil from a dish at parties and guest dinners if you want to reduce fat intake? Solejma legitimises the normative engagement in 'doing healthy' by stating that this way of reducing fat can be done. But by adding 'they do what they want' about somebody from the social network, she also suggests that this nutritionalised eating procedure is slightly inappropriate. Rushy's last statement seems to confirm the inappropriateness of scraping off oil from party food, since she mimics a kind of social control of these 'others' from the shared social network, but she does so with a humoristic touch.

Normative Engagements Positioned

The examples of positionings and negotitions of the normative content of 'doing healthier food' point to the importance of the constant cultural identification and negotiation taking place among the Pakistani-Danish food practitioners. The concrete unfolding of normative engagement in healthier food takes place in a social space where 'doing healthier food' is intersected by constructions of 'doing Pakistani food' and 'doing Danish food'.

Doing Healthier Consumption?

The Danish public discourses on nutrition and food and the related dietary advice, which have been repeatedly produced over the years, seem to have an effect, at least at a discursive level. Across all social differences among the Pakistani-Danish food practitioners, the main elements of such nutritional discourses are reproduced discursively in the sense of which food items to eat more of and which ones to cut down on. However, one of the common critiques raised about public nutritional campaigns in the international literature on food and health in everyday life, and also quoted in the introduction to this chapter, is that *'Nutritional advice typically focuses on what to eat, but seldom on how to fit those recommendations into busy daily lives'* (Jabs and Devine, 2006: 202). I am repeating this point here, because I want to paraphrase it as a way of summing up the main results of the study with Pakistani-Danish food practitioners and their handlings of the nutritional challenges: nutritional discourses typically focus on what and what not to eat, but seldom on how to fit those recommendations into culturally hybridised daily lives.

The basic context, the food practices, is more uniform among the Pakistani-Danish food practitioners than among any of the practitioners in the three other Danish case studies. But the ways of handling the food consumption challenge – nutritionalisation – are just as diverse and complex as, for example, in the case of the young Danes and environmentalisation or in the case of the Danish parents and the risk challenge. Furthermore, a number of conditioning procedural processes in everyday life pull in the direction of both unhealthier and healthier food doings and sayings. Likewise, the normative engagements, positionings and negotiations display a constant double tension between Pakistani food activities as homeland identification but unhealthy food procedures, and Danish food activities as improper food but potentially health enabling. Hence, the handling of nutrition and healthier cooking/eating is much more complex and more socially embedded, conditioned and resourceful than the rational choice and individualised public health studies assume (Aikman et al., 2006; Blanchard et al., 2009; Carrus et al., 2009; Fishbein and Cappella, 2006). The more collectively oriented studies of public health strategies in the food area differ in their basic theoretical outlook from the rational-choice studies, but they share a common assumption about changes of food habits in more nutritionally correct directions as primarily requiring individual self-reflexivity (Coveney, 2000: 18). This study of Pakistani-Danish food practitioners points to the importance of looking at a variety of social conditions and resources in practical food procedures. The study also highlights the significance of the social forms in interaction and communication around healthier food practising, because the social positionings can influence the space for acting for ordinary, multicultural consumers.

What seems to be the consequences for everyday life from the 'nutritionalisation' of food consumption and the various ways in which food practitioners deal with this? Interestingly, the Pakistani-Danish food practitioners do not seem to enact openly critical understandings in relation to the content of the elements of public Danish nutritional discourses. This differs from the findings of the other case studies in this book, where, for example, the parent food practitioners criticise mediated expert discourses on risk for changing all the time, which makes consumer advice impossible to follow, or when the young food practitioners question the environmental effects of public advice to the 'green consumers'.

The questioning of the nutritionalisation of food appears 'only' in relation to the implementation of knowledge on healthier cooking and eating and the daily handling of regulating oneself and the family, while at the same time cooking and eating proper Pakistani food. On the other hand, seen from a practice theoretical perspective, this is where the important reproductions and changes of social life happen – in the ongoing and shared performing of the basic practices.

The culturally hybridised character of the food practices may help to produce practical and social space for adaptation and negotiation in everyday life. Public calls for healthier food habits will be 'translated', adapted, improvised and negotiated culturally into practicalities in order to become integrated in multicultural everyday lives. Cultural identification with cooking and eating works as a strong legitimising element of food activities, understandings, procedures and engagements. Thus, cultural identification with both the practical procedures as well as the normative engagements in changing food routines is necessary if changes are to happen and changes are to be in accordance with consumers' own construction of agency.

Chapter 7
Concluding Consumption Challenged

The initial claim of this book is that there is a discursive framing of the individual ordinary food consumer taking place in medialised societies that ascribes individual consumers with societal responsibility for contributing to solving a number of central societal problems, such as environmental problems and health problems, by changing their own everyday habits. Members of the target group for this type of media discourse and communication campaigns, the ordinary food consumers, respond to such normative contestations of their everyday habits in various ways, because living in a medialised society means that a majority of the population are in contact with, draw upon and use a multiplicity of mediated communications. To put it differently: it is difficult to completely avoid media discourses.

However, as is pointed out in the emerging analytical field of challenged consumption, there are different ways in which consumers respond, and different conditions under which different types of consumer agency are possible, because the context of food consumption and of citizens' communication use in everyday life form a web of complex processes. A mapping of the emerging analytical field around what can be called challenged consumption showed four different types of research: one where the focus is on how to steer consumers in societally 'correct' normative directions with their habits; one of research where it is assumed that consumers can enact societal agency and help change the world; one more pessimistic type where a main assumption is that consumers are being controlled and disciplined through the discourses on consumer agency; and finally, one where the complexities of consumption as everyday life phenomena are acknowledged in order to strike a balance between the enabling and the conditioning processes of this context.

The argumentations and analyses of this book are placed within the everyday life analytical research. The approach used in the book is practice theoretical, thereby assuming that the practical and social performing of activities is the basic constitutive character of everyday life. Everyday life reactions towards four different types of food consumption contestation are analysed and discussed from a practice theoretical perspective. These analyses and discussions are made on the basis of four Danish empirical qualitative case studies about four different topics; namely, handling environmentalisation of food, food-risk handling, cooking from scratch and handling nutritionalisation of food.

The question is now, what can be learned from a comparison of the four different empirical studies of contested food consumption processes, informed by a practice theoretical perspective? The discussion in this concluding chapter falls in three sections. The first discusses the empirical analytical patterns of similarities, differences and difficulties. The second examines the potential analytical consequences of a comparison to the construction of the emerging analytical field of challenged consumption and the discussions characterising this field. The third section discusses a few potential theoretical points from the comparison for the uses of practice theory in consumption research.

Empirical Commonalities and Differences in Everyday Dealings with Contested Food Consumption

The most striking commonality across the four different case studies is the *diversification of handling* each of the normative contestations of food in everyday life. There is not one of the areas of normative contestation that sticks out and can be characterised by one or two main ways of dealing with the contestation processes. Even cooking from scratch, which is the historically oldest kind of everyday performance, cannot be boiled down to one or two kinds. The diversification of dealing with the normativised – mundanely moralised – food consumption in everyday life is noticeable in three respects.

First, it is not possible to establish a simple relationship between food practices and types of challenged consumption performances in any of the four Danish case studies. For example, refusing to practise environmentally friendly food consumption is not systematically linked to only one kind of food practice among the young Danes. Likewise, to handle risk in food in a pragmatic manner is not systematically linked to only one kind of food practice among the Danish parents with young children. Similarly, to take cooking from scratch for granted occurs in each of the different ways of practising cooking. Furthermore, for example the 'fitting in' of healthier eating is carried out in the busier hybridised food practices as well as the more time-consuming ones among the Pakistani Danes.

Second, each of the types within each of the ideal typologies of dealing with contested food consumption represents patterns of doings and sayings across expressions from several participants. The participants' doings and sayings can be in accordance with different ideal-type food consumption performances in different situations and relations in their everyday lives. For example, a father of a young child can be worried regarding food risk in relation to his children, but be irritated with particular kinds of food and handle risk pragmatically in performing particular food work tasks. Or, in other words, the same food practitioner can spend hours hunting down pasteurised egg yolks to make ice cream for his child's birthday, try to ignore the media debate about hormone residues in his beloved beef steak, and automatically wash the surface of imported apples before eating them.

Third, each way of dealing with the four different food consumption contestations is organised by a specific combination of practical procedures and social processes that influence the diversity in carrying out food consumption performances. For example, the practical procedures of handling nutritionalised food among the

Pakistani Danes consist in a mixture of caring, timing and socialising, and each of these three practical procedures can enable less healthy food consumption as well as healthier food consumption. Another example is how the normative content of the category 'cooking from scratch' changes through the social processes of negotiating appropriate cooking among the female food practitioners.

Another obvious commonality across the empirical cases of challenged food is the *similarities* that can be seen between the different *ideal types of dealing with challenged food.* Looking at the constituting elements of the types in the four ideal typologies from a practice theoretical perspective, some of the types share some of the defining elements of the performances across contestation area.

Table 7.1 Comparison of ideal types of handling challenged food consumption across the four Danish case studies

	Defining elements of handlings of challenged food		
Types of performances in different cases of challenged food	**Communicating in network**	**Practical do-ability**	**Criticising public discourses**
	Identifying with environmentalised food	Appropriating environmentalised food	Distancing from environmentalised food
	Worried risk handling	Pragmatic risk handling	Irritated risk handling
	Cooking from scratch is socially expected	Taking cooking from scratch for granted	?
	Proactive engagement in 'healthier' food	Fitting in 'healthier' food	Doing 'healthier' food ambivalently

First, identifying with environmentalised food consumption, worried risk handling, cooking from scratch being expected and proactive engagement in 'healthier' food have in common the importance of interacting and communicating with members of the practitioners' social network about the normative engagement and changes in practical procedures. Second, appropriating environmentalised food, pragmatic risk handling, taking cooking from scratch for granted and fitting in 'healthier' food have in common the importance of the practical do-ability of dealing with contested food consumption. Third, distancing environmentalised food, irritated risk handling and doing 'healthier' food ambivalently share the element of criticising public contestation discourses as important in the understanding of contested food consumption.

There is one last and more specific point of commonality. It is not an unrealistic analytical assumption that the element of engagement would be a decisive element in relation to performing normative consumption. Other everyday life analytical studies point to the importance of meaningful experiences with normative engagement in the life worlds of consumers and the drawing upon discourses of normative engagement. Also, in practice theory, the term engagement is theoretically related to normative emotional orienting in practices (Schatzki, 2002: 77; Warde, 2005: 134). However, it seems as if *practical procedures and social interaction* play equally important parts as normative engagements in the ongoing accomplishment of the different ways of dealing with challenged food consumption.

An example of the practical procedures becoming as important as the normative engagements comes from the case study of environmentalisation of food. The specific combination of routines and reflections in the practical procedures among the young Danes influences how environmentalised food consumption is concretely carried out just as much as any normative engagement expressed as meaningful by the individual food practitioner. An example of the social interaction influencing the content and the stability of normative engagement comes from the case study of the parents with young children. The normative engagement in risk handling becomes adapted and changed through the social interaction of negotiating legitimate exceptions to the normatively appropriate conduct, for example in the negotiation about how to use raw eggs in party desserts.

Turning to the differences in the ways of dealing with challenged food consumption across the four case studies, two sets of analytical differences should be noticed. First, the ideal typology of ways of cooking from scratch differs from the ideal typologies of contested food performances for the other three case studies by not covering a critical or a non-performing type. This could, of course, be related to the character of the sample, which had an overrepresentation of readers of *Isabellas* – the women's magazine representing cooking from scratch in positive texts and images – although the sample did include non-readers and women who did not appreciate such magazines in the focus group part of the data. Another potential explanation could perhaps be the longer and much more practice-integrated historical trajectory of cooking from scratch performances in food practices, compared with the more recent challenges to food consumption from environmentalisation, food risks and nutritionalisation. Furthermore, the normativity and the related social expectations of appropriate conduct of cooking food items and meals from scratch seem to go quite a number of years back when looking at the international literature, e.g. regarding 'a proper dinner' as home-cooked (e.g. Murcott, 1983). In comparison, everyday normativities linked to nutrition and in particular to risk and to environment seem to have had shorter trajectories.

Second, the doings and sayings of environmentalised food performances focus on especially one category of environmentalised food consumption, namely organic food. The doings and sayings of risk handling and of 'healthier' food, however, are expressed around an unfocused multiplicity of categories of food consumption. For risk handling it would be, for example, Danish food, home-grown food, food with fewer additives, food without chemical residues, pasteurised eggs, washing the fruit and keeping raw meat away from other food. For 'healthier' food it would be, e.g. using less oil, cutting down on sugar, using the oven instead of a pot, baking with whole grain flour and steaming vegetables instead of roasting them. This may again be related to the societal trajectories of the specific food contestations, where environmental issues in relation to everyday life have crystallised later as a topic of public campaigns and media discourses than both nutrition issues and risky food issues in relation to everyday life. The longer history of nutrition and risk in relation to public campaigns for changing everyday food routines could imply that incorporating such issues is spread across a broader range of specific categories and processes of shopping, cooking and eating. Currently, the environmental contestation of food consumption is re-surfacing as climate-friendly consumption in media discourses and in public and private communication campaigns, and this will perhaps result in the broadening of categories of environmentally normativised food consumption.

These differences between the case study areas point towards some of the difficulties that arise in comparing the patterns of dealing with challenged food consumption across the four case studies. The comparisons are made across different types of contestation issues, across different types of framings of the contestation issues in media discourses, and across different types of institutions in society. Thus, it is difficult to assess whether it is sufficiently similar analytical phenomena that are compared. Is it the same analytical phenomenon when we are looking at food practitioners taking for granted that they must make their own raspberry preserve, and when we are looking at food practitioners trying to persuade their mates in the college residence hall to buy the organic pork chops for a shared dinner?

Another difficulty with comparison across the four main case studies of dealings with challenged consumption is the differences in types of participating food practitioners. The participating groups of practitioners that are compared are young people, parents with preschool children, female readers of a lifestyle magazine and people belonging to an ethnic minority. The food practices and consumption performances in each of the case studies can vary due to, for example, the food practitioner trajectories being shorter or longer or due to practitioner trajectories being culturally stable or culturally variable. Are we looking at comparable food consumption when we are comparing majority Danish mothers' putting locally grown cucumber in their kids' lunch packets with minority Danish mothers' giving their kids a whole grain chapatti before rushing them off to Koran school?

Taking a practice theoretical perspective, it can be argued that the food practices and the mundane handlings of contested consumption, for example, are the analytical categories that can be compared. Thus, practices and performances can meaningfully be compared across groups of practitioners and types of contestation processes. Parallels can be emphasised because the applied theoretical concepts that inform the analyses of the empirical patterns are the same in the four case studies. These reflections upon comparisons bring us to the next section of the chapter, which deals with the possible analytical implications for the emerging field of challenged consumption from a comparison of the four main case studies in this book.

Implications for the Emerging Field of Challenged Consumption

For each of the four different challenged food consumption case studies, I conclude that the ways in which the food contestation is handled in everyday life is characterised by mundane performances that are not necessarily internally unified. I also conclude that there is no simple relationship between contested food consumption performances and food practices, and that a diversity of both stabilising and dynamic processes contributes to the accomplishment of handling challenged food consumption.

A similar picture of complexity can be painted when the conclusions of each case study are seen in relation to some of the analytical debates of the emerging field of challenged consumption.

In relation to environmentalisation, I discussed whether environmentalised mundane food performances amount to doing political consumption. I suggest that only the 'identifying with environmentalised food' type qualifies analytically to be understood as doing political consumption, insofar as it fulfils criteria often used for political everyday agency, namely intentionality and autonomy (Halkier and Holm, 2008: 669). It is also the only type that qualifies as an integrated practice. But all three types of environmentalised consumption performances come across as diverse and not-unified processes.

In relation to risk handling, I discussed whether a consequence of this contestation process consists in a disciplining of everyday life. I suggest that only worried risk handling, normalising ambivalence procedures and some of the normative negotiations point towards risk-rationalising everyday life. But the other kinds of risk handling, ambivalence procedures and normative negotiations seem to embody anti-disciplining engagements in e.g. the pleasures of food. Furthermore, disciplining should not in itself be seen as a unified process of oppressive control.

In relation to cooking from scratch, I discussed what might be the consequences of the setting that equals cooking from scratch with suitable cooking. I suggest that the type 'taking cooking from scratch for granted' qualifies as an integrated practice, which could strengthen cooking from scratch as social expectation to appropriate cooking. But the other empirical patterns in the analysis (consumption performances, the embodied procedures and the normative negotiations) indicate that cooking from scratch is a fairly flexible, practical and social construction. Thus, there is considerable practical and social space for manoeuvrings and adaptations in accomplishing appropriate cooking in everyday life.

In relation to nutritionalisation, I discussed whether nutritionalised mundane food performances lead to 'healthier' consumption. I suggest that there is a relatively shared, general understanding of what constitutes 'healthier' food across social differences. Both the 'proactive engagement in healthier food' and the 'fitting in healthier food' types pull in the direction of healthier food consumption. But the procedural processes of caring, timing and socialising pull towards both unhealthier and healthier food. Likewise, the social interactions show how engagement in healthier food is conditioned by a constant double-bind positioning between proper food to identify with and proper healthy food.

The current literature about challenged food consumption contains a number of qualitative research studies that are based on some kind of everyday life analytical approach to consumption, as has been shown in Chapter 1 and in the empirical chapters. Such studies also tend to show empirical diversity and analytical complexity around consumers' reactions towards contestation of their routine food consumption. So do practice theory-informed analyses contribute specifically to the analytical knowledge of the emerging field?

First, the everyday life analytical studies of challenged consumption still form a small part of the current literature. There is plenty of room for doing more empirical analyses of this kind in order to gain more knowledge about different sets of diversities and complexities across, for example, different cultural settings.

Second, I will suggest that the additional contribution of a practice theoretical analysis, relative to other everyday approaches in the field, is to underscore the significance of embodied practical procedures and social negotiations in shaping normative acting. A number of the current (and very analytically constructive) everyday life approaches focus on individually bound mental processes of meaning-making as the most important drivers of normative acting. In her qualitative study of English consumers and their relations to organic and functional food, Sally Eden (2009) focuses on consumers' intentional sense-making of labelling information. In her qualitative study of Australian consumers and food risks, Deborah Lupton (2005) focuses on the discourses and beliefs of the participating laypeople. In their qualitative study of Canadian consumers and healthy eating, Svetlana Ristovski-Slijepcevic et al., (2008) also focus on the consumers' sense-making of healthy eating discourses on the basis of the experiences, interpretations and reasoning of the participating consumers. The practice theory-informed analyses of the Danish case studies show that people's reactions to normative contestations of food have just as much to do with embodying how things can practically be done and with negotiating in the social network what is acceptable to do as with individual, mental processes. Thus, other everyday life approaches perhaps tend to underestimate the stability in the embodiment of routine procedures and to overestimate the stability of individual normative sense-making.

However, the bulk of the current literature continues to be dominated by cognitivist studies and by studies building on different versions of cultural structuralism. This seems to be the case both in the areas of environmental, risk and nutrition issues as well as in the general emerging field of challenged consumption. The main analytical problem is that none of the two types of research seems to acknowledge the diversifications and the complexities of everyday practices and handlings of contested consumption. And this analytical problem is related to the more general theoretical problems imbued in the two dominating types of research.

The cognitivist-informed studies assume that changes of consumption habits happen as a result of consumers gaining sufficient information and changing their attitudes in order to change their behaviour. In other words, changes in social life depend upon individualised cognitive dispositions. This way of approaching challenged food consumption is an example of theoretical 'mentalism', where the social is placed in mental activities and mental repertoires of actors' consciousness (see Chapter 2) – an approach that is distinctly different from practice theory. Theoretical mentalism covers both more simplistic versions such as the 'theory of planned behaviour' as well as more sophisticated versions such as some of the dialogical participatory approaches to consumer reflection and involvement.

The studies building on different versions of cultural structuralism assume that changes or reproductions of consumption habits happen as a result of people's social belongings to groups and how the structures of cultural distinctions of such belongings shape consumption activities. In other words, changes in social life depend upon structural conditions outside of the reach of everyday agency. This way of analysing challenged food consumption is parallel to theoretical 'textualism', where the social is placed outside of actors in larger chains of signs, symbols, language and discourses (see Chapter 2), and which practice theory delimits itself from. There are several different versions of theoretical textualism in relation to the emerging field of challenged consumption. There are the segmentation studies where consumers are divided into different lifestyle-based or other segments in order to explain how they react to food contestation processes about for example, the environment and risk. There are also the public health studies in relation to the nutrition contestation where consumers are grouped according to, for example, social marketing concepts and community concepts.

The analytical shortcomings of mentalist- and textualist-inspired approaches in the emerging field of challenged consumption have to do with the inabilities of these approaches to include diversifications and complexities in everyday life into their analyses of potentials for change. The calls in society for normative responsibility of the individual consumer do not link into neat systems of cognitive dispositions, or heroic and unheroic segments of consumer lifestyles. Rather, these calls become entangled in the complicated webs of everyday life practices and conditions. Where does that leave us in relation to the discussions about everyday agency and challenged consumption?

Most mentalist-inspired approaches tend to understand consumer participation in solving societal issues in an optimistic manner, if only consumers get sufficient knowledge. This is *not* to say that all the studies categorised as the optimistic 'empowering consumers' type of research in Chapter 1 are theoretical mentalists, far from it. But the mentalists and the optimists share a positive understanding of individual ordinary consumers as important and capable social actors. The textualist approaches exhibit a more mixed pattern of optimistic and pessimistic understandings of consumer agency in relation to challenged consumption. They see ordinary consumers as capable of participating in changes if the structural conditions they belong to pull in that direction. They also see ordinary consumers as controlling and disciplining themselves through their reactions to the contestations of their food routines. However, both optimists and pessimists in the consumer agency debate tend to miss the point that domestic food consumption activities are complex relational processes, organised in a diversity of ways and situated in the intersections of many different everyday practices and social obligations. The diversities and complexities of everyday life consumption agency ought to inspire to more realistic expectations to consumer responsibilities in society among researchers as well as policy and campaign makers.

These shortcomings of theoretical mentalism and theoretical textualism point in particular to one analytical implication. It is time to get rid of the concept of 'the active consumer' as a generic concept about individual ordinary consumers as actors in society. This has been very sensibly suggested before (Jacobsen and Dulsrud, 2007: 472), and I would like to go further and suggest that we as researchers use different concepts that are more in accordance with the complexities of performed everyday agency. Instead of discussing the active consumer, we ought to discuss different types of do-able performances and what their social and institutional pre-conditions might be. What could practically and socially do-able climate-friendly activities consist in? And what would be the collectively organised and publically regulated context for such activities? This could perhaps also contribute to influencing the public policy debates, communication campaigns and media discourses on ordinary food consumers into less individualised and rationalistic versions.

Reflections on the Use of Practice Theory in Consumption Research

In this section, I want to reflect upon some possible implications for the use of practice theory in social scientific consumption research. In particular, I want to comment upon the theoretical issue of the relationship between practice and consumption. Also, I want to discuss the limitations of using practice theory to inform empirical consumption research.

The relationship between consumption and practices is a theoretical discussion worth having for at least two reasons. A theoretical reason for the discussion is Alan Warde's influential conceptualisation of consumption as an aspect of almost every type of practice in modern societies, whereby consumption is not understood as a form of integrated practice in itself (Warde, 2005: 137). An analytical reason for the discussion is that integrated practices are understood as the most basic unfolding of social life in practice theory. If we accept this premise, then it can be argued that integrated practices and their organising elements are given priority in people's everyday activities. Thus, defining when contested food consumption performances can be understood as integrated practices, and when they cannot, should tell us something about the potentials (or lack thereof) for societal changes coming from everyday life. The closer normatively contested consumption activities are to resembling an integrative practice, the more likely does it seem that such consumption activities will be prioritised in everyday life.

I am sympathetic to Warde's radical conceptualisation of consumption as an element of practices because this conceptualisation takes the practice theoretical critique of theoretical mentalism seriously. It turns upside down the often used mentalist assumption in studies of consumer culture that wants, motives, desires and choices are preludes to consumption activities. This theoretical mentalism is noticeable in the more general approaches to consumption, in seeing consumption as creativity and in some of the approaches seeing consumption as a function of economy (see Chapter 2). In the previous section of this chapter, it was argued that also in the emerging field of researching contested consumption, theoretical mentalism informs a significant proportion of the current studies.

An argument in favour of consumption as an aspect of practices is that most consumption activities take place without being noticed or recognised as being consumption (Warde, 2005: 150). However, the communication campaigns and other media discourses about consumer responsibilities confront people with attempts to make them notice particular consumption activities. A majority of the population in modern societies are in contact with, draw upon and use such medialised knowledges and discourses in their everyday lives (Thompson, 1995). Thus, particular bundles of consumption activities or consumption projects can become highly noticeable as being consumption. The question is then whether these particularly noticeable consumption activities and projects in relation to challenged food consumption can be seen as integrated practices in themselves?

There are two of the contested food consumption performances from the Danish case studies in this book that could be seen to fulfil the criteria for being conceptualised as an integrative practice. It is the 'identifying with environmentalised food' ideal type from Chapter 3 and the 'cooking from scratch as taken for granted' ideal type from Chapter 5.

'Identifying with environmentalised food' covers a large and varied group of activities (doings and sayings) in everyday life. This way of handling environmentalisation is empirically organised systematically by clearly expressed understandings, procedures and engagements – the theoretically basic organising elements of any integrative practice. Furthermore, it clearly works as a socially recognisable category for other food practitioners. The participants know people whom they would categorise as doing this type of consumption, and they relate this type of consumption to expectations about, especially, consumption of organic food. Consumption of organic food is the main category around which a practice project (Schatzki, 2002: 73–74) is build. A practice project of consuming food that is as environmentally friendly as possible combines a strong normative engagement with groups of practical tasks (tasks are groups of activities, concrete doings and sayings), such as using organic food and using food that has not travelled too many food miles.

Earlier studies have shown for a Danish context that the category 'organic consumption' works as a recognisable representation of bundles of consumption doings and sayings (Halkier and Holm, 2008). The socially recognisable 'bundling' of environmentally friendly food consumption activities has probably become sustained by the mainstreaming of organic food in the retail sector in Denmark and the Danish normalisation of the discourses on individual consumer responsibility in the public policies and debates (see Chapter 3). However, qualitative studies of green consumption and identification in everyday life from other national contexts seem to suggest similar rudiments of socially recognisable packages of doing green consumption (Connolly and Prothero, 2008; Evans and Jackson, 2008; Horton, 2003; Lockie et al., 2002).

The recognition of a practice as a practice through its organising elements (activities, understandings, procedures and engagements) is a key feature of the focus on the performative of social life in practice theory. Practices have to be recognised by other practitioners as practices when activities are performed and re-performed. The other empirical example of a consumption candidate for an integrated practice is the 'cooking from scratch as taken for granted' ideal type. This way of handling the normative appraisal of home-made food comprises a large and varied amount of bundles of consumption activities whereby as little ready-made and processed food as possible is used. Although the degree of embodiment and tacitness is high in this consumption project, the explicit normative negotiations from the focus group data show processes of social recognition of cooking from scratch taking place. Parallel processes of social recognition of cooking from scratch as a practical normative category can be found in studies from other national contexts (e.g. Bugge and Almås, 2006; Clarke, 2007; Prim et al., 2007).

Hence, my analytical contention is that it may be necessary to differentiate the conceptualisation of consumption in a practice theoretical approach. There are types of consumption projects – namely, some of the contested food consumption performances – that seem to work in ways similar to integrative practices. This seems to happen when certain 'bundles' of consumption activities become noticed as consumption in discourses and socially recognisable in activities among food practitioners in everyday life.

This is, of course, a suggestion made on the basis of empirical research in the specific field of challenged food consumption with the limitations inherent in such specificity. Also, there is a fine balance between revising theoretical understandings and concepts in the light of empirical complexities and maintaining the analytical clarity of theoretical understandings and concepts.

What then seems to be the current limitations of using a practice theoretical approach to empirical consumption research?

First, social interaction processes as part of practices seem to be either discarded as mental or symbolic exchanges (Reckwitz, 2002: 249), or not explicitly defined in the more general texts (Schatzki, 2002). Although the importance of social interaction is a working assumption in some of the key writings on practice theory use in consumption research (Shove, 2003; 2009; Warde, 2005), social interaction is here mostly treated implicitly, 'dressed' conceptually as recognition or coordination. The Danish case studies of challenged food consumption beg a more explicit understanding of social interaction, because of the significance of communication processes in the societal contestation of food. An attempt to flesh out the social interaction element a bit more is found in the discussion of the concepts of performance and performativity in the theoretical framework (see Chapter 2). Thus, social interactions can be seen as open-ended intersubjectively situated performances, enabled and conditioned by intersecting practical and social do-abilities. Hereby, the interactive element of practising processes becomes slightly more explicit. However, much more conceptual and analytical work is needed in this area of the use of practice theory.

Second, to use applied practice theoretical concepts not just to analyse but also to structure the presentation of empirical case studies runs the risk of chopping up the empirical representations to the degree that they lose their social context. When every detailed empirical expression, pattern or lack of pattern is turned into a diversity of analytical categories and types, the narratives of lived social life are in danger of disappearing. These contextual narratives are usually one of the methodological and analytical prides of qualitative empirical studies. Such contextual empirical narratives also usually serve the purpose of installing reservations to uncritical generalisation of results to other contexts. So although one of the purposes of using practice theory indeed is to bring consumption research closer to the details of carrying out consumption in contexts, there is a risk of de-contextualising lived practices in the presentation of such analysis.

Future Studies of Challenged Consumption

There are many societal issues by which ordinary consumption – not just of food – is becoming and can become contested through communication campaigns and general media discourses. For example, the whole range of ethical issues regarding child labour, animal welfare, economic justice and human rights has not been addressed in this book. Certainly, the emerging field of challenged consumption studies will not have problems finding relevant empirical cases to investigate and discuss. Furthermore, the field of challenged consumption is in need of more collaboration between user-oriented communication research and everyday life-oriented sociology of consumption. Such research collaboration is likely to incorporate the workings of medialisation into the ways in which sociology of consumption captures the processes of practices around and in consumption. Such research collaboration is also likely to ensure an analytical awareness of the social and practical complexities of communication use and communication contexts in research on communication campaigns and communication for social change.

However, there is a danger that the use of a practice theoretical approach may seduce research about challenged consumption in everyday life into remaining at a micro-level, focused on the fascinating diversity of performative processes. What remains vital is to continue to insist that the analysis of challenged consumption comments upon issues of societal power, reproduction and transformation.

References

Aarset, B., S. Beckmann, E. Bigne, M. Beveridge, T. Bjorndal, J. Bunting, P. McDonagh, C. Mariojouls, J. Muir, A. Prothero, L. Reisch, A. Smith, R. Tveteras and J. Young (2004). The European consumers' understanding and perceptions of the 'organic' food regime: The case of aquaculture, *British Food Journal*, 106, 93–105.

Adams, M. (2006). Hybridizing habitus and reflexivity: Towards an understanding of contemporary identity? *Sociology*, 40, 511–28.

Adams, M. and J. Raisborough (2008). What can sociology say about Fair Trade? Class, reflexivity and ethical consumption, *Sociology*, 42, 1165–82.

Ahlgren, M.K., I. Gustafsson and G. Hall (2005). The impact of the meal situation on the consumption of ready meals, *International Journal of Consumer Studies*, 29, 485–92.

Aikman, S.N., K.E. Min and D. Graham (2006). Food attitudes, eating behaviour, and the information underlying food attitudes, *Appetite*, 47, 111–14.

Ajzen, A. (1991). The theory of planned behaviour, *Organizational Behaviour and Human Decision Processes*, 50, 179–211.

Alexander, J.C. and S. Seidman (1990). *Culture and Society. Contemporary Debates*. Cambridge, Cambridge University Press.

Andersson, A. and S. Bryngelsson (2007). Towards a healthy diet: From nutrition recommendations to dietary advice, *Scandinavian Journal of Food and Nutrition*, 51, 31–40.

Ansell, C. and D. Vogel (2006). The contested governance of European food safety regulation, in C. Ansell and D. Vogel (eds): *What's the Beef? The Contested Governance of European Food Safety*. Cambridge Massachusetts, MIT Press.

Antaki, C. (1994). *Explaining and Arguing. The Social Organization of Accounts*. London, Sage.

Appadurai, A. (1996). *Modernity at Large – Cultural Dimensions of Globalization*. Minneapolis, University of Minnesota Press.

Archer, M. (2002). Realism and the problem of agency, *Journal of Critical Realism*, 5, 11–20.

Arnould, E.J. and C.J. Thompson (2005). Consumer culture theory (CCT): Twenty years of research, *Journal of Consumer Research*, 31, 868–82.

Ashley, B., J. Hollows, S. Jones and B. Taylor (2004). *Food and Cultural Studies*. London, Routledge.

Asp, N. and S. Bryngelsson (2007). Health claims in the labelling and marketing of food products: The Swedish food sector's Code of Practice in a European perspective, *Scandinavian Journal of Food and Nutrition*, 51, 107–26.

Aspers, P. (2008). Labelling fashion markets, *International Journal of Consumer Studies*, 32, 633–38.

Atkinson, R. (1998). *The Life Story Interview*. London, Sage.

Atkinson, P. and A. Coffey (2003). Revisiting the relationship between participant observation and interviewing, in J.F. Gubrium and J.A. Holstein (eds): *Postmodern Interviewing*. London, Sage.

Balfe, M. (2007). Diets and discipline: The narratives of practice of university students with type 1 diabetes, *Sociology of Health and Illness*, 29, 136–53.

Bandesha, G. and A. Litva (2005). Perceptions of community participation and health gain in a community project for the South Asian population: A qualitative study, *Journal of Public Health*, 27, 241–45.

Bang, H. and E. Sørensen (2001). The everyday maker: Building political rather that social capital, in P. Dekker and E.M. Uslaner (eds): *Social Capital and Participation in Everyday Life*. London, Routledge.

Barbour, R. (2007). *Doing Focus Groups*. London, Sage.

Bartiaux, F. (2007). Does environmental information overcome practice compartmentalisation and change consumers' behaviours?, *Journal of Cleaner Production*, 16, 1170–80.

Bassett, R., G.E. Chapman and B.L. Beagan (2008). Autonomy and control: The co-construction of adolescent food choice, *Appetite*, 50, 325–32.

Baudrillard, J. (1988). *Selected Writings*. M. Poster (ed.). Cambridge, Polity Press.

Bauman, Z. (1991). *Modernity and Ambivalence*. Cambridge, Polity Press.

Bauman, Z. (2005). *Liquid Life*. Cambridge, Polity.

Bava, C.M., S.R. Jaeger and J. Park (2008). Constraints upon food provisioning practices in 'busy' women's lives: Trade-offs which demand convenience, *Appetite*, 50, 486–98.

Beagan, B., G.E. Chapman, A. D'Sylvia and B.R. Bassett (2008). 'It's just easier for me to do it'. Rationalizing the family division of foodwork, *Sociology*, 42, 653–71.

Beardsworth, A. and T. Keil (1997). *Sociology on the Menu. An Invitation to the Study of Food and Society*. London, Routledge.

Beck, U. (1992). *Risk Society*. London, Sage.

Belk, R., T. Devinney and G. Eckhardt (2005). Consumer ethics across cultures, *Consumption, Markets and Culture*, 8, 275–89.

Bell, D. and J. Hollows (2005). *Ordinary Lifestyles. Popular Media, Consumption and Taste*. Maidenhead, Open University Press.

Bellows, L., K. Cole and J.A. Gabel (2006). Family fun with new foods: A parent component to the food friends social marketing campaign, *Journal of Nutritional Education Behaviour*, 38, 123–24.

Benford, R.D. and D.A. Snow (2000). Framing processes and social movements: An overview and assessment, *Annual Review of Sociology*, 26, 611–39.

Bennett, W.L. and T. Lagos (2007). Logo logic: The ups and downs of branded political communication, *The Annals of the American Academy of Political and Social Science*, 611, 193–206.

Berg, L. (2000). *Trust in Food in Europe: Focus on Consumer Trust in Norway, England and Belgium*. Working Paper no. 15. Oslo, SIFO.

Berger, P. and T. Luckmann (1966/87). *The Social Construction of Reality*. Harmondsworth, Penguin Books.

Bevir, M. and F. Trentmann (2008). Civic choices: Retrieving perspectives on rationality, consumption and citizenship, in K. Soper and F. Trentman (eds): *Citizenship and Consumption*. Houndmills, Palgrave.

Binkley, S. (2003). The seers of Menlo Park: The discourse of heroic consumption in the 'Whole Earth Catalog', *Journal of Consumer Culture*, 3, 283–313.

Blaikie, N. (1993). *Approaches to Social Enquiry*. Cambridge, Polity.

Blake, C.E., C.M. Devine, E. Wethinton, M. Jastran, T.J. Farrell and C.A. Bisogni (2009). Employed parents' satisfaction with food-choice coping strategies. Influence of gender and structure, *Appetite*, 52, 711–19.

Blanchard, C.M., J. Kupperman, P.B. Sparling, E. Nehl, R.E. Rhodes, K.S. Courneya and F. Baker (2009). Do ethnicity and gender matter when using the theory of planned behaviour to understand fruit and vegetable consumption?, *Appetite*, 52, 15–20.

Blok, A., M. Jensen and P. Kaltoft (2006). Regulating pesticide risks in Denmark: Expert and lay perspectives, *Journal of Environmental Policy and Planning*, 8, 309–30.

Blue, G. (2009). Food, publics, science, *Public Understanding of Science*, 18, 01–08.

Blumer, H. (1954). What is wrong with social theory? *American Sociological Review*, 19, 3–10.

Boström, M. and M. Klintman (2008). *Eco-Standards, Product Labelling and Green Consumerism*. Houndmills, Palgrave.

Boström, M., M. Klintman, M. Micheletti and M.P. Sørensen (2005). *Political Consumerism: Its Motivations, Power and Conditions in the Nordic Countries and Elsewhere*. Nordisk Ministerråd, København.

Bourdieu, P. (1984). *Distinction. A Social Critique of the Judgement of Taste*. London, Routledge and Kegan Paul.

Bourdieu, P. (1990). *The Logic of Practice*. Cambridge, Polity Press.

Bove, C.F. and J. Sobal (2006). Foodwork in newly married couples: Making family meals, *Food, Culture and Society*, 9, 69–89.

Bradby, H. (2002). 'Over the top and glamorous': The meaning of the marriage meal among Glasgow Punjabis, *Food and Foodways*, 10, 11–36.

Brembeck, H. (2005). Home to McDonald's. Upholding the family dinner with the help of McDonald's, *Food, Culture and Society*, 8, 215–26.

Brennan, L. and W. Binney (2010). Fear, guilt and shame appeals in social marketing, *Journal of Business Research*, 63, 140–46.

Briceno, T. and S. Stagl (2006). The role of social processes for sustainable consumption, *Journal of Cleaner Production*, 14, 1541–51.

Bugge, A.B. and R. Almås (2006). Domestic dinner. Representations and practices of a proper meal among suburban mothers, *Journal of Consumer Culture*, 6, 203–28.

Burgess, J., T. Bedford, K. Hobson, G. Dvies and C.M. Harrison (2003). (Un)sustainable consumption, in F. Berhout, M. Leach and I. Scoones (eds): *Negotiating Environmental Change: New Perspectives from Social Science*. Cheltenham, Edward Elgar.

Burr, V. (1995). *An Introduction to Social Constructionism*. London, Sage.

Bush, H., R. Williams, H. Bradby, A. Anderson and M. Lean (1998). Family hospitality and ethnic tradition among South Asian, Italian and general population women in the West of Scotland, *Sociology of Health and Illness*, 20, 351–80.

Butler, J. (1990). *Gender Trouble. Feminism and the Subversion of Identity*. New York, Routledge.

Buttel, F.H. (2000). The recombinant BGH controversy in the United States: Towards a new consumption politics of food? *Agriculture and Human Values*, 17, 5–20.

Campbell, C. (1987). *The Romantic Ethic and the Spirit of Modern Consumption*. Oxford, Basil Blackwell.

Caraher, M., H. Baker and M. Burns (2004). Children's views of cooking and food preparation, *British Food Journal*, 106, 255–73.

Carducci, V. (2006). Culture jamming: A sociological perspective, *Journal of Consumer Culture*, 6, 116–38.

Carrus, G., A.M. Neci and P. Caddeo (2009). The role of ethnic identity and perceived ethnic norms in the purchase of ethnical food products, *Appetite*, 52, 65–71.

Certau, M. de (1984). *The Practice of Everyday Life*. Berkeley, University of California Press.

Chaney, D. (2002). *Cultural Change and Everyday Life*. Houndmills, Palgrave.

Chapman, T. (2008). Book reviews of F. Short, 'Kitchen Secrets' and J. Coveney, 'Food, Morals and Meaning', *Sociology of Health and Illness*, 805–7.

Chatriot, A., M.E. Chessel and M. Hilton (2006). *The Expert Consumer. Associations and Professionals in Consumer Society*. Aldershot, Ashgate.

Cherrier, H. (2009). Anti-consumption discourses and consumer-resistant identities, *Journal of Business Research*, 62, 181–90.

Christensen, G. (1998). *Diskursiv Regulering af Ernæringspraksis* [Discursive regulation of nutritional practice]. Phd-thesis, Department of Human Nutrition, The Royal Veterinary- and Agricultural University, Copenhagen.

Christensen, T.H. and I. Røpke (2005). Can practice theory inspire studies on ICT's in everyday life? Paper presented at the 7th European Sociological Association Conference, Torun, Poland, September 9–12.

Christensen, T.H., M. Godskesen, K. Gram-Hanssen, M. Quitzay and I. Røpke (2007). Greening the Danes? Experience with consumption and environment policies, *Journal of Consumer Policy*, 30, 91–116.

Clarke, A.J. (2007). Making sameness: Mothering, commerce and the culture of childrens' birthday parties, in E. Casey and L. Martens (eds): *Gender and Consumption. Domestic Cultures and the Commercialisation of Everyday Life*. Aldershot, Ashgate.

Clarke, N., C. Barnett, P. Cloke and A. Malpass (2007). Globalising the consumer: Doing politics in an ethical register, *Political Geography*, 26, 231–49.

Clegg, S.R. (1989). *Frameworks of Power*. London, Sage.

Coffey, A. and Atkinson, P. (1996). *Making Sense of Qualitative Data*. London, Sage.

Cohen, M. (2001). The emergent environmental policy discourse on sustainable consumption, in M. Cohen and J. Murphy (eds): *Exploring Sustainable Consumption: Environmental Policy and the Social Sciences*. London, Pergamon.

Cohen, M.J. (2006). Sustainable consumption research as democratic expertise, *Journal of Consumer Policy*, 29, 67–77.

Cohen, R. (1997). *Global Diasporas – An Introduction.* London, UCL Press.

Cole, M., M. Miele, P. Hines, K. Zokaei, B. Evans and J. Beale (2009). Animal foods and climate change: Shadowing eating practices, *International Journal of Consumer Studies*, 33, 162–67.

Collins, A.J. (2004). Can we learn to live differently? Lessons from Going for Green: A case study of Merhyr Tydfil (South Wales), *International Journal of Consumer Studies*, 28, 202–11.

Connolly, J. and A. Prothero (2008). Green consumption: Life-politics, risks and contradictions, *Journal of Consumer Culture*, 8, 117–45.

Cova, B. and V. Cova (2001). Tribal aspects of postmodern consumption research: The case of French in-line roller skaters, *Journal of Consumer Behaviour*, 1, 67–76.

Coveney, J. (2000). *Food, Morals and Meaning. The Pleasure and Anxiety of Eating*. London, Routledge.

Cover, R. (2006). Audience inter/active: Interactive media, narrative control and reconceiving audience history, *New Media and Society*, 8, 139–58.

Crawford, R. (1980). Healthism and the medicalization of everyday life, *International Journal of Health Services*, 10, 365–88.

Dahlgren, P. (2006). Doing citizenship. The cultural origins of civic agency in the public sphere, *European Journal of Cultural Studies*, 9, 267–86.

Danmarks Naturfredningsforening (1989). *Den Miljøvenlige Husholdning. Hvad skal jeg Vælge?* [The environmentally friendly household. What shall I choose?] Forlaget Komma.

Dant, T. (2008). The 'pragmatics' of material interaction, *Journal of Consumer Culture*, 8, 11–33.

Davies, B. and R. Harré (1999). Positioning and personhood, in R. Harré and L. van Langenhove (eds): *Positioning Theory*. Oxford, Blackwell.
Day, G. and M. Truninger (2007). Eating locally: A comparative study of three British rural areas. Paper presented at the 8th. European Sociological Association Conference, Glasgow, UK, September 3.–6.
Dean, M. (1999). *Governmentality: Power and Rule in Modern Society*. London, Sage.
Deding, M., M. Lausten and A. Andersen (2006). *Børnefamiliernes Balance mellem Familie- og Arbejdsliv* [The balance between family- and working-life in families with small children]. København, Social Forsknings Instituttet, 06: 32.
De Krom, M.P.M.M. (2009). Understanding consumer rationalities: Consumer involvement in European food safety governance of avian influenza, *Sociologia Ruralis*, 49, 1–19.
Delormier, T., K.L. Frohlich and L. Potvin (2009). Food and eating as social practice – understanding eating patterns as social phenomena and implications for public health, *Sociology of Health and Illness*, 31, 215–28.
DeVault, M. (1994). *Feeding the Family: The Social Organization of Caring as Gendered Work*. Chicago, The University of Chicago Press.
Dervin, B. (2003). Sense-making's journey from metatheory to methodology to method: An example usinginformation seeking and use as research focus'. In B. Dervin and L. Foreman-Wernet (eds): *Sense-Making Methodology Reader: Selected Writings of Brenda Dervin*. Cresskill, NJ, Hampton Press.
Devcich, D.A., I.K. Pedersen and K.J. Petrie (2007). You eat what you are: Modern health worries and the acceptance of natural and synthetic additives in functional foods, *Appetite*, 48, 333–37.
Didier, T. and L. Sirieix (2008). Measuring consumers' willingness to pay for organic and Fair Trade products, *International Journal of Consumer Studies*, 32, 479–90.
Dixon, J. (2008). Operating upstream and downstream: How supermarkets exercise power in the food system, in J. Germov and L. Williams (eds): *A Sociology of Food & Nutrition. The Social Appetite. Third Edition*. Oxford, Oxford University Press.
Dobson, A. (2003). *Citizenship and the Environment*. Oxford, Oxford University Press.
Dodds, R.E., E. Tseëlon and E.L.C. Weitkamp (2008). Making sense of scientific claims in advertising. A study of scientifically aware consumers, *Public Understanding of Science*, 17, 211–30.
Douglas, M. and B. Isherwood (1980). *The World of Goods. Towards an Anthropology of Consumption*. Harmondsworth, Penguin Books.
Douglas, M. and M. Nicod (1974). Taking the biscuit. The structure of British meals, *New Society*, 30, 744–77.

D'Souza, C., M. Taghian, P. Lamb and R. Peretiatko (2006). Green decisions: Demographics and consumer understanding of environmental labels, *International Journal of Consumer Studies*, 31, 371–76.

Eden, S. (2009). Food labels as boundary objects: How consumers make sense of organic and functional foods, *Public Understanding of Science*, 18, 1–16.

Ehn, B. and O. Löfgren (2009). Routines – made and unmade, in E. Shove, F. Trentmann and R. Wilk (eds): *Time, Consumption and Everyday Life. Practice, Materiality and Culture*. Oxford, Berg.

Einseidel, E.F., E. Jelsøe and T. Breck (2001). Publics and the technology table: The consensus conference in Denmark, Canada and Australia, *Public Understanding of Science*, 10, 83–98.

Ekström, M. (1990). *Kost, Klass och Kön* [Food, class and gender]. Umeå, Umeå Universitet.

Ekström, M. (1991). Class and gender in the kitchen, in E. Fürst, R. Prättälä, M. Ekström, L. Holm and U. Kjærnes (eds): *Palatable Worlds. Sociocultural Food Studies*. Oslo, Solum Forlag.

Elkington, J. and J. Hailes (1988). *The Green Consumer Guide*. London, Victor Gollancz.

Erickson, R.J. (2005). Why emotion work matters: Sex, gender, and the division of household labor, *Journal of Marriage and Family*, 67, 337–51.

Eurobarometer (2008). *Attitudes of European Citizens towards the Environment*. Special Eurobarometer 295. European Commission.

EU Commission (2000). *White Paper on Food Safety*. Bruxelles, Commission of the European Communities.

EU Commission (2005). *From Farm to Fork – Safe Food for Europe's Consumers*. Bruxelles, Commission of the European Communities.

Evans, D. and T. Jackson (2008). Sustainable consumption: Perspectives from social and cultural theory, RESOLVE Working Paper 05-08, University of Surrey, UK.

Fagerli, R.Aa., M.E. Lien and M. Wandel (2005). Experience of dietary advice among Pakistani-born persons with type 2 diabetes in Oslo, *Appetite*, 45, 295–304.

Fagt, S., T. Christensen, M.V. Groth, A. Biltoft-Jensen, J. Matthiessen, and E. Trolle. (2008). *Børn og Unges Måltidsvaner 2000-2004*. [Meal habits among children and youth 2000–2004] Fødevareinstituttet, Danish Technological University.

Falbe, J.L. and M. Nestlé (2008). The politics of government dietary advice, in J. Germov and L. Williams (eds): *A Sociology of Food and Nutrition. The Social Appetite*. Third edition. Oxford, Oxford University Press.

Falk, P. (1994). *The Consuming Body*. London, Sage.

Fairclough, N. (1992). *Discourse and Social Change*. Cambridge, Polity Press.

Feagan, R.B. and D. Morris (2009). Consumer quest for embeddedness: A case study of the Brantford Farmers' Market, *International Journal of Consumer Studies*, 33, 235–43.

Featherstone, M. (1990). Perspectives on consumer culture, *Sociology*, 24, 5–22.

Featherstone, M. (1991). *Consumer Culture and Postmodernism*. London, Sage.

Featherstone, H., E. Weitkamp, K. Ling and F. Burnet (2009). Defining issue-based publics for public engagement: Climate changes as a case study, *Public Understanding of Science*, 18, 214–28.

Fennell, D. (2009). Marketing Science. The corporate faces of genetic engineering, *Journal of Communication Inquiry*, 33, 5–26.

Fischler, C. (1988). Food, self and identity, *Social Science Information*, 27, 275–92.

Fishbein, M. and J.N. Cappella (2006). The role of theory in developing effective health communications, *Journal of Communication*, 56, 1–17.

Fiske, J. (1990). *Introduction to Communication Studies*. London, Routledge.

Floyd, J. and L. Forster (2003). *The Recipe Reader: Narratives, Contexts, Traditions*. Aldershot, Ashgate.

Forebyggelseskommissionen (2009). *Vi Kan Leve Længere og Sundere. Forebyggelseskommissionens Anbefalinger til en Styrket Forebyggende Indsats* [We can live longer and more healthy. Recommendations of the Commision for Prevention to a strengthened preventive effort]. København.

Forbrugerstyrelsen [Danish Consumer Agency] (2008). *Forbrugerredegørelse 2008*. [Consumer Review 2008] Copenhagen.

Forster, L. (2003). Liberating the recipe: A study of the relationship between food and feminism in the early 1970s, in J. Floyd and L. Forster (eds): *The Recipe Reader: Narratives, Contexts, Traditions*. Aldershot, Ashgate.

Foucault, M. (1972). *The Archaeology of Knowledge*. London, Tavistock Publications.

Foucault, M. (1978). *The History of Sexuality. Vol. 1*. Harmondsworth, Penguin.

Foucault, M. (1991). Governmentality, in G. Burchell, C. Gordon and P. Miller (eds): *The Foucault Effect: Studies in Governmentality with Two Lectures by and an Interview with Foucault*. Chicago, Chicago University Press.

Fraj, E. and E. Martinez (2007). Ecological consumer behaviour: An empirical analysis, *International Journal of Consumer Studies*, 31, 26–33.

Frame, B. and B. Newton (2007). Promoting sustainability through social marketing: Examples from New Zealand. *International Journal of Consumer Studies*, 31, 571–81.

Frewer, L.J., S. Miles, M. Brennan, S. Kuznesof, M. Ness and C. Ritson (2002). Public preferences for informed choice under conditions of risk uncertainty, *Public Understanding of Science*, 11, 362–72.

Frey, J.H. and A. Fontana (1993). The group interview in social research, in D.L. Morgan (ed.): *Successful Focus Groups*. London, Sage.

Friedman, M. (1996). A positive approach to organized consumer action: The 'buycott' as an alternative to the boycott, *Journal of Consumer Policy*, 19, 439–51.

Gabriel, Y. and T. Lang (1995). *The Unmanageable Consumer. Contemporary Consumption and Its Fragmentations*. London, Sage.

Gabriel, Y. and T. Lang (2007). New faces and new masks of today's consumer, *Journal of Consumer Culture*, 8, 321–40.
Garfinkel, H. (1967/1984). *Studies in Ethnomethodology*. Cambridge, Polity Press.
Giddens, A. (1991). *Modernity and Self-Identity*. Cambridge, Polity Press.
Giddens, A. (1984). *The Constitution of Society*. Cambridge, Polity Press.
Goffman, E. (1967). *Interaction Ritual: Essays on Face-to-Face Behaviour*. New York, Doubleday Anchor.
Goodman, D. and M. Redclift (1991). *Refashioning Nature. Food, Ecology and Culture*. London, Routledge.
Goul Andersen, J. and M. Tobiassen (2004). Who are these political consumers anyway? Survey evidence from Denmark, in M. Micheletti, A. Follesdal and D. Stolle (eds): *Politics, Products and Markets. Exploring Political Consumerism Past and Present*. London, Transaction Publishers.
Gram-Hanssen, K. (2007). Practice theory and the green energy consumer. Paper presented at the 8th European Sociological Association Conference, Glasgow, UK, September 3–6.
Gram-Hanssen, K. (2008). Consuming technologies – developing routines, *Journal of Cleaner Production*, 16, 1181–89.
Greenberg, C. (2004). Political consumer action: Some cautionary notes from African American history, in M. Micheletti, A. Follesdal and D. Stolle (eds): *Politics, Products and Markets. Exploring Political Consumerism Past and Present*. London, Transaction Publishers.
Gregory, S. (2005). Living with chronic illness in the family setting, *Sociology of Health and Illness*, 27, 372–92.
Gregson, N. and G. Rose (2000). Taking Butler elsewhere: Performativities, spatialities and subjectivities, *Environment and Planning D: Society and Space*, 18, 433–52.
Griffin-Foley, B. (2004). From tit-bits to big brother: A century of audience participation in the media, *Media, Culture and Society*, 26, 533–48.
Gronow, A. (2008). The over-or the under-socialized conception of man? Practice theory and the problem of intersubjectivity. *Sociology*, 42, 243–59.
Gronow, J. (1993). Taste and fashion: The social function of fashion and style, *Acta Sociologica*, 36, 89–100.
Gronow, J. (1997a). *The Sociology of Taste*. London, Routledge.
Gronow, J. (1997b). The risks and dangers of eating: Trust and legitimacy. Paper presented at the 3rd European Sociological Association Conference, Essex, UK, 27–30. August.
Gronow, J. and L. Holm (2008). The perpetual concept of choice: Reflections on a dominant theoretical construct in the field of food consumption. Paper presented at the ESA Research Network, Sociology of Consumption, interim workshop, Helsinki, Finland, 27–30. August.
Gronow, J. and A. Warde (2001). *Ordinary Consumption*. London, Routledge.

Grøn Information (1995). *Mod Gift* [Against poison]. København, Grøn Information.
Guerro, L., M.D. Guardia, J. Xicola, W. Verbeke, F. Vanhonacker, S. Zakowska-Biemans, M. Sajdakowska, C. Sulmont-Rossé, S. Issanchou, M. Contel, M.L. Scalvedi, B.S. Granli and M. Hersleth (2009). Consumer-driven definition of traditional food products and innovation in traditional foods. A qualitative cross-cultural study, *Appetite*, 52, 345–54.
Gulyas, E. (2008). Interpretations of ethical consumption, *Review of Sociology*, 14, 25–44.
Habermas, J. (1984). *The Theory of Communicative Action. Vol. 1*. Cambridge, Polity Press.
Habermas, J. (1987). *The Theory of Communicative Action. Vol. 2*. Cambridge, Polity Press.
Hagemann, K. and J. Scholderer (2007). Consumer versus expert hazard identification: A mental models study of mutation-bred rice, *Journal of Risk Research*, 10, 449–64.
Halkier, B. (1999). Consequences of the politicization of consumption: The example of environmentally friendly consumption practices, *Journal of Environmental Policy and Planning*, 1, 25–41.
Halkier, B. (2001a). Consuming ambivalences. Consumer handling of environmentally related risks in food, *Journal of Consumer Culture*, 1, 205–24.
Halkier, B. (2001b). Risk and food: Environmental concerns and consumer practices, *International Journal of Food Science and Technology*, 36, 801–12.
Halkier, B. (2003). The challenge of qualitative generalisations in communication research, *Nordicom Review*, 24, 115–24.
Halkier, B. (2004). Handling food-related risks: Political agency and governmentality, in M.E. Lien and B. Nehrlich (eds): *The Politics of Food*. Oxford, Berg.
Halkier, B. (2006). Preserving preserving? Cooking practices in medialised everyday life. Paper presented at the ESA Research Network, Sociology of Consumption, interim workshop, Durham, UK, 30.8–1.9.
Halkier, B. (2009). Suitable cooking? Performances and positionings in cooking practices among Danish women, *Food, Culture and Society*, 12, 3, 357–77.
Halkier, B. (2010). Focus groups as social enactments: Integrating interaction and content in the analysis of focus group data, *Qualitative Research*, 10, 71–89.
Halkier, B. and L. Holm (2004). Tillid til mad – forbrug mellem dagligdag og politisering [Trust in food – consumption between everyday life and politicisation], *Dansk Sociologi*, 15, 9–26.
Halkier, B. and L. Holm (2006). Shifting responsibilities for food safety in Europe: An introduction, *Appetite*, 47, 127–33.
Halkier, B. and L. Holm (2008). Food consumption and political agency: On concerns and practices among Danish consumers, *International Journal of Consumer Studies*, 32, 667–74.

Halkier, B., L. Holm, M. Domingues, P. Magaudda, A. Nielsen and L. Terragni (2007). Trusting, complex, quality conscious or unprotected? Constructing the food consumer in different European national contexts, *Journal of Consumer Culture*, 7, 379–402.

Hall, S. (1992). The question of cultural identity, in S. Hall, D. Held and T. McGrew (eds): *Modernity and its Futures*. Cambridge, Polity Press.

Hall, S. (1997). The work of representation, in S. Hall (ed.): *Representation. Cultural Representations and Signifying Practices*. London, Sage.

Hammersley, M. and P. Atkinson (1995). *Ethnography. Principles in Practice*. London, Routledge.

Hanpää, L. (2007). Consumers' green commitment: Indication of a postmodern lifestyle? *International Journal of Consumer Studies*, 31, 478–86.

Hansen, K. (1992). *Den Lille Grønne* [The little green one]. København, Høst og Søn.

Hansen, J., L. Holm, L. Frewer, P. Robinson and P. Sandoe (2003). Beyond the knowledge deficit: Recent research into lay and expert attitudes to food risks, *Appetite*, 41, 111–21.

Hargreaves, T., M. Nye and J. Burgess (2007). 'Work in progress': Analysing facilitated behaviour change process through the lens of social practice theory. Paper presented at the 8th European Sociological Association Conference, Glasgow, UK, 3–6 September.

Harré, R. and L. van Langenhove (1999). *Positioning Theory*. Oxford, Blackwell.

Heath, J. and A. Potter (2004). *Nation of Rebels: Why Counterculture Became Consumer Culture*. New York, Harper Business.

Hebdige, D. (1988). *Hiding in Light*. London, Routledge.

Heck, M. de C. (2003). Adapting and adopting: The migrating recipe, in J. Floyd and L. Forster (eds): *The Recipe Reader: Narratives, Contexts, Traditions*. Aldershot, Ashgate.

Heisley, D.D. and S.J. Levy (1991). Autodriving: Photoelicitation technique. *Journal of Consumer Research*, 18, 257–72.

Held, D. (1987). *Models of Democracy*. Cambridge, Polity Press.

Helle-Valle, J. (2009). Consumption and gender: a late-Wittgensteinian view. Paper presented at the 9th European Sociological Association Conference, Lisboa, Portugal, 2–5 September.

Hermes, J. (1995). *Reading Women's Magazines: An Analysis of Everyday Media Use*. Cambridge, Polity Press.

Hermes, J. (2005). *Re-reading Popular Culture*. Oxford, Blackwell.

Hertzler, A.A. and F.A. Bruce (2002). Cooking, recipe use and food habits of college students and nutrition educators, *International Journal of Consumer Studies*, 26, 340–45.

Hewitt, M. (1991). Bio-politics and social policy: Foucault's account of welfare, in M. Featherstone, M. Hepworth and B.S. Turner (eds): *The Body: Social Processes and Cultural Theory*. London, Sage.

Hirschman, A.O. (1970). *Exit, Voice and Loyalty*. Massachusetts: Harvard University Press.
Hjarvard, S. (1999). *TV-Nyheder i Konkurrence* [Television news under competition]. Frederiksberg, Samfundslitteratur.
Hjarvard, S. (2002). Seernes reality [Reality of the viewers], *Mediekultur*, 34, 92–109.
Hogg, M.K., E.N. Banister and C.A. Stephenson (2009). Mapping symbolic anti-consumption, *Journal of Business Research*, 62, 148–59.
Holbrook, M.B. (1995). *Consumer Research. Introspective Essays on the Study of Consumption*. London, Sage.
Hollows, J. (2003). Feeling like a domestic goddess. Postfeminism and cooking, *European Journal of Cultural Studies*, 6, 179, 202.
Hollows, J. (2007). The feminist and the cook. Julia Child, Betty Friedan and domestic femininity, in E. Casey and L. Martens (eds): *Gender and Consumption. Domestic Cultures and the Commercialisation of Everyday Life*. Aldershot, Ashgate.
Holm, L. (1996). Identity and dietary change, *Scandinavian Journal of Nutrition*, 40, supplement 31, S95–8.
Holm, L. (2003a). Blaming the consumer: On the free choice of consumers and the decline in food quality in Denmark, *Critical Public Health*, 13, 139–54.
Holm, L. (2003b). Food health policies and ethics: Lay perspectives on functional foods, *Journal of Agricultural and Environmental Ethics*, 16, 531–44.
Holm, L. (2004). *Mad, Mennesker og Måltider – Samfundsvidenskabelige Perspektiver* [Food, people and meals – social scientific perspectives]. København, Munksgaard.
Holm, L. and B. Halkier (2009). EU food safety policy: Localising contested governance, *European Societies*, 11, 473–93.
Holm, L., C. Brombach, S. Jansson and A. Murcott (2003). Lay conceptions of food and health – evidence from four European cities. Working paper, Royal Veterinary- and Agricultural University, Copenhagen.
Holm, L. and H. Kildevang (1996). Consumers' views on food quality: A qualitative interview study, *Appetite*, 27, 1–14.
Holstein, J.A. and J.F. Gubrium (2003). Active interviewing. In J.F. Gubrium and J.A. Holstein (eds): *Postmodern Interviewing*. London, Sage.
Holtzman, J.D. (2006). Food and memory, *Annual Review of Anthropology*, 35, 361–78.
Holzer, B. (2006). Political consumerism between individual choice and collective action: Social movements, role mobilization and signalling, *International Journal of Consumer Studies*, 30, 405–15.
Horton, D. (2003). Green distinctions: The performance of identity among environmental activists, *Sociological Review*, 51, 63–77.
Howard, P.H. and P. Allen (2006). Beyond organic: Consumer interest in new labelling schemes in the central coast of California, *International Journal of Consumer Studies*, 30, 439–51.

Hughner, R.S., J.K. Maher, N.M. Childs and W.E. Nganje (2009). Fish: Friend or foe? Food policy and subpopulation warnings for consumers, *Food Policy*, 34, 185–97.

Hurdley, R. (2007). Focal points: Framing material culture and visual data. *Qualitative Research*, 7, 355–74.

Hustvedt, G. and J.C. Bernard (2008). Consumer willingness to pay for sustainable apparel: The influence of labelling for fibre origin and production methods, *International Journal of Consumer Studies*, 32, 491–98.

Hustvedt, G., H.H. Peterson and Y. Chen (2008). Labelling wool products for animal welfare and environmental impact, *International Journal of Consumer Stuides*, 32, 427–37.

Irwin, A. (2001). Constructing the scientific citizen: Science and democracy in the biosciences, *Public Understanding of Science*, 10, 1–18.

Jabs, J. and C.M. Devine (2006). Time scarcity and food choices: An overview, *Appetite*, 47, 196–204.

Jacobsen, E. and A. Dulsrud (2007). Will consumers save the world? The framing of political consumerism, *Journal of Agricultural and Environmental Ethics*, 20, 469–82.

Jagers, S.C. (2009). In search of the ecological citizen, *Environmental Politics*, 18, 18–36.

Jamal, A. (1998). Food consumption among ethnic minorities: The case of British-Pakistanis in Bradford, UK, *British Food Journal*, 100, 221–27.

Jensen, I. and B. Halkier (2008). Conceptualising network communication from a practice theoretical perspective: Starting-point in a case-study of food habits and nutritional communication. Paper presented at the ECREA Conference, Barcelona, Spain, 25–28 November.

Jensen K.O., H.N. Larsen, J.P. Mølgaard, J. Andersen, A. Tingstad, P. Marckmann og A. Astrup (2001). Økologiske fødevarer og menneskets sundhed: rapport fra vidensyntese udført i regi af Forskningsinstitut for Human Ernæring [Organic food stuff and human health: Report from a knowledge synthesis carried out under Research Institute for Human Nutrition], KVL. Foulum: Forskningscenter for Økologisk Jordbrug.

Jensen, T.Ø and U. Kjærnes (1997). Designing the good life: Nutrition and social democracy in Norway, in P. Sulkunen, J. Holmwood. H. Radner and G. Schulze (eds.): *Constructing the New Consumer Society*. Houndmills, Macmillan.

Jerslev, A. (2005). *Performative Realism*. København, Museum Tusculanum Press.

Johnson, G.J. and P.J. Ambrose (2006). Neo-tribes: The power and potential of online communities in health care, *Communications of the ACM*, 49, 107–13.

Johnston, J. (2008). The citizen-consumer hybrid: Ideological tensions and the case of Whole Foods Market, *Theory and Society*, 37, 229–70.

Jubas, K. (2007). Conceptual con/fusion in democratic societies: Understandings and limitations of consumer-citizenship, *Journal of Consumer Culture*, 7, 231–54.

Julier, A.P. (2004). Entangled in our meals. Guilt and pleasure in contemporary food discourses, *Food, Culture and Society*, 7, 13–21.

Keum, H., N. Devanathan, S. Despande, M.R. Nelson and D.V. Shah (2004). The citizen-consumer: Media effects at the intersection of consumer and civic culture, *Political Communication*, 21, 369–91.

Kilbourne, W.E., S. Beckmann and E. Thelen (2002). The role of the dominant social paradigm in environmental attitudes. A multinational examination, *Journal of Business Research*, 55, 193–204.

Kjærnes, U. (2001). *Eating Patterns. A Day in the Lives of Nordic Peoples*. Professional Report no. 7. Oslo, SIFO.

Kjærnes, U. (2006). Trust and distrust: Cognitive decisions or social relations? *Journal of Risk Research*, 9, 911–32.

Kjærnes, U., M. Harvey and A. Warde (2007). *Trust in Food. A Comparative and Institutional Analysis*. Houndsmill, Palgrave.

Kline, S. (2005). Countering children's sedentary lifestyles. An evaluative study of media-risk education approach, *Childhood*, 12, 239–58.

Klintman, M. (2006). Ambiguous framings of political consumerism: Means or end, product or process orientation? *International Journal of Consumer Studies*, 30, 427–38.

Klintman, M. and M. Bostöm (2006). Editorial, *International Journal of Consumer Studies*, 30, 401–04.

Knight, A.J (2009). Perceptions, knowledge and ethical concerns with GM foods and the GM process, *Public Understanding of Science*, 18, 177–88.

Knorr-Cetina, K. (2001). Objectual practice, in T. Schatzki, K. Knorr-Cetina and E. von Savigny (eds): *The Practice Turn in Contemporary Theory*. London, Routledge.

Kolandai-Matchett, K. (2009). Mediated communication of 'sustainable consumption' in the alternative media: A case study exploring a message framing strategy, *International Journal of Consumer Studies*, 33, 113–25.

Kotler, P. N. Roberto and N. Lee (2002). *Social Marketing: Improving the Quality of Life* (2nd ed.). London, Sage.

Kristensen, S.T. and L. Holm (2006). Modern meal patterns: Tensions between bodily needs and the organization of time and space, *Food and Foodways*, 14, 151–73.

Kronenberg, J. (2007). Making consumption 'reasonable', *Journal of Cleaner Production*, 15, 557–66.

Kvale, S. (1996). *Inter Views. An Introduction to Qualitative Research Interviewing*. London, Sage.

Laclau, E. (1996). Deconstruction, pragmatism, hegemony, in S.Critchley and C. Mouffe (eds.): *Deconstruction and Pragmatism*. London, Routledge.

Lang, T. and M. Heasman (2004). *Food Wars. The Global Battle for Mouths, Minds and Markets*. London, Earthscan.

Langenhove, van L. and R. Harré (1999). Introducing positioning theory in R. Harré and L. van Langenhove (eds): *Positioning Theory*. Oxford, Blackwell.

Latour, B. (1993). *We Have Never been Modern*. Cambridge, Massachusetts: Harvard University Press.

Latour, B. (2005). *Reassembling the Social. An Introduction to Actor-Network Theory*. Oxford, Oxford University Press.

Lefebvre, R.C. (2007). The new technology: The consumer as participant rather than target audience, *Social Marketing Quarterly*, 13, 31–42.

Lien, M.E. (2004). The politics of food: An introduction, in M.E. Lien and B. Nehrlich (eds): *The Politics of Food*. Oxford, Berg.

Lin, C.J., K.L. Jensen and S.T. Yen (2005). Awareness of foodborne pathogens among US consumers, *Food Quality and Preference*, 16, 401–12.

Lindén, A. and M. Nyberg (2009). The workplace lunch room: An arena for multicultural eating, *International Journal of Consumer Studies*, 33, 42–48.

Livingstone, S. and E.J. Helsper (2006). Does advertising lieteracy mediate the effects of advertising on children? A critical examination of two linked research literatures in relation to obesity and food choice, *Journal of Communication*, 56, 560–84.

Lizardo, O. (2009). Is a 'special psychology' of practice possible? From values and attitudes to embodied dispositions, *Theory and Psychology*, 19, 1–15.

Lockie, S. (2002). 'The invisible mouth': Mobilizing 'the consumer' in food production-consumption networks, *Sociologia Ruralis*, 42, 278–94.

Lockie, S., K. Lyons, G. Lawrence and K. Mummery (2002). Eating 'green': Motivations behind organic food consumption in Australia, *Sociologia Ruralis*, 42, 23–40.

Lofstedt, R.E. (2006). How can we make food risk communication better: Where are we and where are we going?, *Journal of Risk Research*, 9, 869–90.

Luckmann, T. (1989). On meaning in everyday life and sociology, *Current Sociology*, 37, 17–30.

Luhmann, N. (1995). *Social Systems*. California, Stanford University Press.

Luke, T. (1997). Environmentality as green governmentality, in E. Darier (ed.): *Discourses of the Environment*. Oxford, Blackwell.

Lull, J. (2007). *Culture-on-demand: Communication in a Crisis World*. Oxford, Blackwell.

Lund, A.K. og Grandjean, F. (1997). *Skån Miljøet – og Spar 23.600 kr. om Året* [Spare the environmentment – and save 23.600 kr. per year]. DR Multimedie, Copenhagen.

Lupton, D. (1996). *Food, Body and the Self*. London, Sage.

Lupton, D. (1999). *Risk*. London, Routledge.

Lupton, D. (2005). Lay discourses and beliefs related to food risks: An Australian perspective, *Sociology of Health and Illness*, 27, 448–67.

Lyon, P., A. Colquhoun and E. Alexander (2003). Deskilling the domestic kitchen: National tragedy or the making of a modern myth? *Food Service Technology*, 3, 167–75.

Macnaghten, P. (2003). Embodying the environment in everyday life practices, *Sociological Review*, 51, 63–84.

Macnaghten, P. and J. Urry (1998). *Contested Natures*. London, Sage.
Maffesoli, M. (1996). *The Time of the Tribes. The Decline of Individualism in Mass Society*. London, Sage.
Magnusson, M.K., A. Arvola, U.K. Hursti, L. Åberg and P. Sjödén (2003). Choice of organic foods is related to perceived consequences for human health and to environmentally friendly behaviour, *Appetite*, 40, 109–17.
Mäkela, J. and P. Timonen (2007). Active consumers and ethical food consumption in Finland. Paper presented at the 8th European Sociological Association Conference, Glasgow, UK, September 3–6.
Maniates, M. (2002). Individualization: Plant a tree, buy a bike, save the world?, in T. Princen, M. Maniates and K. Conca (eds): *Confronting Consumption*. London, The MIT Press.
Marsden, T., A. Flynn and M. Harrison (2000). *Consuming Interests. The Social Provision of Foods*. London, UCL Press.
Marshall, D. and R. Bell (2003). Meal construction: Exploring the relationship between eating occasion and location, *Food Quality and Preference*, 14, 53–64.
Martens, L. and S. Scott (2006). Under the kitchen surface: Domestic products and conflicting constructions of home, *Home Cultures*, 3, 39–62.
Martens, L., D. Southerton and S. Scott (2004). Bringing children (and parents) into the sociology of consumption: Towards a theoretical and empirical agenda, *Journal of Consumer Culture*, 4, 155–82.
Masullo, A. (2009). Sociological theories and food insecurity: A practice theory approach. Paper presented at the 9th European Sociological Association Conference, Lisboa, Portugal, 2–5 September.
McCracken, G. (1988). *Culture and Consumption*. Bloomington, Indiana University Press.
McDonald, S., C. Oates, M. Thyne, P. Alevizou and L. McMorland (2009). Comparing sustainable consumption patterns across product sectors, *International Journal of Consumer Studies*, 33, 137–45.
McEachern, M.G. and P. McClean (2002). Organic purchasing motivations and attitudes: Are they ethical? *International Journal of Consumer Studies*, 26, 85–92.
McKenzie-Mohr (2000). Promoting sustainable behaviour: An introduction to community-based social marketing, *Journal of Social Issues*, 56, 543–54.
McKie, L., S. Bowlby and S. Gregory (2004). Starting well: Gender, care and health in the family context, *Sociology*, 38, 593–611.
McNair, B. (2000). *Journalism and Democracy. An Evaluation of the Political Public Sphere*. London, Routledge.
Mellin-Olsen, T. and M. Wandel (2005). Changes in food habits among Pakistani immigrant women in Oslo, Norway, *Ethnicity and Health*, 10, 311–39.
Mennell, S., A. Murcott and A. van Otterloo (1992). *The Sociology of Food: Eating, Diet and Culture*. London, Sage.

Michaelidou, N. and L.M. Hassan (2008). The role of health conciousness, food safety concern and ethical identity on attitudes and intentions towards organic food, *International Journal of Consumer Studies*, 32, 163–70.
Micheletti, M. (2003). *Political Virtue and Shopping. Individuals, Consumerism and Collective Action*. Houndmills, Palgrave.
Micheletti, M., A. Follesdal and D. Stolle (2004). *Politics, Products and Markets. Exploring Political Consumerism Past and Present*. London, Transaction Publishers.
Miele, M. (2006). Consumption culture? The case of food, in P. Cloke, T. Marsden and P. Mooney (eds): *The Handbook of Rural Studies*. London, Sage.
Miller, D. (1998). *A Theory of Shopping*. Cambridge, Polity.
Millstone, E. and P.v Zwanenberg (2007). Mad cow disease – painting policy making into a corner, *Journal of Risk Research*, 10, 661–91.
Misztal, B.A. (1996). *Trust in Modern Societies. The Search for the Bases of Social Order*. Cambridge, Polity Press.
Moisander, J. (2007). Motivational complexity of green consumerism, *International Journal of Consumer Studies*, 31, 404–9.
Moisio, R., E.J. Arnould and L.L. Price (2004). Between mothers and markets. Constructing family identity through homemade food, *Journal of Consumer Culture*, 4, 361–84.
Mol, A.P.J. and G. Spaargaren (2000). Ecological modernisation theory in debate: A review, in A.P.J. Mol and D.A. Sonnenfeld (eds): *Ecological Modernisation Around the World: Perspectives and Critical Debates*. London, Frank Cass.
Moloney, M. and S. Fenstermaker (2002). Performance and accomplishment: Reconciling feminist conceptions of gender, in S. Fenstermaker and C. West (eds): *Doing Gender, Doing Difference. Inequality, Power and Institutional Change*. New York, Routledge.
Morgan, D.L. (1997). *Focus Groups as Qualitative Research*. London, Sage.
Mortensen, N. (1991). Modsætninger og forsoninger mellem strukturer og aktører [Contradictions and reconciliations between structures and actors], *Politica*, 23, 42–59.
Mortensen, N. (1992). Future norms, in P. Gundelach and K. Siune (eds): *From Voters to Participants*. Aarhus, Politica.
Mouzelis, N. (1995). *Sociological Theory. What Went Wrong?* London, Routledge.
Murcott, A. (1983). 'It's a pleasure to cook for him': Food, mealtimes and gender in some South Wales households, in E. Garmanikow, D. Morgan, J. Purvis and D. Taylorson (eds): *The Public and the Private*. London, Heinemann.
Murcott, A. (1993). Talking of good food: An empirical study of women's conceptualizations, *Food and Foodways*, 5, 305–18.
Murcott, A. (2000). Is it still a pleasure to cook for him? Social changes in the household and the family, *Journal of Consumer Studies and Home Economics*, 24, 78–84.

Murdoch, J. and M. Miele (1999). 'Back to nature': Changing 'worlds of production' in the food sector, *Sociologia Ruralis*, 39, 466–83.
Nash, H.A. (2009). The European Commission's sustainable consumption and production and sustainable industrial policy action plan, *Journal of Cleaner Production*, 17, 496–98.
Newman, F. and M. Gibson (2005). Monoculture versus multiculinarism: Trouble in the Aussie kitchen, in D. Bell and J. Hollows (eds): *Ordinary Lifestyles. Popular Media, Consumption and Taste*. Maidenhead, Open University Press.
Newman, J. and E. Kuhlmann (2007). Consumers enter the political stage? The modernization of health care in Britain and Germany, *Journal of European Social Policy*, 17, 99–111.
Nicholls, A. and C. Opal (2005). *Fair Trade. Market Driven Ethical Consumption*. London, Sage.
Nielsen, A. (2006). Contesting competence – change in the Danish food safety system, *Appetite* 47, 143–151.
Nielsen, A. (2008). *Keeping it Down and Getting it Right. A Sociological Analysis of Weight Control and Dietary Change in an Experimental Setup*. Phd-thesis. Department of Human Nutrition, University of Copenhagen.
Niva, M. and P. Timonen (2001). The role of consumers in product-oriented environmental policy: Can the consumer be the driving force for environmental improvements?, *International Journal of Consumer Studies*, 25, 331–38.
Nofsinger, R.E. (1991). *Everyday Conversation*. London, Sage.
Ozcaglar-Toulouse, N., E. Shiu and D. Shaw (2006). In search of fair trade: Ethical consumer decision making in France, *International Journal of Consumer Studies*, 30, 502–14.
Paterson, M. (2004). *Consumption and Everyday Life*. London, Routledge.
Pattie, C., P. Seyd and P. Whiteley (2003). Citizenship and civic engagement: attitudes and behaviour in Britain, *Political Studies*, 51, 443–68.
Peattie, K. and S. Peattie (2003). Ready to fly solo? Reducing social marketing's dependence on commercial marketing theory, *Marketing Theory*, 3, 365–86.
Peattie, K. and S. Peattie (2009). Social marketing: A pathway to consumption reduction?, *Journal of Business Research*, 62, 260–68.
Pechmann, C. and M.D. Slater (2005). Social marketing messages that may motivate irresponsible consumption behaviour, in S. Ratneswar and D.G. Mick (eds): *Inside Consumption. Consumer Motives, Goals and Desires*. London, Routledge.
Pedersen, L.H. (2000). The dynamics of green consumption: A matter of visibility? *Journal of Environmental Policy and Planning*, 2, 193–210.
Pepper, M., T. Jackson and D. Uzzell (2009). An examination of the values that motivate socially conscious and frugal consumer behaviours, *International Journal of Consumers Issues*, 33, 126–36.
Peretti, J. (2004). The Nike sweatshop email: Political consumerism, internet and culture jamming, in M. Micheletti, A. Follesdal and D. Stolle (eds): *Politics,*

Products and Markets. Exploring Political Consumerism Past and Present. London, Transaction Publishers.
Petersen, L.K. (2008). Autonomy and proximity in household heating practices: The case of wood-burning stoves, *Journal of Environmental Policy and Planning*, 10, 423–38.
Phillips, L. (2000). Mediated communication and the privatization of public problems, *European Journal of Communication*, 15, 171–207.
Phillips, L. and M. Jørgensen (2002). *Discourse Analysis as Theory and Method*. London, Sage.
Piggford, T., M. Raciti, D. Harker and M. Harker (2008). Young adults' food motives: An Australian social marketing perspective, *Young Consumers: Insights and Ideas for Responsible Marketers*, 9, 17–28.
Polkinghorne, D.E. (2007). Validity issues in narrative research, *Qualitative Inquiry*, 13, 471–86.
Potter, J. (1996). *Representing Reality. Discourse, Rhetoric and Social Construction*. London, Sage.
Potter, J. (2007). *Discourse and Psycology*. London, Sage.
Poulsen, M.S. (2006). Vi skal spise! [Dinner's served!], *Samvirke*, 12, 36.
Prim, M.K., I. Gustafsson and G. Hall (2007). The appropriateness of ready meals for dinner, *Journal of Foodservice*, 18, 238–50.
Puchta, C. and J. Potter (2005). *Focus Group Practice*. London, Sage.
Qin, W. and J.L. Brown (2007). Public reactions to information about genetically engineered foods: Effects of information formats and male/female differences, *Public Understanding of Science*, 16, 471–88.
Ratneshwar, S. and D.G. Mick (2005). *Inside Consumption. Consumer Motives, Goals and Desires*. London, Routledge.
Reckwitz, A. (2002). Toward a theory of social practices. A development in culturalist theorizing, *European Journal of Social Theory*, 5, 243–63.
Renn, O. (2006). Risk communication – consumers between information and irritation, *Journal of Risk Research*, 9, 833–49.
Rindfleish, J. (2005). Consuming the self: New age spirituality as 'social product' in consumer society, *Consumption, Markets and Culture*, 8, 343–60.
Ristovski-Slijepcevic, S., G.E. Chapman and B.L. Beagan (2008). Engaging with healthy eating discourse(s): Ways of knowing about food and health in three ethnocultural groups in Canada. *Appetite*, 50, 167–78.
Ritzer, G. (1993/2008). *The McDonaldization of Society 5*. Los Angeles, Pine Forge Press.
Roe, B. and M.F. Teisl (2007). Genetically modified food labelling: The impacts of message and messenger on consumer perceptions of labels and products, *Food Policy*, 32, 49–66.
Rokka, J. and L. Uusitalo (2008). Preference for green packaging in consumer product choices – do consumers care? *International Journal of Consumer Studies*, 32, 516–25.

Rowe, G., D. Rawsthorne, t. Scarpello and J.R. Dainty (2009). Public engagement in research funding: A study of public capabilities and engagement methodology, *Public Understanding of Science*, 19, 255–39.

Salih, S. and J. Butler (2004). *The Judith Butler Reader*. Oxford: Blackwell Publishing.

Sanden, M.C.A van der and F.J. Meijman (2008). Dialogue guides awareness and understanding of science: An essay on different goals of dialogue leading to different science communication approaches, *Public Understanding of Science*, 17, 89–103.

Sandikci, Ö. and A. Ekici (2009). Politically motivated brand rejection, *Journal of Business Research*, 62, 208–17.

Sandlin, J.A. and J.L. Callahan (2009). Deviance, dissonance and detournesment: Culture jammers' use of emotion in consumer resistance, *Journal of Consumer Culture*, 9, 79–115.

Sanjuan, A.I., M. Sanchez, J.M. Gil, A. Gracia and F. Soler (2003). Brakes to organic market enlargement in Spain: Consumers' and retailers' attitudes and willingness to pay, *International Journal of Consumer Studies*, 27, 134–44.

Sassatelli, R. (2001). Tamed hedonism: Choice, desires and deviant pleasures, in J. Gronow and A. Warde (eds): *Ordinary Consumption*. London, Routledge.

Sassatelli, R. (2007). *Consumer Culture. History, Theory and Politics*. London, Sage.

Schatzki, T. (1996). *Social Practices. A Wittgensteinian Approach to Human Activity and the Social*. Cambridge, Cambridge University Press.

Schatzki, T. (2001). Practice minded orders, in T. Schatzki, K. Knorr-Cetina and E. von Savigny (eds): *The Practice Turn in Contemporary Theory*. London, Routledge.

Schatzki, T. (2002). *The Site of the Social. A Philosophical Account of the Constitution of Social Life and Change*. Pennsylvania, Pennsylvania State University Press.

Schibecci, R. and J. Harwood (2007). Stimulating authentic community involvement in biotechnology policy in Australia, *Public Understanding of Science*, 16, 245–55.

Schütz, A. (1975). *Hverdagslivets Sociologi* [The sociology of everyday life]. København, Hans Reitzel.

Sellerberg, A. (1991). In food we trust? Vitally necessary confidence – and unfamiliar ways of attaining it, in E. Fürst, R. Prättälä, M. Ekström, L. Holm and U. Kjærnes (eds): *Palatable Worlds: Sociocultural Food Studies*. Oslo, Solum Forlag.

Seyfang, G. (2006). Ecological citizenship and sustainable consumption: Examining local organic food networks, *Journal of Rural Studies*, 22, 383–95.

Shaw, D. and C. Moraes (2009). Voluntray simplicity: An exploration of market interactions, *International Journal of Consumer Studies*, 33, 215–23.

Short, F. (2006). *Kitchen Secrets. The Meaning of Cooking in Everyday Life*, Oxford, Berg.

Shove, E. (2003). *Comfort, Cleanliness and Convenience. The Social Organisation of Normality*. Oxford, Berg.

Shove, E. (2009). Everyday practice and the production and consumption of time, in E. Shove, F. Trentmann and R. Wilk (eds): *Time, Consumption and Everyday Life. Practice, Materiality and Culture*. Oxford, Berg.

Shove, E. and M. Pantzar (2005). Consumers, producers and practices: Understanding the invention and reinvention of Nordic walking, *Journal of Consumer Culture*, 5, 43–64.

Shove, E., F. Trentmann and R. Wilk (2009). *Time, Consumption and Everyday Life. Practice, Materiality and Culture*. Oxford, Berg.

Sibbel, A. (2008). Consumer science: A science for sustainability, *International Journal of Consumer Studies*, 27, 240.

Silverman, D. (2006). *Interpreting Qualitative Data*. London, Sage.

Simmons, P. (1997). The construction of environmental risks: Eco-labelling in the European Union, in P. Sulkunen, J. Holmwood, H. Radner and G. Schulze (eds): *Constructing the New Consumer Society*. Houndmills, Macmillan.

Sirieix, L., G. Grolleau and B. Schaer (2008). Do consumers care about food miles? An empirical analysis in France, *International Journal of Consumer Studies*, 32, 508–15.

Sjørslev, I. (2007). *Scener for Samvær: Ritualer, Performance og Solidaritet*. [Scenes of being together: Rituals, performance and solidarity] Århus: Århus Universitetsforlag.

Slater, D. (1997). *Consumer Culture and Modernity*. Cambridge, Polity.

Slovic, P. (1999). Trust, emotion, sex, politics and science: Surveying the risk-assessment battlefield, *Risk Analysis*, 19, 689–701.

Soper, K. (2007). Re-thinking the 'Good Life': The citizenship dimension of consumer disaffection with consumerism, *Journal of Consumer Culture*, 7, 205–29.

Soper, K. and F. Trentmann (2008). *Citizenship and Consumption*. Houndmills, Palgrave.

Southerton, D. (2006). Analysing the temporal organization of daily life: Social constraints, practices and their allocation, *Sociology*, 40, 435–54.

Southerton, D., A. Warde and M. Hand (2004). The limited autonomy of the consumer: Implications for sustainable consumption, in D. Southerton, H. Chappells and B. van Vliet (eds): *Sustainable Consumption: The Implications of Changing Infrastructures of Provision*. Cheltenham, Edward Elgar.

Spaargaren, G. (2000). Ecological modernization theory and domestic consumption, *Journal of Environmental Policy and Planning*, 2, 323–35.

Spaargaren, G. and A.P. Mol (2008). Greening global consumption: Redefining politics and authority, *Global Environmental Change*, 18, 350–59.

Spradley, J.P. (1979). *The Ethnographic Interview*. Fort Worth, Holt, Rinehart and Winston.

Stevenson, N. (2002). Consumer culture, ecology and the possibility of cosmopolitan citizenship, *Consumption, Markets and Culture*, 5, 305–19.

Stolle, D., M. Hooghe and M. Micheletti (2005). Politics in the supermarket: Political consumerism as a form of political participation, *International Political Science Review*, 26, 245–69.
Storey, J. (1999). *Cultural Consumption and Everyday Life*. London, Arnold.
Storstad, O. and H. Bjørkhaug (2003). Foundations of production and consumption of organic food in Norway: Common attitudes among farmers and consumers?, *Agriculture and Human Values*, 20, 151–63.
Sulkunen, P. (1997). Introduction: The new consumer society – rethinking the social bond, in P. Sulkunen, J. Holmwood. H. Radner and G. Schulze (eds): *Constructing the New Consumer Society*. Houndmills, Macmillan.
Sulkunen, P. (2009). *The Saturated Society: Governing Risk and Lifestyles in Consumer Culture*, London, Sage.
Sulkunen, P. (2010). Autonomy against intimacy. On the problem of governing lifestyle related risks, *Telos*, forthcoming.
Sullivan, O. and T. Katz-Gerro (2007). The omnivore thesis revisited: Voracious cultural consumers, *European Sociological Review*, 23, 123–37.
Terragni, L. and U. Kjærnes (2005). Ethical consumption in Norway: Why is it so low? In Boström, M., M. Klintman, M. Micheletti and M.P. Sørensen (eds): *Political Consumerism: Its Motivations, Power and Conditions in the Nordic Countries and Elsewhere*. Nordisk Ministerråd, København.
Thomas, J. (2008). Using social marketing techniques to tackle alcohol issues, *Journal of Communication in Heath Care*, 1, 382–96.
Thompson, C.J. and G. Coskuner-Balli (2007). Enchanting ethical consumerism: The case of community supported agriculture, *Journal of Consumer Culture*, 7, 275–303.
Thompson, J.B. (1995). *Media and Modernity. A Social Theory of the Media*. Cambridge, Polity.
Thøgersen, J. (2006). Norms for environmentally responsible behaviour: An extended taxonomy, *Journal of Environmental Psychology*, 26, 247–61.
Thøgersen, J. and F. Ölander (2003). Spillover of environment-friendly consumer behaviour, *Journal of Environmental Psychology*, 23, 225–36.
Trentmann, F. (2007). Citizenship and consumption, *Journal of Consumer Culture*, 7, 147–58.
Truninger, M. (2009). Cooking with Bimby. Paper presented at the 9th European Sociological Association, Lisboa, Portugal, 2–5 September.
Tukker, A., E. Stö and C. Vezzoli (2008). The governance and practice of change of sustainable consumption and production. Editorial, *Journal of Cleaner Production*, 16, 1143–45.
Tulloch, J. and D. Lupton (2002). Consuming risk, consuming science: The case of GM foods, *Journal of Consumer Culture*, 2, 363–83.
Turner, B.S. (1984). *Kroppen I Samfundet. Teorier om Krop og Kultur* [Body in society. Theories about body and culture]. København, Hans Reitzels Forlag.
Turner, S. (1994). *The Social Theory of Practices: Tradition, Tacit Knowledge and Presuppositions*. Cambridge, Polity Press.

Turner, S. (2001). Throwing out the tacit rule book: Learning and practices, in T. Schatzki, K. Knorr-Cetina and E. von Savigny (eds): *The Practice Turn in Contemporary Theory*. London, Routledge.

Ureña, F., R. Bernabéu and M. Olmeda (2007). Women, men and organic food: Differences in their attitudes and willingness to pay. A Spanish case study, *International Journal of Consumer Studies*, 32, 18–26.

Vallgårda, S. (2001). Governing people's lives. Strategies for improving the health of the nations in England, Denmark, Norway and Sweden, *European Journal of Public Health*, 11, 386–92.

Ventakesh, A. and L.A. Meamber (2008). The aesthetics of consumption and the consumer as aesthetic subject, *Consumption, Markets and Culture*, 11, 45–70.

Vermeir, I. and W. Verbeke (2006). Sustainable food consumption: Exploring the consumer 'attitude-behavioral intention' gap, *Journal of Agricultural and Environmental Ethics*, 19, 169–94.

Vittersø, G. (2003). *Environmental Information and Consumer Practices. A Case Study of Households in Fredrikstad*. Professional Report 4-2003, Oslo, SIFO.

Wacquant, L. (2004). *Body and Soul: Notes of an Apprentice Boxer*. Oxford, Oxford University Press.

Wahlström, M. and A. Peterson (2006). Between the state and the market: Expanding the concept of 'political opportunity structure', *Acta Sociologica*, 49, 363–77.

Walker, G. and E. Shove (2007). Ambivalence, sustainability and the governance of socio-technical transitions, *Journal of Environmental Policy and Planning*, 9, 213–25.

Warde, A. (1997). *Consumption, Food and Taste*. London, Sage.

Warde, A. (2002). Setting the scene: Changing conceptions of consumption, in S. Miles, A. Anderson and K. Meethan (eds): *The Changing Consumer*. London, Routledge.

Warde, A. (2005). Consumption and theories of practice, *Journal of Consumer Culture*, 5, 131–53.

Warde, A., L. Martens and W. Olsen (1999). Consumption and the problem of variety: Cultural omnivorousness, social distinction and dining out, *Sociology*, 33, 105–27.

Warin, M., K. Turner, V. Moore and M. Davies (2008). Bodies, mothers and identities: Rethinking obesity and the BMI, *Sociology of Health and Illness*, 30, 97–111.

West, C. and S. Fenstermaker (1995). Doing difference, *Gender and Society*, 9, 8–37.

West, C. and D.H. Zimmerman (1987). Doing gender, *Gender and Society*, 1, 125–51.

Wilk, R. (2001). Consuming morality, *Journal of Consumer Culture*, 1, 245–60.

Wilk, R. (2009). The edge of agency: Routines, habits and volition, in E. Shove, F. Trentmann and R. Wilk (eds): *Time, Consumption and Everyday Life. Practice, Materiality and Culture*. Oxford, Berg.

Willis, P. (1990). *Common Culture. Symbolic Work at Play in the Everyday Cultures of the Young*. Buckingham, Open University Press.
Windahl, S, B. Signitzer and J.T. Olson (1998). *Using Communication Theory. An Introduction to Planned Communication*. London, Sage.
www.coop.dk
www.dsg.dk
www.ecolabel.dk
www.fedtfattig.dk
www.food.dtu.dk
www.forbrug.dk/erdetfarligt
www.foedevarestyrelsen.dk
Ziehe, T. (1988). *Ambivalenser og Mangfoldighed* [Ambivalences and diversity]. København, Politisk Revy.
Zoller, H.M. (2005). Health activism: Communication theory and action for social change, *Communication Theory*, 15, 341–64.
Zukin, S. and J.S. Maguire (2004). Consumers and consumption, *Annual Review of Sociology*, 30, 173–97.

Index